EARLY COOPER AND HIS AUDIENCE

Early Cooper and His Audience

JAMES D. WALLACE

P. 106
P. 121
P. 161

COLUMBIA UNIVERSITY PRESS

New York   1986

As a manuscript this book was awarded the Bancroft Dissertation Award by a committee of the faculty of the Graduate School of the Arts and Sciences of Columbia University.

Columbia University Press
New York   Guildford, Surrey
Copyright © 1986 Columbia University Press
All rights reserved

Printed in the United States of America

Library of Congress Cataloging in Publication Data
Wallace, James D., 1946–
Early Cooper and his audience.
Bibliography: p.
Includes index.
1. Cooper, James Fenimore, 1789–1851—Criticism and interpretation.   2. Cooper, James Fenimore, 1789–1851—Appreciation.   3. Authors and readers—United States.   4. Books and reading—United States—History—19th century.   I. Title.
PS1438.W33   1986   813'.2   85-12810
ISBN 0-231-06176-5

This book is Smyth-sewn.

CONTENTS

PREFACE

My study of James Fenimore Cooper began with a simple observation: if Cooper had to invent "the American novel," he also had to invent an audience for it. Who knew, in 1820, how to read an American novel? Despite earlier novels by Charles Brockden Brown, Royall Tyler, John Neal, and a host of others, there simply was no audience whose taste could respond to an indigenous American fiction when Cooper began to write. The fiction that Americans read was entirely imported: the epistolary novels of Richardson and his epigons at the Minerva Press; the moral fictions of Hannah More and Amelia Opie; the provincial romances of Edgeworth and Scott; Byron's Oriental tales. Brown is only the most famous of those original creative talents whose ambition to become great novelists (or at least to support themselves by their writing) foundered on the indifference of the reading public. Yet in a surprisingly short time, Cooper succeeded in transforming both his art and his audience from awkward imitations of the English into something triumphantly American; in the process, he created the audience which represented the reading public for every American author through most of the nineteenth century, the audience to which Hawthorne, Melville, Stowe, and Twain tried (at least intermittently) to appeal and which determined the commercial success or failure of every American novel. How did he do it?

My question was a perfectly ordinary one for an Americanist, a literary historian, but no one engaged in critical writing in this era of poststructuralist polemics can escape methodological questions. The contemporary dissatisfaction with traditional literary history is well represented by a parable by Roman Jakobson, who compared literary historians to "police who are supposed to arrest a certain person, arrest everybody and carry off everything they find in the house, and all the people who pass by chance in the street. Thus the historians of literature appropriate everything—the social setting, psychology, politics, philosophy. Instead of literary scholarship we got a conglomeration of derivative disciplines."[1] If literary history isn't really literary scholarship but biography, metrics, politics, sociology, intellectual history, philosophy, theology, and psychoanalysis, who can take seriously the dabbling of a mere dilettante? Each of those disciplines has real practitioners, specialists whose knowledge bears real authority, and to these we must turn for a proper understanding of the issues so irresponsibly raised by the literary historian. In addition, Jakobson's parable suggests that there is something unpleasantly authoritarian and repressive about traditional literary history: innocent passersby fall victim to the blind malevolence of the agents of political terror. What Jakobson means is that literary history has too often been warped to nationalistic political and social purposes; the history of world literature is surveyed in order to illustrate how we have arrived at the present perfection of neoclassical epic, Christian lyric, or Socialist Realism and to ridicule and punish any artist who dares to ignore the evolutionary theory that finds its *telos* in the present perfection of a form toward which all literature has been groping since the first subhuman band gathered around the fire to narrate their heroics in the last successful hunt.

Recent attempts to purge literary history of nationalist bias and to establish a coherent method for historical scholarship have focused on the role of the reader in a contractual relation to texts. Over the last decade, the reader—actual, implied, enscripted, encoded, Super, Absolute—has attracted a vast body of criticism, much of it fascinating, epistemologically sophisticated, and polemically accomplished.[2] For literary history, the most relevant of these investigations is Hans Robert Jauss' concept of *Rezeptionsästhetik,* an aesthetics of reception in which the act of reading is seen as a negotiation between text and reader. Every text, argues Jauss, establishes a *"literarische Erwartungshorizont,"* a literary horizon of expectations which confronts the reader's preexisting social horizon of expectations, i.e., the reader's social values, mores, taboos, and literary taste. In the negotiation between text and reader a fusion of the two horizons may or may not take place. If it does not, the work is simply a failure (it may have to wait, as *Moby-Dick* did, for a generation of readers whose social horizons are capable of entering into negotiation with it); if the fusion does take place, the work has literary value according to how much it changes the reader's social horizon. Some works merely fulfill the reader's existing expectations; these will be commercial successes but have no literary value. Other works have a norm-breaking impact and actually change their readers' horizon of expectations; the greater that change, the greater the literary value.[3] The task of literary history, then is to record those changes in the social horizon of expectations and to analyze the textual conventions that stimulated those changes. Jauss' work has been provocative, and it has the virtue of focusing critical attention on methods of literary history amid the debate over poststructuralist critical ideology. Jauss himself, however, is more interested in what he calls *"Gipfelebene"* (peak-level) readers—authors reading authors, Goethe reading Racine—than in the *"mittlere Ebene"* (middle level) of cultured readers or *"präreflexive Ebene"* (naive level) of common readers in a mass audience. In addition, Jauss' literary history is subject to the same objection as older versions: how can we establish the social horizon of expectations in, say, early nineteenth-century New York, without creating the same patchwork of sociology, philosophy, and psychology that Jakobson scorned?[4]

   Still, the concept of a negotiation between text and reader is a useful one, and it connects suggestively to one of the more powerful formulations of a method for literary history in the American tradition. In 1949 William Charvat called for a literary history that would recognize the triangular relation of reader, writer, and book trade and would develop methods to increase our understanding of the ways in which writers have produced and communicated.[5] The methods Charvat had in mind—close examination of relations between authors and publishers, the economics of the book trade, and the response of common readers to an author's works—were best demonstrated in his own essays on Longfellow and Melville. But Charvat's hope for a new literary history that would be both more historical and more literary than the traditional has gone largely unfulfilled.

My study of Cooper and his audience is intended to be a contribution to the literary history Charvat envisioned. By "audience" I mean neither the implied reader of Iser nor the statistical reader of literary sociology (though neither concept is irrelevant to my discussion); rather I have tried to deal with idea of an audience as Cooper himself conceived it. While Cooper adopted the tone, matter, and thematic concerns (and thus the implied reader) of the Opie novel, he was immediately interested in enlarging his audience beyond that rather narrow scope and sought to create new modes of narrative that would appeal in the first instance to readers he knew and respected and beyond them to a broad-based national readership. Similarly, though he knew the book market well, followed reviews and sales of his books closely, and thought deeply about the reasons for his successes and failures, he refused to compromise his principles for popularity and labored mightily to improve his readers' taste and to serve what he perceived to be the cultural needs of his nation. This combination of the abstract and the concrete, of the practical and the ideal, is the outstanding feature of Cooper's thinking about his audience, and that is what I have focused on in this study. In other words, beginning with the concept of the contractual relation between text and reader, I have tried to focus on Cooper's understanding of that relation and his attempts to generate fictions which would both fulfill his prescribed role as author and modify the terms of the existing horizon of expectations. Although neither Jauss' nor Charvat's work fully succeeds in establishing an unassailable foundation for methods of literary history, nevertheless they have provided important suggestions for undertaking the kind of investigation that my initial question seemed to entail.[6]

The first chapter of this study attempts to sketch the horizon of expectations that existed when Cooper began to write in 1820. There were extensive debates over the prospects for a republican literature in both Europe and America; critical ideology espoused the moral and social aims of Common Sense philosophy; and the decentralized publishing industry made it virtually impossible for a writer to connect with any audience large enough to support him or her. The second chapter discusses the reasons for the failure of Charles Brockden Brown, who aspired to become the first professional man of letters in America but who never succeeded in devising techniques for engaging readers or for distributing his books. The third chapter traces the evolution of Cooper's art from his first imitation British novel, *Precaution,* to his first American novel, *The Spy,* and of the attention Cooper gave to details of publication and commercialization. The fourth chapter demonstrates the full maturing of Cooper's powers in *The Pioneers* and examines the literary structures by which Cooper attempted to control his readers' responses to an indigenous American fiction. The final chapter summarizes what Cooper actually achieved in creating an audience that would determine the course of American fiction throughout the nineteenth century. I have been especially concerned with Cooper's theory of fiction, his publishing practices and techniques of commercialization, his experiments with the incorporation of popular literary forms, and the reception of his works.

During the course of preparing for and writing this study, I have benefited from more help and encouragement than I can well acknowledge. Sacvan Bercovitch and Werner Sollors read it, pointed out my worst errors, prodded me onward, and generously supplied moral support when it was most needed. Elizabeth Kowaleski-Wallace, my best auditor and critic, provided intellectual, moral, and other, nameless, enrichment for my labors. I have learned much from discussions with many friends, including Hannah Bercovitch, Max Rudin, Paul Royster, Larry Rothfield, and a host of others. But my greatest debt is to my daughter Becky, who cares nothing for Cooper or literary history, but cares for my caring.

CHAPTER ONE

Toward a Democratic Fiction

"**R**eading, which always enters so naturally into country life, was a regular resource for the evening hours and rainy days, at Angevine. It is needless to observe that the books on every table were, at that day, almost exclusively English. The roll of all the contemporary authors in the country, of any note, might have been called over in a trice; and if, among these, there were already several brilliant pens, yet the united influence of the whole class on the nation was still very slight indeed."[1]

So Susan Fenimore Cooper begins her account of the night that her father found his vocation. She goes on to describe the excitement that attended the arrival of a packet carrying new books from England; orders immediately went out to the New York bookseller for the latest work by Scott, Byron, Edgeworth, Wilberforce, or Hannah More. Cooper's favorite reading was Shakespeare, and "Pope, Thomson, Gray, were also in favor. . . . But new books were, of course, in particular request; and rapidly as the great Scotch novels succeeded each other, something more was needed to fill up all those quiet evening hours at Angevine."[2]

A number of interesting conditions may be gleaned from this account. Cooper's family may not have been entirely representative, but the craving for new fiction that it felt was widespread, as the demand for Scott's novels suggests.[3] To satisfy that craving, the American audience had to rely on English novels reprinted in New York and elsewhere; few American works were available at all, and fewer still were of any interest to novel readers. Excitement was stirred by something new, but taste was based on Pope, Gray, Thomson, and (above all) Shakespeare. When Cooper tried his hand at his first novel in the spring of 1820, these are the conditions that confronted him.

Yet reading habits represent only a small part of the unusual complex of pressures, restrictions, and ambitions that Cooper faced. The European debate over the possibility of a republican literature cast a powerfully ideological gloom over American writing even while pressures mounted for American writers to validate the experiment in democracy with an indigenous democratic fiction. Contemporary literary theory placed severe restrictions on every author's creative imagination and demanded a stringently moral and social art. The decentralized publishing industry virtually guaranteed that no mere writer would be able to support himself by his craft. Together these factors created an atmosphere of anxious expectation and erected formidable hurdles in the path of the would-be writer in America.

I

While the majority of modern studies are concerned to define what is uniquely *American* about American literature, citing the devotion to such qualities as the genre of romance, to folklore, to antifeminism, or to anxiety over authority and genealogy as the characteristic traits, the conditions of the early Republic discouraged American writers from considering themselves unique in any way. To be sure, Royall Tyler, Charles Brockden Brown, John Neal, and a host of others called for an indigenous American fiction and designed programs for it, but the very redundancy of their demands and the fact that each tended to see himself as the sole true exemplar of an American school serve as an acknowledgement that English models dominated. Margaret Fuller, reflecting on the state of American letters as late as 1846, could only detect "the first faint streaks" of a dawning era: "It is sad for those that foresee, to know they may not live to share its glories, yet it is sweet, too, to know that every act and word uttered in the light of that foresight may tend to hasten or ennoble its fulfill-ment." Fuller lamented the economic and social conditions that seemed to militate against American writers at midcentury, and she summarized fifty years of struggle to create a native literature:

> The ranks that led the way in the first half century of this republic were far better situated than we, in this respect. The country was not so deluged with the dingy page reprinted from Europe, and patriotic vanity was on the alert to answer the question, "Who reads an American book?" And many were the books written as worthy to be read as any out of the class in England. They were, most of them, except in their subject matter, English books.[4]

As Howard Mumford Jones reminds us, republican nationalism and anti-British sentiment united in the nineteenth century to produce a vague theory of American literature:

> Yet whereas most writers before 1850 denounced or envied British literature as the chief obstacle to native genius; and despite the hostility between the British upper class and the North during the Civil War—a hostility which, added to previous controversies, might reasonably be expected to increase American distrust of Brit-ish criticism—almost every history of American literature from the sixties to 1913, when John Macy published his *Spirit of American Literature* and inaugurated the modern interpretation of the sub-ject, not only insisted upon measuring American writers by British standards, but also claimed that American literature was a branch of English letters, a subordinate, if locally interesting, expression of the Anglo-Saxon spirit.[5]

In many ways American literature was such a branch of English letters, as studies of Godwin's influence on Brown, or Scott's on Cooper, or Bentham's on Neal suggest. From an English perspective, however, American literature must have seemed an extreme example of tendencies within Britain itself, tendencies whose political and cultural implications many British observers had already deplored. The rise of democracy and of industrialism in the years between 1757 and 1827 effected major changes in English life, and these changes were reflected in new ideas concerning art, the artist, and the artist's place in society. Raymond Williams lists five major points regarding the artist's new role: 1) a major alteration in the nature of the relationship between the writer and the reader; 2) a different habitual attitude among artists toward their public; 3) a concept of the production of art as one of a number of specialized kinds of production; 4) an increasing emphasis on the "superior reality" of art as the seat of imaginative truth; and 5) an increasing emphasis on the idea of the independent creative writer, the autonomous genius.[6] The rise of a middle-class reading public and the end of the patronage system meant that the artist had a new independence from personal responsibility for his work, but it also meant that he had to please a new, impersonal public in a "literary marketplace."

One direct result of these changes was the artist's tendency to hold his public in contempt even as he labored to attract it. A second result, more far-reaching in its implications, was that market forces exerted an unprecedented influence on literary production. Appropriately enough, Adam Smith had already noted this effect in a draft of *The Wealth of Nations:* "In opulent and commercial societies to think or reason comes to be, like every other employment, a particular business, which is carried on by a very few people, who furnish the public with all the thought and reason possessed by the vast multitudes that labor."[7]

The threat to traditional European culture in this change was thus twofold: it concentrated the creation of cultural artifacts in the hands of a minuscule minority, obviating the concept of the "cultured gentleman" who manages his tenant farm, supports a parish, stands for Parliament, brings out a volume of his own decorous verse, and befriends a better poet from his love of poetry; and it dangerously democratized the dissemination of culture, transforming Milton's "fit audience though few" into a mass market whose members had little in common save the power to starve an artist by ignoring this product. Carlyle's Teufelsdröckh brilliantly animated this change in *Sartor Resartus:*

He who first shortened the labour of Copyists by device of *Moveable Types* was disbanding hired Armies, and cashiering most Kings and Senates, and creating a whole new Democratic world: he had invented the Art of Printing. The first ground handful of Nitre, Sulphur, and Charcoal drove Monk Schwartz's pestle through the ceiling; what will the last do? Achieve the final indisputed prostration of Force under Thought, of Animal courage under Spiritual. A simple invention it was in the old-world Grazier,—sick of lugging his slow Ox about the country till he got it bartered for corn or oil,—to take a piece of Leather, and thereon scratch or stamp the mere Figure of an Ox (or *Pecus*); put it in his pocket, and call it *Pecunia*, Money. Yet hereby did Barter grow Sale, the Leather Money is now Golden and Paper, and all miracles have been outmiracled: for there are Rothschilds and English National Debts; and whoso has sixpence is Sovereign (to the length of sixpence) over all men; commands cooks to feed him, philosophers to teach him, kings to mount guard over him—to the length of sixpence.[8]

The evils of the Industrial Revolution are all here: the popular dissemination of culture dooms existing political forms and produces democracy; the invention of gunpowder gives the weak unnatural power over their aristocratic superiors; the invention of money turns culture into a marketplace and renders artists and kings mere hirelings. A few years later, in his 1840 lecture on "The Hero as Man of Letters: Johnson, Rousseau, Burns," Carlyle abandoned the irony of *Sartor Resartus* and made clear his acceptance of the change wrought in culture by the "Ready-writing which we call *Printing*," but at the same time he emphasized the strange metamorphosis that had replaced his poetic heroes, Shakespeare and Dante, with the humble laborer in the marketplace of letters: "He, with his copy-rights and copy-wrongs, in his squalid garret, in his rusty coat; ruling (for this is what he does), from his grave, after death, whole nations and generations who would, or would not, give him bread while living,—is a rather curious spectacle! Few shapes of Heroism can be more unexpected."[9]

      Carlyle's capacity for appreciating the "curious spectacle" of the Industrial Man of Letter represents the end of half a century of rancorous debate over the projected effect on culture of democratic institutions. German writers (Herder, Lessing,

Schiller, and Friedrich Schlegel) taught methods of reading literature as an expression of the dynamics of a culture and society, as
an index of a national *Zeitgeist.* In these terms it was natural for
Europeans to look to America for the art of the future: here the
European tradition was freely available, owing to the immigrant
character of the American population; at the same time the frontier condition of the country, the physical separation from Europe,
and the American Revolution and the merging of many national-
ities into one provided sufficient cultural distance from the past to
enable the Americans to make themselves wholly new.

What, precisely, would be the character of art in a
democracy? For those Europeans such as Rousseau, Condorcet,
Madame de Staël, and others who brought the greatest urgency to
this question, the answer depended on a particular political vision,
for art served political ends above all. Each of them projected a
vision of an American literature that contributed to the atmosphere of intense expectation and commensurate disappointment
that prevailed in the United States in the first decades of the nineteenth century, and each indicated a direction for American writers to explore.

Rousseau rejected the functions of art altogether in his
search for the immediacy of personal experience. Jean-Jacques,
the tutor of the titular hero of *Emile,* presents his pupil with one,
and only one, book before Emile's adulthood. Jean-Jacques prefaces his gift with a digression to the reader in which he reveals his
loathing for all books (especially the Bible) for their tendency to
distort the natural relation between men and things and for their
capacity to stimulate artificially desires, hopes, and fears. When
Jean-Jacques at last presents his gift, it is *Robinson Crusoe,* a new
Bible of man's original condition and true relation to nature—a
kind of anti-book, and the most stubbornly bourgeois, Protestant,
and mercantile of European novels.[10]

The literature produced by Rousseau's natural man
would be natural, too: primal and fecund, less literate than mythic.
Intellectual positions can have surprising consequences, and, as
Richard Slotkin has shown, Rousseau's fiction prepared an enthusiastic reception in a circle of European intellectuals for an Ameri-

can swindler named Gilbert Imlay.[11] Imlay had fled from Kentucky in order to escape massive indebtedness (he owed money to most of the state's leading citizens, including Daniel Boone). Once in Paris he published *A Topographical Description of the Western Territory of North America* (London, 1792), a work that took its form from Jefferson's *Notes on the State of Virginia* and its content from John Filson's *The Discovery, Settlement and Present State of Kentucke.* He also made contact with Parisian Americanist circles and shortly became the lover of Mary Wollstonecraft, who described him as "an unspoiled child of nature, an incarnation of Rousseau's Emile."[12] Together, Imlay and Wollstonecraft wrote *The Emigrants* (1794), an epistolary novel based on Filson's narrative of the life of Daniel Boone.

For a brief period, Imlay exercised extraordinary influence over European intellectual life. One of the readers of *A Topographical Description* was François-René de Chateaubriand. Chateaubriand used Imlay's book as background for his own *Les Natchez,* the book which probably did more than any other to disseminate the popular image of the Noble Savage and to prepare European readers for the reception of Cooper's novels. Imlay was also the primary source of information about America for Coleridge and Southey, who not only planned to establish their pantisocratic community in the Ohio Valley, but also took their model constitution and marriage laws from *The Emigrants.* Imlay's influence might have grown still greater had he been able to sustain his role as an unspoiled child of nature, but in 1796 he abandoned Wollstonecraft, and William Godwin subsequently made sure that Imlay disappeared into obscurity.

Imlay's brief ascendancy is a literary curiosity, but it illustrates the peculiar blend of naive wonder and desire with which even sophisticated liberal Europeans regarded the new nation across the sea. For the burgeoning European bourgeoisie whose economic and political aspirations were frustrated by the oppression following the French Revolution, America came to represent every freedom they were denied. William Blake could link resurrection, rebirth, and freedom in a visionary paraphrase of the Declaration of Independence in *America a Prophecy* (1793):

The morning comes, the night decays, the watchmen leave their
   stations;
The grave is burst, the spices shed, the linen wrapped up;
The bones of death, the cov'ring clay, the sinews shrunk & dry'd.
Reviving shake, inspiring move, breathing! awakening!
Spring like redeemed captives when their bonds & bars are burst;
Let the slave grinding at the mill, run out into the field;
Let him look up into the heavens & laugh in the bright air;
Let the unchained soul shut up in darkness and in sighing,
Whose face has never seen a smile in thirty weary years;
Rise and look out, his chains are loose, his dungeon doors are open.
And let his wife and children return from the oppressor's scourge;
They look behind at every step & believe it is a dream.
Singing. The Sun has left his blackness, & has found a fresher
   morning
And the fair Moon rejoices in the clear & cloudless night;
For Empire is no more, and now the Lion & Wolf shall cease.[13]

In Germany, where police measures and censorship
decrees characterized literary life, one method for tacitly engaging
in political discussion was to write about America; the resulting
body of literature is known as the *Amerika-Thematik*.[14] By 1800
there were already three German periodicals exclusively devoted to
the United States, and in the first half of the nineteenth century at
least fifty books were published to cater to the huge market of
would-be German emigrants: "The *Amerika-Thematik* was not
only a means to take a disguised position on the political situation
and to oppose restrictions on democratic freedom in the police
states, but it was partly the cause and partly the result of a general
need to learn about that exotic, strange land."[15]

Rousseau's legacy was a widespread hunger for information about America. The form in which this information came
hardly mattered; from Coleridge and Wollstonecraft to the
humblest German burger, liberal Europeans converted raw American materials into their own utopian dreams of freedom.

Condorcet, more sanguine than Rousseau about the
effects of art, ended the tenth stage of his *Progress of the Human
Mind* (1795) with a noble vision of the future perfection of democratic society in its laws, sciences, philosophy, education, domestic

bliss, and artistic expression. Denying the conservative argument that the classical periods of Greece, Italy, and France had exhausted art's resources and condemned it to a monotonous repetition of its former glory, Condorcet projected a new era, one made possible by the cheap availability of works of art on a massive scale. Yet even Condorcet's optimism was strangely muted; unable to foresee Carlyle's men of letters in their rusty coats, he imagined instead an anonymous art, depersonalized from both producer and consumer:

> If the more reflective pleasure of comparing the products of different ages and countries and admiring the success and energy of the effort of genius will probably be lost, the pleasure to be derived from the actual contemplation of works of art as such will be just as vivid as ever, even though the author may no longer deserve the same credit for having achieved such perfection. As works of art genuinely worthy of preservation increase in number, and become more perfect, each successive generation will devote its attention and admiration to those which really deserve preference, and the rest will fall into oblivion; the pleasure to be derived from the simpler, more striking, more accessible aspects of beauty will exist no less for posterity although they will be found only in the latest works.[16]

Condorcet's teleology demanded that works of art successively become "more perfect," but his commitment to democratic culture required that they also reflect the "simpler, more striking, more accessible aspects of beauty," and despite his optimism about the future of mankind, there is a decided anticlimax in the notion that the audience of the future will appreciate only "the latest works." Those more perfect works of art will be merely transitory, after all. Condorcet tacitly accepted the strictures of conservative critics and, making virtue of necessity, suggested that the feebler democratic art would be justified by its political importance.

Madame de Staël's *Influence of Literature upon Society* (1800; a translation appeared in the United States in 1811) represented a more analytical approach to the problem of a democratic literature. For Staël, literature is the best mode for undertaking a critical examination of society and its irrational prejudices; philosophical literature is "the chief stay and most permanent pledge of liberty," and indeed, in the eyes of monarchs, "political and religious philosophy would rise up in the shape of the most formidable insurrection."[17] Poetry, it is true, has often served the ends of tyranny by diverting the minds of readers from *all* ideas, by lulling "to intoxication, to sleep and to death." In a democratic republic, then, art must adopt a new character. Staël argued that the institution of democracy has divested both satire and tragedy of one of their major purposes—the reformation of the social order. Consequently, the art of the future will focus inward, away from social subjects: satire must attack "the vices of the human heart," and comedy must develop toward "the most philosophical of all the works of the imagination, and that which presupposes the most profound and extensive knowledge of the human heart." The social field, rationalized and constricted by republican institutions, ceases to be an adequate subject for modern writers, who therefore will find little of interest in the subjects treated by ancient authors and their imitators; in place of those subjects modern tragedians must strive to "awaken and recall individual recollections: for nothing can excite such deep emotions as these." A non-aristocratic art must employ "philosophy and sensibility" as its means:

> Life glides away, as it were, unperceived by the happy; but in affliction, reflection enlarges itself to search for some hope, or to discover a motive for regret; it examines the past, and tries to drive into the future; and this faculty of observation, which, when the mind is at ease, turns entirely upon exterior objects, in misfortune is exercised only upon the impressions we feel. The ceaseless operation of uneasiness upon the mind causes in the heart, a fluctuation of ideas and sentiments, which agitate our internal feelings, as if every moment were teeming with some new event. What an inexhaustible source of reflection does this afford to genius.

This introspective turn may seem to deprive literature of real matter and to invite the fantastic figures of mythology to occupy the writer's imagination, but modern taste makes it impossible that imagination should be assisted by "illusion": "it is necessary that reason should always approve and comprehend what enthusiasm renders charming." The modern writer must rather follow Rousseau and seek his subject in the close observation of nature, "In its relations to the sentiments with which it inspires man. . . . Providence has so closely connected physical objects with the moral existence of man, that nothing can be added to the study of the one, which does not at the same time lend to farther knowledge of the other." Particularly interesting to Staël in this connection was the development of a new romance of manners and characters, a species of art that was "frequently the means of conveying more knowledge respecting the human heart, than history itself."[18]

Staël's influence in American literary circles was widespread, and although she wrote too late to influence the work of Charles Brockden Brown, she may have helped to prepare the more respectful reception given his novels after 1820. Certainly her axioms for republican literature shrewdly forecast two closely connected characteristics of the nascent American tradition—the introspective quest for "the truth of the human heart," and the focus on nature as an image of psychic states—but these would not be fully developed until Hawthorne, Melville, and Thoreau became active. Perhaps most important for her American readers in the first decades of the nineteenth century was Staël's insistence that progress is historically inevitable, that it leads to liberty, and that liberty necessarily creates and depends upon a moral, Christian literature. Although her prescriptions for the literature of liberty were addressed to a French audience, she used American oratory as a preliterary model:

> I think it always interesting to examine what would be the prevailing character of the literature of a great and enlightened people, in whose country should be established liberty, political equality, and manners in unison with its institutions: there is but one nation in the world to whom some of these reflections may be applied at the present day;—America. The American literature, indeed, is not yet formed; but when their magistrates are called upon to address themselves on any subject to the public opinion, they are eminently gifted with the power of touching all the affections of the heart, by expressing simple truth and pure sentiments; and to do this, is already to be acquainted with the most useful secret of elegant style.[19]

In 1800 Staël could dream of the glorious future of American letters; by 1820 the dream seemed in danger of a cold awakening indeed. Jeffersonian optimism about the growth of republican cultural institutions had largely given way to an edgy anxiety regarding the continuing American dependence on and deference to European, and especially British, institutions.[20] Into this nervous atmosphere fell like a thunderbolt a scathing attack on American cultural life by the Reverend Sydney Smith. The attack must have been all the more galling for its unlikely source; Smith was a Whig, "favorably disposed with regard to American theories of government and liberal institutions."[21] Nevertheless, reviewing Adam Seybert's *Statistical Annals of the United States of America* in *The Edinburgh Review* for January 1820, Smith denied absolutely any intellectual or cultural achievement by any American whatever:

> The Americans are a brave, industrious, and acute people; but they have hitherto given no indications of genius, and made no approaches to the heroic, either in their morality or character. They are but a recent offshoot indeed from England; and should make it their chief boast, for many generations to come, that they are sprung from the same race with Bacon and Shakespeare and Newton. Considering their numbers, indeed, and the favourable circumstances in which they have been placed, they have yet done marvellously little to assert the honour of such a descent, or to show that their English blood has been exalted or refined by their republican training and institutions. Their Franklins and Washingtons, and all the other sages and heroes of their revolution, were born and bred subjects of the King of England—and not among the freest or most valued of his subjects: And, since the period of their separation, a far greater proportion of their statesmen and artists and political writers have been foreigners, than ever occurred before in the history of any civilized and educated people. During the thirty or forty years of their independence, they have done absolutely nothing for the Sciences, for the Arts, for Literature, or even for the statesmanlike studies of Politics or Political Economy.[22]

Smith's attack is notable for its tone of contemptuous dismissal and its determination to deny American culture any possible avenue of expression. It is less an intellectual position than an act of internecine hostility, and so it was taken at the time. Smith's notorious question, "In the four quarters of the globe, who reads an American book?"[23] became a rallying cry for American critics, though it was not Smith's attitude (nothing new, after all) that turned his question into a slogan, but the happy coincidence that Irving's *Sketch Book,* Cooper's *The Spy,* and Bryant's 1821 *Poems* suddenly appeared as ready rejoinders.

The European debate over republican literature was partly a continuation of the "battle of the books" between advocates of ancient and of modern writers, in which America took the role of an avant-garde. More generally, the debate indicated the political and economic anxieties of the Industrial Revolution, nationalistic ambitions, and class conflict. The effect of the debate on American writers, not surprisingly, was the anxiety of high expectations and disappointment, political passion and party conflict, open or undeclared war.

II

While the debate over republican literature went on in Europe, American observers were primarily engaged in attempts to understand why Americans wrote so little of recognizable value and to propose solutions for the impasse in the growth of a national culture. John Adams had proposed that the first generation of Americans born after the Revolution were employed at "the mechanic arts" so that the second would have the leisure to pursue the fine arts:

> I must study politics and war, that my sons have liberty to study mathematics and philosophy, geography, natural history and naval architecture, navigation, commerce, and agriculture, in order to give their children a right to study painting, poetry, music, architecture, statuary, tapestry, and porcelain.[24]

But by the first decade of the nineteenth century the grace period was clearly drawing to a close, and no American literature seemed in prospect. In 1801 Noah Webster's *Commer-*

cial Advertiser began publishing a series entitled "Letters of Shahcoolen, a Hindu Philosopher, Residing in Philadelphia; to His Friend El Hassan, an Inhabitant of Delhi." The series was the work of Benjamin Silliman, a tutor at Yale College and later the founder and editor of *The American Journal of Science.* As a Federalist, Silliman was largely engaged in a satiric attack on Republicanism in the "Letters," but he was also an amateur poet, and his "Letter Seventh" was devoted to a serious consideration of the American indifference to poetry:

> This does not arise from a deficiency of poetical talents but from the state of society. For I have conversed with many Americans, whose souls were elevated by the purest poetical fire; whose minds were familiar with every dreadful, and every pleasing scene; who had been accustomed to contemplate, every thing which is "awfully vast, or elegantly little;" and to whom nature had opened her most copious stores of language.

Silliman cited two social evils that prevented Americans from either writing or reading poetry: business and politics. No American is a poet because "every man is here a man of business. So universally is this true, that no American poet, *by profession,* can be found in the list of their literary men." Similarly, no proper audience exists for poetry because of the debasement of public taste: "Party-spirit, and the lust of gain, rule the American nation with such undivided sway, as to engross every passion, and inlist every propensity." Silliman could foresee a time when poets would possess the means for sufficient leisure and when literary taste would improve to the point "that poetry will be so far cultivated and encouraged in America that the fame of American Poets will be equally great, and their names equally respectable, with those of Great Britain." But the time had not yet come.[25]

Silliman's analysis of the American literary scene was echoed dozens of times over subsequent decades by everyone from George Watterston and Samuel Lorenzo Knapp to Cooper and Richard Henry Dana. Behind the analysis, however, is the assumption that poetry (like all the arts) is antithetical to "party-spirit and the lust of gain"—that is, to post-industrial social forms. For most Europeans, America represented the future of Europe, a future they might welcome and embrace or loathe and assail. But at the same time, by one of those paradoxes that seem to govern relations between the Old World and the New, for many Americans, Europe represented the future of America. The United States was, or had recently been, a "primitive" society which in time would develop the social forms of eighteenth-century England.

Such at least was the argument of most Federalists. Perhaps the most forceful expression of this argument was in an address by Fisher Ames, representative from Massachusetts, to the first U.S. Congress, on "American Literature":

> But the condition of the United States is changing. Luxury is sure to introduce want; and the great inequalities between the very rich and the very poor will be more conspicuous and comprehend a more formidable host of the latter. The rabble of great cities is the standing army of ambition. Money will become its instrument and vice its agent. Every step, and we have taken many, towards a more complete, unmixed democracy is an advance towards destruction; it is treading where the ground is treacherous and excavated for an explosion. Liberty has never yet lasted long in a democracy; nor has it ever ended in any thing better than despotism. With the change of our government, our manners and sentiments will change. As soon as our emperour has destroyed his rivals and established order in his army, he will desire to see splendour in his court and to occupy his subjects with the cultivation of the sciences.[26]

This is gloomy indeed; but Ames' Napoleonic vision of the birth of American arts and sciences is merely the most extreme form of what Federalists assumed to be the inevitable progress of American society. One way or another the unstable egalitarianism of the early Republic would have to yield to great concentrations of wealth in a few hands, and a golden age of art would ensue. In the meanwhile, the debased taste of the public made it impossible for the artist to find an audience that would patronize his or her best efforts.

The Republican perspective on the problem of a national culture was quite different, as Alexis de Tocqueville discovered. In assessing the influence of democracy on the intellectual life of the United States, Tocqueville relates the following anecdote:

> When I arrived for the first time at New York, by that part of the Atlantic Ocean which is called the East River, I was surprised to perceive along the shore, at some distance from the city, a number of little palaces of white marble, several of which were of classic architecture. When I went the next day to inspect more closely one which had particularly attracted my notice, I found that its walls were of white-washed brick, and its columns of painted wood. All the edifices that I had admired the night before were of the same kind.[27]

Tocqueville's experience epitomizes early American art. The classical temple of white marble proves, on closer examination, to be a warehouse of painted native brick and wood. The fundamental duality that Tocqueville saw as the consequence of democracy in America—the duality between the weakness of the individual and the strength of the state, between hard-headed practicality and vaunting idealism, between the cramped squalor of private dwellings and the gigantic splendor of public monuments—was inherent in American intellectual life and came eventually to be seen as the prevailing genius of American culture. Another manifestation of Tocqueville's temples was Monticello, the "portico facing the wilderness," in which Thomas Jefferson's own ambiguity was strikingly exposed: "The mind fluctuated between [Monticello's] antithetical meanings, those that were past and reminiscent of the Old World, those that were new in the American vernacular."[28] The classical architecture confronted the American forest and contained American gadgets and curiosities. To contemporary observers, puzzling over the cultural implications of democracy, Monticello and its equivalents seemed a vainglorious effort at forcing America to become a classical nation by imposing Roman form on native materials:

> The poetry at Monticello, in landscape, architecture, and interior decor, was more persuasive than its practical mechanism; the sense of the archaic more powerful than the sense of the modern; the impression of the Old World order and refinement more compelling than the impression of New World life. But the portico, after all, faced the wilderness. There was the riddle.[29]

The riddle of Monticello is traceable to the curious paradox of American radical thought: "Jefferson's radicalism was, like so much of American radicalism, retrospective. He ruled, as Henry Adams had said, with a Golden Age in view; but it was set in the past." The result of this paradox was a shrewd combination of idealism and practicality "in a creative outlook all the world has since taken to be the characteristically American outlook of 'Practical Idealism.'"[30]

The spirit of "retrospective radicalism" and "Practical Idealism" had direct consequences for literary theory. In most of the discussion of the possibility of a national literature, the question addressed is how to utilize American materials in poetry and fiction. The question of form and language rarely arises outside the writings of Noah Webster.[31] For example, Neal Frank Doubleday has shown that between 1815 and 1826 the *North American Review* consistently developed a doctrine for fiction, but the development consisted exclusively of enlarging the body of materials considered suitable for treatment.[32] In 1815 William Tudor recommended colonial history as a subject; in 1818 John Knapp added the Revolution; in 1822 William Howard Gardiner identified three suitable epochs for an American historical romance: those of the first settlements, the Indian Wars, and the Revolution. With the advent of Scott's novels a similar extension was recommended in the treatment of manners. John Gorham Palfry (1817), Edward Tyrell Channing (1818), and Jared Sparks (1825) praised Scott's picturesque topography, provincial characters, and verisimilitude and helped to nourish a nascent realism in American fiction.

The sense that motivated such projects was that America's history constituted a "heroic age" comparable to the classical eras of Greece and Rome. The substance of that heroic age was worthy of preservation, regardless of the form. Rufus Choate, then a Congressman, articulated the prevailing opinion in a lecture on "The Importance of Illustrating New-England History by a Series of Romances Like the Waverley Novels" (Salem, 1833). Every lover of America and every lover of literature would wish for one thing, according to Choate:

> He would wish to see such a genius as Walter Scott, (*exoriatur aliquis*), or rather a thousand such as he, undertake in earnest to illustrate that early history, by a series of romantic compositions, "in prose or rhyme," like the Waverley Novels, the Lay of the Last

Minstrel, and the Lady of the Lake,—the scenes of which should be laid in North America, somewhere in the time before the Revolution, and the incidents and characters of which should be selected from the records and traditions of that, our heroic age. . . . He would wish to see him begin with the landing of the Pilgrims, and pass down to the war of Independence, from one epoch and one generation to another, like Old Mortality among the graves of the unforgotten faithful, wiping the dust from the urns of our fathers,—gathering up whatever of illustrious achievement, of heroic suffering, of unwavering faith, their history commemorates, and weaving it all into an immortal and noble national literature,— pouring over the whole time, its incidents, its actors, its customs, its opinions, its moods of feeling, the brilliant illustration, the unfading glories, which the fictions of genius alone can give to the realities of life.

Choate went on to emphasize repeatedly the historical value of such fictions, and he clinched his point with a reference to Homer: "The Iliad and the Odyssey of Homer,—what are they but great Waverley Novels! And yet what were our knowledge of the first 400 years of Grecian history without them!"[33]

 Unfortunately, the problem of finding an audience for an American historical fiction proved far more complex than Choate's oritund phrases allowed. Too often such attempts as Barlow's *The Vision of Columbus* (1787) proved on close inspection to be, like Tocqueville's temple, composed of painted brick and wood rather than white marble. Further, Choate's enthusiasm caused him to overlook the fact that history is not a fixed business of dates and names but a fluid perspective, subject to differing interpretations, and that those interpretations are shaped by nonrational political allegiances. Cooper's *Lionel Lincoln* excited the people of Boston, where it was set, but all his painstaking research into the battles at Lexington, Concord, and Bunker Hill found no favor in the rest of the country, and the novel was Cooper's first unqualified failure.

 The conflicting literary theories of Federalists and Republicans share a common impulse toward classicism and a common assessment of America's heroic past. In the anxious political atmosphere of the time, however, it was not easy to see how those common elements could be realized in literature. Instead of agreement and applause, writers before 1820 confronted indifference or hostility. Some, like Philip Freneau, endured artistic crises precipitated by political events; some, like Charles Brockden Brown, were forced to take on hack work to survive. In retrospect we can appreciate the characteristic American genius represented by Monticello; at the time the inherent intellectual contradictions were more apparent.

III

In 1766 the trustees of the College of New Jersey (later Princeton), hoping to retain the conservative Calvinist tenor of Jonathan Edwards against the inroads of the Moderate party, invited a Scottish theologian named John Witherspoon to be their sixth president. The trustees had not found a true Calvinist, but in his sturdy way Witherspoon was to transform the intellectual climate of his new country. Over the course of his thirty-six year tenure at Princeton, Witherspoon gave an unchanging series of lectures on Scottish Common Sense philosophy. As a signer of the Declaration of Independence he was a sort of minor hero of the early Republic, and he became "the most admired and even loved of college presidents in the Revolutionary era."[34] His lectures proved popular,[35] and his apostles carried their creed to Harvard, Andover, and Yale. By the second decade of the nineteenth century, the Common Sense philosophy was the dominant mode of American intellectual life in the North.

The triumph of Common Sense philosophy was an important factor in the development of American literature because the overwhelming majority of periodical critics were ministers, lawyers, physicians, or teachers. "In no other period in American history," wrote William Charvat, "has our culture been so completely and directly dominated by the professional classes," and this dominance accounts for what Charvat identified as "the two major characteristics of the criticism of the period: its judicial and its moral tone."[36] The Americanization of Common Sense philosophy was a process of simplification intended to validate republican and Protestant institutions. Special emphasis was given to the moral sense, which "was not a mere sentiment or feeling, but a rational faculty implanted by the creator [and] which made correct judgments in the field of ethics even more trustworthy than in any other." This moral sense validated the perceptions and judgments of the rational being against the skepticism of Hume and obviated the phenomenology of Kant. In theology it was used to reconcile natural religion and revelation; in law it meant that moral obligation rather than tradition or custom was paramount; in political economy it justified laissez-faire individualism.[37] Aesthetically, it meant

> that literature is primarily social, and that the artist must adjust his work to the desires of the established society. This fact alone makes the history of the reception of romanticism in the early nineteenth century comprehensible. It accounts for the rejection of Godwin, Shelley, and Keats; for the partial acceptance of Byron, Wordsworth, and Coleridge; for the complete acceptance of Scott.[38]

Commitment to this concept of literature resulted in a body of criticism that displays regular features. Charvat has summarized them in six basic critical principles.

First, the critic thought of himself as the watchdog of society. His task was to condemn and punish any writer who offended the status quo, and he prescribed measures for the improvement of public taste and literary performance.

Second, literature was not to condone rebellion of any kind against the existing social and economic order. Most critics of the time were allied with the Federalist party and shared its fears of excessive democracy. Godwin, Thomas Paine, Philip Freneau, Rousseau, and Madame de Staël were regularly assailed in the pages of *The Christian Spectator, The North American Review,* and the *Port Folio* for their radical idealism and "depredations on private property."

Third, literature was not to contain anything implicitly or explicitly derogatory to religious ideals or moral standards.

Byron's private life (but not his poetry), Thomas Moore's "coldly voluptuous" verse, and the novels of Fielding and Sterne were all condemned.

Fourth, literature was encouraged to be optimistic, and it certainly was not to condone philosophical pessimism or skepticism. Gloom was considered dangerous to the social order; cheer, conducive to social health. Charvat emphasizes the point: "This admittedly American principle has not been given its proper importance as a critical force."

Fifth, literature was to deal with the intelligible, not the mystical or obscure. Of course, the definitions of "intelligible" and "mystical" gradually changed, but the effect of this principle was to discourage innovative or visionary writing. Wordsworth and Coleridge were marginal cases, but Shelley and Keats were beyond the pale.

Sixth—and in this principle is the basis for all the others—literature was to be social in point of view, not ego-centric.[39]

There may have been other consequences of the spread of Common Sense philosophy as well. Tocqueville had noted the tendency of American writers to avoid the particular and individual in favor of the general and universal.[40] Benjamin T. Spencer has argued that this tendency derives from the influence of the Common Sense philosopher Lord Kames:

> By Kamesian doctrines American modes and materials were suitable only so long as they conformed to that "standard of taste" common to all nations; American idiom was admissible only to the extent that it moved within "certain inflexible laws." . . . Intimidated by these canons, many a native writer turned away from his own experience and milieu toward the abstract plane of universals.[41]

Whether the source of this tendency is democracy itself, or the philosophy that democracy adopted and modified to its own ends, or (as Anne Bradstreet's nightingales suggest) the pressure of a vast body of traditional literature on the products of colonial writing hardly matters. The principle of generality was as important as the principles Charvat summarizes. Cooper, reassessing *The Pioneers* in 1832, found its scenes and characters somewhat too particular and asserted that in fiction "delineations of principles and of characters in their classes" are preferable to "a too fastidious attention to originals."[42]

Such were the critical principles that ruled the quest for a national literature. Ordinarily, we might question their impact on writers; too often the reception of a work seems to have nothing to do with the kinds of reviews it gets, and a general condemnation on moral grounds can propel a book into bestsellerdom. The peculiar circumstances of intellectual life in early nineteenth-century America, however, generally prevented any such thing from happening. The critics were moral and intellectual leaders in their communities, not "professional critics." The book-buying public (as opposed to the book-renting public) consisted of people very much like the critics in social standing, education, and opinion. There was no American author with a reputation that could weather bad reviews, and cheap British reprints with supporting raves from the *Edinburgh Review* and *Blackwood's* were readily available. In the anxious atmosphere of the quest for a national literature, the moralistic critics, backed by the diffusion of Common Sense philosophy, enforced their principles relentlessly.

IV

Howard Mumford Jones has referred to the circumstances of publication as "the threefold tensions of public production":

> the judgment of the author in creating the work and submitting it for publication; the judgment of the publisher both of the aesthetic or philosophic importance of the manuscript and of its potential sales; and the judgment of the reading public, expressed in opinion and purchase, on the validity of the work as amusement, edification, or illumination.[43]

At the center of this triad is the publisher, on whose professional competence everything else depends. The history of publishing in America is complex, but it is also crucial to the growth of American society; Benjamin Franklin is one of our first cultural heroes, and it is significant that his career of invention, statesmanship, philosophy, and *belles lettres* began in a printshop. The self-image of the new nation was created and confirmed in the printed word.[44]

Before 1820 there were no publishers as such in America. When William Cullen Bryant published *Poems* in 1821 he had to pay for the printing of it, pay a "publisher" a commission for handling it, and allow bookstores to take it on consignment. Bryant's publisher was a bookseller in Boston. As a dealer he believed it more profitable to monopolize sales than to sell to other dealers in the same city at a discount. The result was a very narrow distribution of *Poems:* of 750 copies retailing at 37½ cents, only 270 were sold in two years.[45] Whatever his qualities as a poet, Bryant was the victim of the limitations of publishing in his time. The key factors in the limitations of the book industry in 1820 were localized publishing, transportation, the absence of international copyright, and financial arrangements among authors, printers, distributors, and sellers.

Localized publishing was the regular practice of the time. Thomas Paine's *Common Sense* appeared in forty-six separate editions in the eighteenth century. Exactly half of these appeared in New England, but only two were published in Boston; Providence and Newport each published four. There were also twenty-three separate editions of *Charlotte Temple* published in New England between 1794 and 1840; of these, two were issued in Boston compared to thirteen in Hartford.[46] Clearly, publishing was very much a local industry, and publishers considered their markets to be very small.

Similarly, writers generally published wherever they happened to live, but this often meant that the circulation of their works would be minuscule. Such was the case with Royall Tyler, who had the misfortune to live in Walpole, New Hampshire. A more dramatic example is that of John Neal, a man with boundless faith in his talent as a novelist, who made a fateful decision in

1827. He had just returned from England and intended to settle in New York, but he went first to Portland, Maine, to see his mother and sister. When local wags tried to drive him out of town, the belligerent Neal determined to stay, and there he remained until his death in 1876. Neal's literary production in Portland was extraordinary: he founded and edited *The Yankee* magazine, wrote several novels and tales (including *Rachel Dyer*), lectured on everything from Christian redemption to women's rights, tried his hand at a play, and encouraged the young Edgar Allan Poe with friendly reviews and letters. Yet he died, and remains, in almost total obscurity. Margaret Fuller struck the proper note in a letter to Neal when she called him "a great man of a little town" who would have few distractions "except such trifling divertisements, such as attending Portland sidewalks, chastising inhuman teamsters, [and] prosecuting the study of Phrenology, Magnetism. . . ."[47]

From time to time ambitious publishers tried to devise plans that would overcome the decentralized nature of their industry. In 1800 a few of the larger publishers in the country (Mathew Carey and Benjamin Franklin of Philadelphia, Hugh Gaine of New York, and Samuel Hall, Greenleaf & West, and Thomas & Andrews of Boston) began to issue catalogues of their own publications and those available from other firms. The same year a letter was circulated among the major publishing houses; it proposed that they enter into a "Company of Stationers of North America" and cooperate in refraining from issuing competing editions of classics and popular works:

> The present State of the morals of Booksellers in the United States requires something of this kind to keep them honest, punctual & willing to serve each other. If in process of time Men should grow better, there would be no occasion for associations. We must fit ourselves and our institutions to the times, since we cannot alter the Manners and Morals of Nature in a sudden.
>
> I am told that in general 500 copies of any book will pay the expenses and a decent profit, if so, what a vast number of books must be reprinted if booksellers would only be punctual and honest to each other.[48]

An association called "The American Company of Booksellers" was actually formed in 1802, and for a few years it succeeded in creating an atmosphere of cooperation, but it could not withstand the competition from publishers outside the Company:

> The less important and more remote publishers produced large editions of popular works on cheap paper and with worn and broken type, with which, by means of the exchange [i.e. of stock between different booksellers], they flooded the country. Naturally the more prominent publishers, the leaders in the company, who had in many cases good editions of these books on hand, soon withdrew, and the movement collapsed.[49]

Between 1800 and 1810 over half the native fiction published in America was issued outside New York and Philadelphia; between 1840 and 1849 the figure was only eight percent. The centralization of publishing that these figures represent was largely the result of enterprising publishers who took advantage of the transportation facilities of those two cities. Before the thirties and the advent of railroads, transportation of goods was almost exclusively by water (stagecoach was faster, but far more expensive). Any mercantile center required a deep port for coastal shipping and one or more navigable rivers for shipping into the interior. Thus Boston, the oldest intellectual center in the country, did not become a major publishing center until the fifties, when the railroads connected the city to the rest of New England: "much of the famous New England flowering before 1850, took place, as far as publishing was concerned, in New York and Philadelphia."[50] Navigable rivers and canals opened huge new markets in the West and South, markets that not only fueled the economic boom that began in the twenties but also became an important source of profits in the book trade. Because the waterways were closed in winter, seasonal publishing became an important practice. Poor timing could cause a book to fail:

> Cooper hurried his London publishers so that the sheets of his novel *The Bravo* would get to [Mathew] Carey during the summer of 1831. But the American edition was delayed until November 29, and Carey wrote him the following January, "*The Bravo* has been much

liked, but the unfortunate close of our navigation immediately after it was published has prevented it from reaching over half the interior towns and has affected its sale."[51]

Access to interior markets not only resulted in the centralization of publishing in the New York-Philadelphia axis, it also brought about a reciprocity between provincial readers and urban writers that was unique to America. The concentration of literary talent and its audience that was the norm in London, Paris, or Rome never existed in America. Instead, writers and publishers had to consider a market that extended from New York to Louisville. *Graham's Magazine* paid James Russell Lowell less for his poetry than it paid Longfellow and Bryant because, as George Graham explained to Longfellow,

> [Lowell] is well known in New England and appreciated there but has not a tythe of the reputation *South* and *West* possessed by yourself and Bryant. This of course I *know*—it is no guess work, for with a thousand exchange papers scattered all over the whole Union I should be a dolt in business not to see who is most copied and praised by them.[52]

As publishing became a centralized business in the New York-Philadelphia axis, taste became decentralized (and perhaps democratized) and publishers increasingly sought to exercise control over their authors' writing to insure popularity, as the careers of Poe, Hawthorne, and Melville amply illustrate.

The absence of international copyright meant that American publishers could issue editions of English novels without paying royalties; it was a highly profitable operation. In May 1826 Mathew Carey's cost book showed a projected profit of $2,306.55 on an edition of 9,000 of Scott's latest novel, *Woodstock*. Each two-volume set of the novel sold for 75 cents. The following winter Carey published Cooper's *Red Rover*. The first printing of 5,000 copies sold at $1.50 per set, and Carey's profit after royalties was $93.00.[53] Even so popular an author as Cooper was a financial liability to an American publisher, and when the young Longfellow wrote to Carey in 1828 to propose an Irvingesque "Sketch Book of New England," Carey turned him down on the grounds that the lack of international copyright had made original books unprofitable: "so much so, that it appears to us there is less inducement for writing now than ten years since."[54] American writers competed on unequal terms with the English for an American audience: American works cost twice as much at the bookstore, and the reception of English novels was prepared for by their popularity in England. It was a condition that galled every American novelist from the time of Charles Brockden Brown until 1891, when an international copyright law was at last passed.

Financial arrangements among authors, printers, distributors, and sellers also affected the distribution of American books. The essence of the problem was the rate of discount a publisher could offer to booksellers, and since the discount determined the seller's profit margin, it materially affected his willingness to handle a work.

In 1829 Carey printed a list of his prices to the trade: Scott's, Disraeli's, and Moore's works were discounted at from 50 per cent to 66⅔ per cent—Cooper's oldest works at 50 per cent, a later one at 40 per cent, and two new ones at 25 per cent. In Boston, the situation was even worse. A 20 per cent discount on American works was common, and in the early forties Emerson decreed discounts as small as 10 per cent on some of his books. It is small wonder that the reputation of many New England writers before 1850 was local: booksellers outside the area could not make a reasonable profit on their books.[55]

Financial arrangements for native works were so tight that very little advertising was done. Promotion was generally limited to free copies of new works to newspaper editors, who duly provided a "notice" for each such work. Only if the author or publisher had a friend on the staff of the paper could he count on a longer notice (known as a "puff"). Otherwise, the book had to make its own way in the world, even though the power of advertising was known: Winifred Gates, who sold Carey's books in Raleigh, North Carolina, on commission, wrote him in 1800 that although his last shipment to her had been a "very unsaleable one," she would "immediately advertise them, by giving the Title of each Book in the Paper, and if anything will sell them this will."[56] Before 1820 no publisher had sufficient capital to work advertising into his budget.

Every condition of American publishing and distribution in the early nineteenth century served to constrict a writer's access to an audience and to dictate the direction of his or her creative work. The effort involved in accommodating or circumventing these conditions was no trivial affair for aspiring writers. On the contrary, it was for the most part inextricably bound up with the creative process, if by "creative process" we mean the conscious effort to write for an audience.

The dilemma of the early American writer was manifold. The expectations for a republican culture were high and generated lofty ambitions; the prevailing American culture was a chimerical amalgam of classical forms and native materials, a blend that was puzzling at best, and at times, hilarious; critical theory was conservative, moralistic, and stringently enforced; and the conditions of publication made it doubtful whether even the most talented author could find and maintain an audience or survive on earnings from his or her writing. The blighting effect of the dilemma can best be seen in the career of Charles Brockden Brown, the most ambitious and productive of American novelists before Cooper.

CHAPTER TWO

The Failure of
Charles Brockden Brown

On March 14, 1798, the Philadelphia *Weekly Monitor* carried an announcement of and an extract from a new novel entitled *Sky Walk, or, The Man Unknown to Himself. An American Tale* by "a native and resident of this city." The announcement posited three goals for the American novelist: first, he must spurn the argument that America is immature and that American art must consequently be immature as well; second, he must treat America's "ecclesiastical and political system," and its "domestic and social maxims" as distinct from their European equivalents in order to "lay some claim to the patronage of his countrymen"; finally, he must write not merely to amuse "the idle and thoughtless" but to satisfy those who seek "lofty eloquence," the "exhibition of powerful motives, and a sort of audaciousness of character." The audience he seeks is, in fact, in the very forefront of American cultural and political development: "The world is governed, not by the simpleton, but by the man of soaring passions and intellectual energy. By the display of such only can we hope to enchain the attention and ravish the souls of those who study and reflect."[1]

The writer was Charles Brockden Brown. *Sky Walk* was never published (Brown's Philadelphia publisher fell victim to the yellow fever epidemic of 1798), but Brown's program for that first attempt served as the basis for all his fiction. He never gave up hope of winning an audience—the simpleton as well as the man of soaring passions and intellectual energy—for a mature, indigenous American novel. His failure to accomplish this goal has often been seen as an epitome of the dilemma of the early American novelist. Max Schultz sees Brown's failure as the result of his "recoil from some bleak implications of fanaticism and bloodlust in the national character." Paul Witherington argues that "Brown simply found that imagination was revolutionary, that it threatened the values of benevolence he wanted to preserve." William Hedges notes that at the center of Brown's work "there exists an ambivalence or ambiguity so deep and intense that it seems partly pathological," an ambivalence that Hedges locates in the "culture of contradictions" of Federalist America. Michael Bell has recently argued that the plots and narrative strategies of Brown's first four novels trace his development away from his early championing of the imaginative power of fiction, "the deviant, theoretical radicalism of his youth," toward a skeptical Federalism and a "renunciation of the ravishing power of fiction."[2] That Brown's fiction embodies a profound ambivalence is undoubtedly true, but it is questionable that this ambivalence is the cause of Brown's failure to find an audience or of his subsequent decision to abandon the novel as a form. Brown insisted on the moral potential of fiction, and both his failure and his renunciation were largely circumstantial. His rejection of a legal career in favor of a career as a man of letters, the conditions in which he wrote and published, his lack of any adequate conception of an audience in his writing, and his failure to find an appropriate method for marketing his work are all factors that must be considered if we want to understand the disappointment of Brown's ambition to become America's first professional man of letters.

I

The story of Brown's unhappy tenure as a law student is well known. At the outset he seems to have been convinced that the law offered the perfect outlet for his talents and aspirations. He led a "law-society" and became known among his fellow students for the "acuteness and copiousness of his arguments."[3] In an essay published anonymously in 1789 (his first year as a law student) Brown hinted at his current occupation in glowing terms: "My ambition has already devoted me to the service of my country, and the acquisition of true glory."[4] Despite this early enthusiasm, however, Brown was poorly suited to the law. His Quaker upbringing had had little effect on his sense of religious duty, but it had left him with an almost fanatical regard for the plain truth. The same early essay that revealed his ambitions also displayed his moral earnestness:

> I speak seriously, when I affirm that no situation whatsoever will justify a man in uttering a falsehood. . . . My scruples in this respect, have been ridiculed by my friends, as absurd and extravagant, and I am well aware that it is a common weakness of the human character to wander into extremes; but I am also sensible that we are much less liable to depart from the true medium in favor of the truth, than of falsehood.[5]

As we shall see, his three years of immersion in the language of legal documents convinced him that the law constituted a vast system whose essence was the deliberate suppression of the plain truth.

In addition, Brown had already committed himself to imaginative writing. Before settling on a career in law, Brown had sketched plans for three epics—on the discovery of America and the conquests of Peru and Mexico.[6] His first known contribution to a periodical was published on February 26, 1789, shortly after his eighteenth birthday, in *The State Gazette of North Carolina.*[7] It was a poem addressed to Benjamin Franklin, but as Brown recorded in his journal,

> The blundering printer, from zeal or ignorance, or perhaps from both, substituted the name of Washington. Washington therefore stands arrayed in awkward colors; philosophy smiles to behold her darling son; she turns with horror and disgust from those who have won the laurel victory in the field of battle, to this her favorite candidate, who had never participated in such bloody glory, and

whose fame was derived from the conquest of philosophy alone. The printer by his blundering ingenuity made the subject ridiculous. Every word of this clumsy panegyric was a direct slander upon Washington, and so it was regarded at the time.[8]

It is tempting to discover in every aspect of Brown's career an allegory of the fate of the American writer simply because he stands at the threshold of the American Renaissance, but the fate of his effusion to Franklin is altogether too exemplary to resist. An aspiring young writer turns away from the standard subject of American poetry to seek a broader cultural awareness in Franklin, the printer, man of letters, ambassador, and philosopher; but the poet's quest is sabotaged by another printer, who insists on substituting the trite figure for the fresh one and who thereby transforms the eulogy into a satire. The episode is an uncanny foreshadowing of the forces that would frustrate Brown throughout his career.

The full extent of Brown's uneasiness regarding his legal studies emerges in an abortive epistolary romance, nine installments of which he published in the Philadelphia *Weekly Magazine* from April 21 to June 2, 1798. The letters are exchanged between Henry D——, a young man studying law in Philadelphia, and his sister Mary in Burlington, New Jersey. In her first letter Mary chides Henry for his snobbery and remarks that a tailor or an usher "rank as high on the scale of utility as he whose business it is, instead of enlightening, to perplex and bewilder the human understanding—as he who makes a trade of weaving together subtleties and sophisms calculated to mislead the consciousness of justice implanted in every human being"—i.e., as a lawyer.[9] Henry is provoked to a defense of his choice of the law as a career; he reminds Mary that she recommended it to him:

It was the road to honor, you said. Men annex different degrees of respect to different occupations. The highest degree has been annexed to the law. The qualifications and exercises which it requires from its pupils are wholly intellectual. It is a science, and the investigation of truth is always delightful to ingenuous minds. It was the regulator of the claims and conduct of men in society. It was the instrument of wealth, and wealth was not to be despised by us whether we be studious of our own happiness or that of others. It is the shortest and safest road to the possession of power, and power must be desireable by bad men for its own sake, and by good men for the sake of the beneficial employment of it. Nothing more common than the transition from the province of interpreting to that of enacting laws. This then was the suitable road whether reputation, riches, or power were the object of our search. (p. 108)

Yet Henry has to admit his own difficulties with the law as a subject of study. It is very far from representing the working of plain truth:

A fortnight's reading can give me no information as to the merits or demerits of the *trade*. It shews me, in a slight degree, of what materials the *science* is composed. They are sufficiently refractory and rugged. Wrapt up in barbarous jargon, a spurious and motley compound of obsolete French and Latinized English. My poor head has been honored by you, with the epithet of metaphysical; but as skilful a dissecter as I am of complex ideas, and as nice a weigher of abstruse distinctions, I fear I shall never untie legal knots or disenvolve from this maze my already bewildered understanding. (p. 109)

Mary returns an explanation that is meant to calm her brother's anxieties, but the explanation itself is broadly ambivalent. In a perfect society the innate sense of justice would rule, she argues, and lawyers would be unnecessary, but since no perfect society yet exists, there must be lawyers. "The conduct of individuals is regulated by institutions whose written language is, to a large majority, without a meaning. It is therefore unquestionably *right* that some one should be capable of interpreting it to them" (p. 112). Since lawyers are necessary, the best we can hope for is that they be men like Henry:

You, my brother, possess splendid talents, and your integrity is founded on a broad basis. You excel in those graces of person and address which are so peculiarly advantageous to the orator. The emoluments arising from this exercise of your talents will, I trust, in our hands, be employed in the promotion of beneficial purposes. For you, therefore, and such as you, the profession of the law is eligible. (p. 113)

It is clear that Mary regards lawyers as a necessary *evil*, and Henry's reaction to her reasoning is heavily ironic. He finally proposes that they close the subject for a year so that he can learn enough about it to judge it objectively. However, he immediately reverts to his studies, and it appears that he will never learn enough law to judge it at all. Not only does he harbor doubts about the moral basis of legal language, but he also finds it impossible to curb his intellectual energies to the task at hand:

> I find vigorous efforts are necessary to keep my attention from straying from a page, which seems to me replete with frivolous subtleties and injurious distinctions. When my task is finished with the day, it leaves me listless and melancholy. I perceive that I have retained little of the day's reading, and am haunted by a kind of presentiment that what is wearisome to-day will be still more so to-morrow, and will at length become insupportable. (p. 116)

In this state, Henry begins to take an interest in the story of a Miss Beddoes and her relationship with three sisters who apparently are prostitutes. It would seem that Brown proposed to make Miss Beddoes the central figure in a tale of seduction, though the novel breaks off at this point. In Henry D—, Brown created a portrait of his own apostasy from the legal profession—a young man who abandons law for the imaginative appeal of a tale which he must learn indirectly, gradually, through his own powers of detection. In addition, it appears that Brown intended to make Henry's curiosity the agent for the salvation of his sister, who has already begun to respond to the charms of a Mr. Beddoes (she draws a fascinated verbal portrait of Beddoes' face in a passage that prefigures Clara's reaction to Carwin's face in *Wieland*). In Mary and Henry, Brown represented the bifurcation of the imaginative and the rational powers of a single mind; their debate over the moral basis for legal rhetoric embodies the terms of his own, internal debate, and Henry's apostasy to his chosen profession would evidently have resulted in his redeeming Mary, the image of his own imaginative capacity, from the blandishments of another in Brown's gallery of "double-tongued deceivers," for Beddoes is an early version not only of Carwin but of Welbeck in *Arthur Mervyn* and of Ormond.

The significance of Brown's rejection of the law and of legal rhetoric is that it was bound to offend the critics of his day, many of whom were practicing lawyers and virtually all of whom subscribed to the political and religious orthodoxy that gave early nineteenth-century criticism its judicial and moral tone, as William Charvat has shown (see chapter 1 above). William Hickling Prescott, for example, found Brown's rejection to law troubling enough to devote two pages of his sixty-four page article on Brown's life for Jared Sparks' American Biography series to a refutation of Brown's criticism of the legal profession, and he notes with satisfaction that "from one of his letters in later life, he appears to have clearly recognized the value of the profession he had deserted. But his object was, at this time, to justify himself in his fickleness of purpose, as he best might, in his own eyes and those of his friends."[10] For Prescott, himself trained in the law, the rejection had to be retracted before Brown could be given the friendly treatment that his biographical essay includes. Brown's contemporary readers, denied the benefit of the retraction, must have found his attacks on legal rhetoric too radical to be in good taste.

II

Between 1792 and 1798 Brown worked for his father's hardware business and devoted himself to literature. His plans were formidable, but his accomplishment was something less. He began a "Philadelphia novel" in 1795 but abandoned it after fifty pages because the style was "feeble and diffuse."[11] In 1796 he began and abandoned two political narratives, "Sketches of a History of Carson" and "Sketches of a History of the Carrils and Ormes."[12] In 1797 he left unfinished a dramatization of a novel by Robert Bage, *Hermsprong*. As Harry Warfel notes, "His trunk was crammed with unfinished manuscripts."[13] Throughout this period of apprenticeship Brown was encouraged by the friends he had made when a student: Elihu Hubbard Smith, a physician and the editor of *American Poems* (1793), and William Dunlap, a dramatist and theater manager. Smith became the leading spirit of the "Friendly Society" of New York City, a group that met from 1793 to 1798, when Smith died. In addition to Brown and Dunlap its membership included James Kent, the future Chancellor of New York, Samuel Latham Mitchill, a scientist at Columbia College, and Samuel Miller, a leading Presbyterian minister. Together this circle read Condorcet, Volney, Mary Wollstonecraft, and Godwin. Most were deists and were devoted to the principles of the Revolutionary Enlightenment; Smith especially admired Godwin's *Political Justice,* a work that certainly left its mark on Brown's writing. Yet nearly all the Friendly Society were Federalists; Smith "distinguished between democracy in general (in its pure Godwinian form), and 'the common idea of democracy which prevails in the United States (i.e. anarchy).'"[14]

Between 1793 and 1798 Brown spent long periods in New York with Smith and Dunlap, reading them his works in progress and attending meetings of the Society. In 1797 Smith encouraged Brown to send something to Joseph Dennie, then editor of *The Farmer's Weekly Magazine,* on the grounds that Dennie might be willing actually to pay Brown for his work. On August 7, 1797 Brown sent Dennie *Alcuin,* parts 1 and 2. When Dennie failed to respond, Smith had the work published at his own expense on April 27, 1798. Brown, meanwhile, had already begun printing *Alcuin* serially in the *Weekly Magazine* of Philadelphia (March 17 to April 7, 1798). On March 17 the *Weekly Magazine* also carried Brown's advertisement for *Sky Walk.* Apparently *Sky Walk* was actually set in type when the death of the publisher caused the project to be dropped. Thus Brown's first books have a curious history—one suffering a double birth, the other stillborn. Either because of his dissatisfaction with the Philadelphia publishing scene or because the yellow fever soon would reach epidemic proportions there, Brown left Philadelphia for New York in July 1798. He brought with him the opening chapters of a new novel: *Wieland.* This time Smith was able to sell Brown's work to Hocquet Caritat, owner of a circulating library and bookshop.[15]

Caritat was one of those colorful characters who enliven the history of the early republic. A distant relative of Condorcet and a citizen of France, Caritat set out for America to make his fortune in 1792. Immediately his wife denounced him to the authorities, evidently in order to obtain a quick divorce and possession of his property. In the meantime Caritat's trade in New York and Philadelphia netted him enough profit so that he was able to purchase a sloop, the *Polly of Hudson,* on June 6, 1793, and to outfit it as a privateer, renamed *Le Republicain,* for the purpose of raiding British sea traffic from American ports. The sloop was issued a letter of marque by the French minister in America, Citizen Genet. Unfortunately for Caritat, Washington had declared American neutrality in the French-British war, and *Le Republicain* was seized at the direction of Secretary of War Henry Knox. The whole affair generated great excitement in the United States and provided the instance many Federalists had been seeking to repudiate the French Republic. Genet was expelled from the country, the pro-French party was embarrassed, and Caritat spent over a year in the courts trying to recover his investment.[16]

Caritat had already made a connection with a staunch republican and disciple of Paine: John Fellows, a Yale graduate and proprietor of a bookstore that served as a center of republican sentiment in New York. In June 1793 Caritat and Fellows opened a circulating library in Water Street. It was to be "devoted to the propaganda of the new liberalism." The business prospered enough to allow Caritat to return to France in 1795, but he was detained there for two years by the legal tangles resulting from his wife's denunciation. When he finally came back to New York in 1797 he found that the circulating library had fallen on hard times, at least partly as a result of the poor economic conditions created by England's war with France. He purchased the library's stock from Fellows, and on May 1, 1797, he opened at 93 Pearl Street with "about twenty-five hundred volumes, five hundred of which were chiefly novels added in less than a fortnight before the opening."[17]

This heavy infusion of novels signaled the beginning of Caritat's campaign to overcome the prevailing prejudice against novel reading. There were two primary tactics in the campaign: first, to convince readers that novels were not only pleasurable but profitable to read, and that they had a *bona fide* educational function; second, that novel reading was after all respectable and not merely a lower-class pleasure. To the first end he published a catalogue for his library, the *Repository of Useful and Entertaining Knowledge,* in order to "prepare the reader for an easy choice of his books, and a suitable disposition to relish and be pleased with them."[18] By 1800 the new title of Caritat's catalogue reflected his library's comfortable popularity: *The Feast of Reason and the Flow of the Soul* was the new catalogue, and its appearance was in itself a publishing event in New York.

Even more important for the success of his enterprise was Caritat's determination to lift the circulating library out of the sleazy atmosphere of its beginnings. Pearl Street was known as a good place for business, but the population lived in slum conditions, and the smell arising from outdoor privies, fish stalls, and the East River gave the street a reputation as a breeding ground for yellow fever. On May 1, 1798, Caritat opened at a more fashionable location, 153 Broadway, near the City Hotel, St. Paul's Church, and a new theater. The better surroundings encouraged new business, as did Caritat's offer of special rates for subscribers who lived outside the city. During the epidemic of 1798 Caritat was able to keep his library open and made special arrangements to deliver books to city inhabitants who had fled to farms or villages in the surrounding countryside.

All these measures brought Caritat considerable success. From his initial 2,500 volumes the library had grown to 5,500 by July 1799; in addition, he had opened a bookstore, most of whose stock was also available for borrowing by library patrons, so that a total of twenty thousand volumes was in circulation. By comparison, the Columbia College library, which of course was not open to the public, owned 2,249 volumes in 1800, and the private Society Library had some 6,500 volumes.[19] Caritat had succeeded in establishing his library as a center of decorous novel reading and literary taste during a period of plague and economic depression.

For these reasons, Caritat's circulating library attracted the attention of the Friendly Society, and many of the circle were known to Caritat personally. It was perhaps natural that at the time of Brown's decision to move to New York and devote himself entirely to writing, Smith should approach Caritat with a proposal to publish *Wieland*. William Charvat has remarked with some irony, "Closely associated with Caritat, Brown must have acquired the illusion that there was a commercial future for the author of novels as well as for the distributor, and Caritat must have shared the illusion—for he published and advertised at his own expense Brown's *Wieland* and *Ormond*."[20] But Caritat had already proved that a market indeed existed for novels in America if only readers could be assured that they were behaving decorously, and after his library and bookshop had become so profitable, publishing an original novel must have seemed a logical next step. On the basis of the chapters then complete, he agreed to publish *Wieland*.

Exactly how much of *Wieland* was complete when Caritat undertook its publication is not known; Dunlap had first heard of the novel in a letter Smith showed him on March 29, 1798, and when Dunlap visited Brown in Philadelphia on April 12 he noted merely that *Wieland* was substantially under way.[21] After Brown's move to New York the novel was still incomplete; on July 19 Smith read eighty-four pages of manuscript, and as late as July 22, the day before the first installment went to the printers, Dunlap read a "continuation" of the unfinished novel.[22]

On July 23, 1798, Brown delivered the "greater part" of *Wieland* to Thomas and James Swords, Caritat's printers. Brown received fifty dollars at that time and was to receive "the rest" of his money upon delivery of "the remaining sheets."[23] In the next month Brown continued to write even as he was correcting proof, which was returning from the printers with remarkable speed and regularity. Dunlap found Smith and Brown correcting the first gathering of twelve pages on July 25, only two days after the manuscript had been delivered.

As Joseph Katz notes, Brown's agreement with Caritat involved an investment of time and energy the budding author may not have anticipated: "His cost was the need to function primarily as producer rather than as artist," and the physical details of the printing placed severe restrictions on Brown's creative freedom. The consequences for the final form of *Wieland* were enormous. As Katz has shown, the formal defects which critics were to note and deplore for the next 180 years were the direct result of the control Brown surrendered in his arrangement with Caritat:

> Since the printer must have had most of the extant manuscript after 23 July, and retained it until at least 5 September, and since the rush of time probably did not permit Brown to copy for himself new material before he sent it to the printer, seriatim composition and proof correction by the forme meant that he never had access to the entire book at any time after printing began. One clue to his having only memory to rely on for early details of the novel is the confusion in the names of Major Stuart's wife for which he has been criticized: before her marriage she is "Louisa Conway" and after it she is "Lady Jane Conway." Under the circumstances, the wonder is not that he blundered but that he blundered so little.[24]

An additional difficulty arose from the fact that the Swords' shop was a small one—two presses and six to eight hands—and generally had more work than it could easily handle. Katz therefore concludes that the Swords must have followed the common practice of the time: a complete book could not stand in type at once; rather, when the compositor received corrected proof, he would make the indicated corrections and release the forme to the pressman, who would immediately print the number of sheets required for the edition and then redistribute the type. It was impossible for Brown to revise earlier sections of the novel to conform to later changes in creative intent. He could not even make substantial changes in proof as he read it without the risk of upsetting subsequent gatherings that were already in the printer's hands.[25] Whatever creative decisions he made after July 23 necessarily appear as disjunctions in the final text. The two most notable examples are the Maxwell-Stuart material and Clara's *postscriptum* to attain a happy ending, both of which have often drawn critics' fire. Alexander Cowie is particularly harsh:

> It seems very likely that the last "ten or twelve" page addition was the ill-fated last chapter (27), in which after burning down Clara's house and tying up loose ends regarding herself and Pleyel and

Carwin, Brown has Clara ramble on about the Stuart-Maxwell im-
broglio, for the ostensible reason that it too needs to be wrapped
up. As if himself aware of how little relevance any of this had, Brown
jams Maxwell's "evils" in with Carwin's to point the concluding
moral.[26]

Cowie's tone is unfair to Brown, who was after all struggling hero-
ically to accomodate his creative vision to the mechanical forms
imposed on him by the means of production. Nevertheless, the
defects undeniably are there: as Katz puts it, "The justification
required by an episode that no longer had a place in *Wieland*
ruined the novel."[27]

III

What are the qualities of the work Brown produced in
these less than desirable conditions? On September 3, 1798, Brown
wrote the "Advertisement" that serves as his preface to *Wieland.* He
chose to emphasize the following points: 1) the necessity of a
popular reception for his work; 2) the veracity of his portrayal of
ventriloquism; 3) the veracity of his portrayal of Wieland's mental
disturbance and its consequences; 4) the epistolary form and the
pre-Revolutionary setting of the novel. The first and last sentences
of the "Advertisement" promise further works from Brown's pen,
"which the favorable reception of this will induce the Writer to
publish" and which "will be published or suppressed according to
the reception which is given to the present attempt." This direct
appeal to the reader's patronage is accompanied by guides for
reading the work: "The incidents related are extraordinary and
rare," but they are *real* for all that. "It is hoped that the intelligent
reader will not disapprove of the manner in which the appearances
are solved, but that the solution will be found to correspond with
the known principles of human nature." Ventriloquism is rare but
is supported by historical evidence; Wieland's delusions may seem
impossible, but "the Writer must appeal to Physicians and to men
conversant with the latent springs and occasional perversions of

the human mind." Besides, "most readers will probably recollect an authentic case, remarkably similar to that of Wieland." These delusions may also be rare, but "If history furnishes one parallel fact, it is a sufficient vindication of the Writer." In other words, Brown is hinting at sensational incidents in the novel in an effort to arouse the browsers' interest—here we have the Gothic mode made real, powers and perversions on the margin of the actual— yet at the same time he is concerned to keep his seriousness of purpose in the reader's view: "His purpose is neither selfish nor temporary, but aims at the illustration of some important branches of the moral constitution of man." The sensational is here not for the usual purpose—to exploit the popular taste for the Gothic—but "because it is the business of moral painters to exhibit their subject in its most instructive and memorable forms."[28]

It is clear from the treatment he gives them that Brown expected the public interest in ventriloquism and in Wieland's delusion to be high and controversial. In the "Advertisement," in footnotes to the text, and in the 1801 review of *Wieland* he reverts to these and to the elder Wieland's spontaneous combustion as if clarifying the public's understanding of them were the key to securing the broad acceptance he sought. An interesting corollary is his stress on the epistolary form of the novel. He seems not to have anticipated at all the sense of claustrophobic obsession and demonic brooding that most readers have taken from the novel. These qualities are powerful enough to have generated doubts about Brown's own ability to believe in the moral quality of his fiction, doubts that constitute the modern orthodoxy in Brown criticism. Paul Witherington may be taken as a representative reader:

The titles of Charles Brockden Brown's novels suggest the steps backward his fiction took from 1798 to 1801, and the failure of his plan for an American literature. The mythic sounding *Sky-Walk* is lost to us today. . . . *Wieland* and *Ormond,* the next novels, offer romance and exotic singularity. *Arthur Mervyn* and *Edgar Huntly* take up everyday names, which *Clara Howard* and *Jane Talbot* turn toward the women's market, Brown's last effort to come to terms with fiction. There was no failure of imagination. Brown simply found that imagination was revolutionary, that it threatened the values of benevolence he wanted most to preserve.[29]

In *Wieland,* Witherington argues, Carwin's ventriloquism adumbrates both the disjunction between appearance and reality and the "seductiveness of art. Ventriloquism represents the pose of fiction itself, the split between author and actor, doubleness in point of view and tone. Mimicry, Carwin's other talent, represents the artist's ability to copy reality. Together—Carwin never separates them—they form the artist's paradox of distance (the 'thrown' voice) and involvement (mimesis)." Carwin, then, is the irresponsible artist who precipitates tragedy through the well-meaning but misdirected exercise of his powers. The writing of *Wieland* alerted Brown to the paradox at the center of his art and frightened him back to more conventional modes of fiction.[30] Thus the descending curve of Brown's career: Carwin's renunciation of his ventriloquism foreshadows Brown's eventual renunciation of fiction.

The teleological reading of Brown's career depends upon assumptions that are possible only in the twentieth century. Our interest in the novel as a major literary form, for example, leads us to regard *Jane Talbot* as Brown's farewell to literature. In fact, however, Brown gave up the writing of novels because he couldn't earn a living from it. As editor (and principal writer) for a series of magazines between 1800 and 1810 he went on writing fiction as well as fact; he remained a man of letters until his death. The existence on library shelves of the six slender volumes of Brown's novels blinds us to the remarkable quantity of writing he produced in his short life.

Yet his project for an American novel certainly failed. Further, Brown undeniably gives serious consideration to the moral implications of art in *Wieland.* His tormented renunciation of his law career indicates that he could not have taken the role of artist in society lightly. The primary clue to his judgment of the artist, however, does not lie in Carwin alone. If we follow the guides in his "Advertisement" we find not one but three artists in

Wieland: Wieland himself and Clara, as well as Carwin. One function of the novel is a comparative assessment of each of these as artists; within the symbolic structure of the novel, Carwin and Wieland are literally reduced to silence. The artist whose voice remains and who communicates with the reader is Clara.

Certainly Carwin's personal magnetism, the limitless power of his voice, and his boundless curiosity (after all, he is a voyeur, not a rapist) are attributes of the artist. He speaks of his power in the way we might expect to hear an artist speak: "I have handled a tool of wonderful efficacy without malignant intension, but without caution" (p. 198). Further, he is motivated by the same feelings as at least some artists; he speaks of the "rooted passion which possesses me for scattering around me amazement and fear" (p. 209) and explains why he leads Pleyel to believe in Clara's duplicity in the same terms: "I must fly; but let me leave wonder and fear behind me" (p. 209). When he admits the consequences of his deceptions, he draws a "black catalogue" of effects that would be the envy of many a novelist:

> I had inspired you with the most vehement terrors: I had filled your mind with faith in shadows and confidence in dreams: I had depraved the imagination of Pleyel: I had exhibited you to his understanding as devoted to brutal gratifications and consummate in hypocrisy. The evidence which accompanied this delusion would be irresistible to one whose passion had perverted his judgment, whose jealousy with regard to me had already been excited, and who, therefore, would not fail to overrate the force of this evidence. (p. 211)

It is tempting to see Carwin as Brown himself and to see Brown's notion of the artist in that moment when Clara looks down the stairs and sees Carwin's weirdly distorted face while behind her a disembodied voice cries, "Hold! Hold!"

Equally certain, however, is the judgment passed on Carwin by the symbolic moral scheme of *Wieland.* Confronted by Wieland in Clara's bedroom Carwin is doomed to a condition that is fatal to the artist: speechlessness. "Carwin, irresolute, striving in vain for utterance, his complexion pallid as death, his knees beating against one another, slowly obeyed the mandate and withdrew" (p. 220). Ultimately, he is banished to a bucolic life in a remote district of Pennsylvania, virtually under a vow of silence: "The innocence and usefulness of his future life may, in some degree, atone for the miseries so rashly or so thoughtlessly inflicted" (p. 239).

But Carwin is not the only artist in *Wieland*. As Michael Butler points out, the tale of the elder Wieland that is related in the first two chapters of the novel prepares the reader to understand him as a frustrated artist.[31] Wieland is a relative of Christoph Martin Wieland (1733–1813), a novelist and poet, but his station in life has denied him the opportunity for wide education or acquaintance with art:

> He did not hold his present occupations in abhorrence because they withheld him from paths more flowery and more smooth, but he found in unintermitted labour, and in the sternness of his master, sufficient occasions for discontent. No opportunities of recreation were allowed him. He spent all his time pent up in a gloomy apartment, or traversing narrow and crowded streets. His food was coarse, and his lodging humble. (p. 7)

In these images of constriction and repression the elder Wieland grows stunted, and he soon begins to display symptoms of a pathological discontent: "His heart gradually contracted a habit of morose and gloomy reflection. He could not accurately define what was wanting in his happiness. . . . yet every engagement was irksome, and every hour tedious in its lapse" (pp. 7–8). In this state the elder Wieland encounters what is apparently the first book he has ever read, the tract on Camisard theology: "His mind was in a state peculiarly fitted for the reception of devotional sentiments. The craving which had haunted him was now supplied with an object" (p. 8).

The elder Wieland's creative impulse is now released, but only in various oddly constrained and distorted forms: his "art," like his reading of the Bible, must be expressed "through a medium which the writings of the Camisard apostle had suggested. His constructions of the text were hasty, and formed on a narrow scale. Everything was viewed in a disconnected position"

(p. 9). First he remakes himself in the image of his new theology: "The empire of religious duty extended itself to his looks, gestures, and phrases. All levities of speech, and negligences of behaviour, were proscribed" (p. 9). Then he sets out for America to do missionary work, but he pauses long enough to become a wealthy farmer (on the labor of African slaves) and to begin a family. Eventually his sense of duty returns, and he does go out to preach to Native Americans; he suffers enough persecution to satisfy his inner voice, returns to his home and designs the fateful temple. Some time before his death he composes the memoirs which Clara mentions in chapter 9:

> The narrative was by no means recommended by its eloquence; but neither did all its value flow from my relationship to the author. Its style had an unaffected and picturesque simplicity. The great variety and circumstantial display of the incidents, together with their intrinsic importance, as descriptive of human manners and passions, made it the most useful book in my collection. (p. 83)

Brown has represented the elder Wieland as constrained, bound, limited, and distorted in every way; the repressions and distortions that result are a deliberate preparation for his death. The spontaneous combustion seems to be an explosion of the repressed energies he contains. We can best appreciate this strategy on Brown's part by comparing Wieland's death with the circumstances of the source Brown used; significantly, the one respect in which Brown departed from his source is in speculation about the cause of the combustion. Messrs. Merille and Muraire had noted

> that those subjected to such accidents were, for the most part, advanced in years, remarkably fat, and had been much addicted to use of spirituous liquors, either in their drink, or applied in frictions to the body; whence they have concluded, that these people had perished by their whole substance spontaneously taking fire, the principal seat of which had been the entrails or the epigastric viscera, and that the exciting cause was naturally found in the phlogiston of the animal humours, called forth by that of the spirituous liquors combined with the latter.[32]

That Brown omitted all this from a model which he otherwise follows with meticulous care (even to the inexplicable detail of the sensation of a blow on the arm) indicates that for the effects of "spirituous liquors" he has substituted Wieland's own repressed creative energies.

Brown's purpose in dwelling on the story of the elder Wieland is to emphasize the parallels between father and son.[33] Theodore's personality, like that of his father, "bespoke a sort of thrilling melancholy," reports Clara. "I scarcely ever knew him to laugh" (p. 23). Despite the embellishments of literature, Wieland limits himself as severely as his father had:

> the chief object of his veneration was Cicero. He was never tired of conning and rehearsing his productions. To understand them was not sufficient. He was anxious to discover the gestures and cadences with which they ought to be delivered. He was very scrupulous in selecting a true scheme of pronunciation for the Latin tongue, and in adapting it to the words of his darling writer. His favorite occupation consisted in embellishing his rhetoric with all the properties of gesticulation and utterance. (p. 24)

Wieland's education has changed the author, but in fact he is doing exactly what his father did: obsessively remaking himself in the image of a single book. His emphasis on gesticulation and embellishment suggests the qualities Brown despised in legal rhetoric: the employment of means without attention to matter. When Wieland hears a call from God, it is a repetition of the pattern of his father's life.

Again like his father, Wieland composes a memoir, though it is in front of a courtroom rather than on paper. Clara's uncle tells her that Wieland spoke "with significance of gesture and a tranquil majesty which denoted less of humanity than godhead. Judges, advocates and auditors were panic-struck and breathless with attention" (p. 163). Here at last Wieland has become a lawyer, but it is not only his presence that sways people; when Clara has finished reading the deposition, *she finds herself convinced by it:* "surely there was truth in this appeal: none but a command from heaven could have swayed his will; and nothing but unerring proof of divine approbation could sustain his mind in its present elevation" (p. 181).

Wieland is a powerful artist whose energies have been released through his madness, but they are still distorted and constrained by a paradox: so long as he remains mad, he will be serene; if sanity is restored to him, the knowledge of his crimes will drive him mad. When Carwin's last deception does restore Wieland to sanity, he metaphorically fulfills the last element in the pattern of his father's doom: "His eyes were without moisture, and gleamed with the fire that consumed his vitals" (p. 231).[34] He does not spontaneously combust, but he stabs himself in the throat, a gesture in which we may see an image of the failed artist cutting off his voice forever, as when the captured Iago silences himself at the end of *Othello:* "Demand me nothing. What you know you know. / From this time forth I never will speak word" (V.302–3).

Carwin and Wieland represent two images of the artist: the double-tongued deceiver and the inspired lunatic. These images would seem to confirm Witherington's hypothesis that Brown found the creative imagination too threatening to the values of benevolence to be sustained. There is, however, still another artist in *Wieland:* Clara. It is she who writes the novel, in the form of a long letter, and by doing so she attains a degree of self-knowledge and inner peace that both her brother and her father lacked. It is the writing of *Wieland* that allows Clara to escape the hereditary doom of the Wielands.

Clara is perfectly aware that the stories of her father and brother suggest a genetic flaw that she may share. Reading Wieland's deposition, she reflects on "the change which a moment had effected in my brother's condition":

> Now I was stupified with tenfold wonder in contemplating myself. Was I not likewise transformed from rational and human into a creature of nameless and fearful attributes? Was I not transported to the brink of the same abyss? Ere a new day should come, my hands might be embrued in blood, and my remaining life be consigned to a dungeon and chains. (pp. 179–80)

Yet, unlike father and brother, Clara is aware of her creative energies and puts them to positive use. Wieland errs on the side of reserve and melancholy, Pleyel on the side of levity and skepticism, but Clara is irreproachable. Pleyel says,

> I have questioned whether the enchantments of your voice were more conspicuous in the intricacies of melody, or the emphasis of rhetoric. I have marked the transitions of your discourse, the felicities of your expression, your refined argumentation, and glowing imagery; and been forced to acknowledge, that all delights were meagre and contemptible, compared with those connected with the audience and sight of you. (pp. 121–22)

Further, while her father and brother dedicated themselves to the exemplification of a single book in a manner that obviates self-examination, Clara has always kept a journal in which she has habitually tested her own thoughts and action. This is the journal Carwin discovers and of which he says, "You know what you have written. You know that in this volume the key to your inmost soul was contained" (p. 206).

The writing of the long letter which is the text of *Wieland* corresponds to the habit of this journal, for a goodly portion of it is given over to self-analysis. Clara debates her reaction to Pleyel's overtures and accusations in a manner that transforms the conventions of the sentimental novel; she examines the common assumptions of conventional morality, such as the notion that virtue alone is sufficient defense against the possibility of rape; she struggles to understand her relationship to her brother; she tests her own attitude to suicide and death. In all these examples Brown is illustrating the means for developing the conventions of the novel into avenues of moral knowledge. Out of the terror and suffering she records, Clara does finally manage to attain an understanding of herself which is both painful and purging. Before she tells us that she has decided to kill Wieland if he attacks her, she pauses to write,

> Alas! nothing but subjection to danger, and exposure to temptation, can show us what we are. . . . I stand aside, as it were, from myself; I estimate my own deservings; a hatred, immortal and inexorable, is my due. I listen to my own pleas, and find them empty and false: yes, I acknowledge that my guilt surpasses that of mankind: I con-

fess that the curses of a world, and the frowns of a deity, are inadequate to my demerits. Is there a thing in the world worthy of
infinite abhorrence? It is I. (pp. 222–23)

The intense pain of this sort of self-knowledge leads Clara to expect
that when her story is told, she will die, but in fact it is the
preparation for a rebirth. In the *postscriptum* to her letter she
tells us,

> My uncle earnestly dissuaded me from this task [writing her experi-
> ences]; but his remonstrances were as fruitless on this head as they
> had been on others. They would have withheld from me the imple-
> ments of writing; but they quickly perceived that to withstand
> would be more injurious than to comply with my wishes. Having
> finished my tale, it seemed as if the scene were closing. A fever
> lurked in my veins, and my strength was gone. (p. 235)

The fever is the manifestation of the hereditary fire of the Wielands, and Clara lapses into a repetition of her father's passive
waiting for death. But instead a transformation occurs: her house
burns, recapitulating her father's spontaneous combustion, but
Clara awakes from her dream of fire in time to escape its reality.
Only after this purging is Clara at last able to accept both the
events of the past and the knowledge they have brought. "The
memory of the past did not forsake me; but the melancholy which
it generated, and the tears with which it filled my eyes, were not
unprofitable. My curiosity was revived, and I contemplated with
ardour the spectacle of living manners and the monuments of past
ages" (p. 237). Thus the "happy ending" of the novel, for which
Brown has been chastized by so many critics, is integral to the
meaning of the whole. The double-tongued deceiver and the inspired lunatic are condemned to silence, but the honest seeker for
self-knowledge writes on.

IV

On September 5, 1798, Caritat secured the copyright
for *Wieland,* and on September 14 he announced it for sale at one
dollar "handsomely bound" or at twelve shillings "elegantly

bound." The advertisement appeared in at least six New York news-papers (*The Daily Advertiser, The New-York Gazette and General Advertiser, The Spectator, Argus, Greenleaf's New Daily Advertiser,* and the *Commercial Advertiser*), but contrary to Brown's practice in his announcement for *Sky-Walk,* Caritat provided no extracts from the novel and made no attempt to supply any notion of its plot other than quoting Brown's "Advertisement" to the effect that "the incidents related in it [*Wieland*] are extraordinary and rare."[35] In any case there were few New Yorkers interested in new novels; the yellow fever epidemic was at its height, and just one week later Elihu Hubbard Smith, Brown's staunchest supporter through his years of vocational uncertainty, died of it at the age of twenty-seven. Brown himself and another friend, attorney William John-son, contracted a milder form of the disease; as soon as they were sufficiently recovered they fled the city for William Dunlap's house at Perth Amboy, Brown carrying a copy of *Wieland* and the opening pages of a new novel, *Memoirs of Stephen Calvert*.[36] There were few buyers for *Wieland,* and the first review did not appear until November 10, 1798. This review, in *The Spectator,* was apparently the work of one of Brown's associates; it was primarily concerned with the apathetic response to the first published novel of Amer-ica's first professional writer:

> Shall it be said that America, whose citizens have been famed for their superior knowledge and love of letters, were so destitute of liberality, as to refuse or neglect patronizing an attempt like the present? And shall this stigma in a particular manner, rest upon our city, whose commercial intercourse is so extensive, and whose *young men* are so justly celebrated? Forbid it patriotism; forbid it all that has a connection with science and *Amor Patria[e]*.[37]

The reviewer then considered Brown's use of the "powers of ven-triloqution" in the novel and adduced the example of a New Jersey man who could "mimic the tone of almost any individual, and even the sound of musical instruments." After considering the portraits of the characters, he concluded, "we may venture to assert, the writer has established his reputation as a man of genius, tho his bookseller may fail of that encouragement to which he is justly entitled."[38] The tone of this review—an appeal to the patriotism and social conscience of the buying public—would become a familiar one over the next half century of American literary history, but it was no more effective in 1798 than it would be in 1850. The factual basis of ventriloquism, so important to Brown in his effort to bend Gothic means to serious ends, was treated as a kind of sideshow phenomenon and could have sparked little interest. No rush to the bookshop followed the *Spectator* review.

Caritat may have concluded that the yellow fever was responsible for the slow sales of *Wieland;* in any case he did not wait for the novel to sell but went ahead with the publication of *Ormond; or, The Secret Witness.* It was announced as "in the press" on December 19, 1798. Since Brown had committed all his time at Perth Amboy to *Stephen Calvert,* and since he did not return to New York until November 15,[39] *Ormond* was produced in an even narrower time frame than *Wieland.* The day after Caritat's announcement, Brown wrote to his brother James,

> Some time since I bargained with the publisher of *Wieland* for a new performance, part of which only was written, and the publication commencing immediately, I was obliged to apply with the utmost diligence to the pen, in order to keep pace with the press. Absorbed with this employment, I was scarcely conscious of the lapse of time, and when the day's task was finished, felt myself thoroughly tired and unfit for a continuance of the same employment in any new shape.[40]

Caritat, meanwhile, had begun to hatch plans for making Brown a saleable commodity. At his urging, on December 15, 1798, Brown made a dramatic attempt to secure a major endorsement for *Wieland:* he presented a copy to Thomas Jefferson, then Vice President of the United States and the most prominent literary man in the nation. Brown's letter to Jefferson maintains a species of diffident pride in his accomplishment. On the one hand he doubts that a man like Jefferson is disposed to indulge any weakness for "mere works of imagination and invention," supposing that

> this form of composition may be regarded by you with indifference or contempt, that social and intellectual theories, that the history of facts in the processes of nature and the operations of government

may appear to you the only laudable pursuits; that fictitious narratives in their own nature or in the manner in which they have been hitherto conducted may be thought not to deserve notice, and that, consequently, whatever may be the merit of my book as a fiction, yet it is condemned because it is a fiction.

On the other hand, Brown is fully aware that to ask Jefferson to read a book that isn't worthy of being read would be "an uncommon proof of absurdity," and he marks the chief characteristics of the proffered volume as "an artful display of incidents, the powerful delineation of characters and the train of eloquent and judicious reasoning." He hopes that Jefferson will not find the reading time "tediously or uselessly consumed"; but the true purpose of his letter emerges only in his farewell to Jefferson:

> That he will be pleased to any uncommon degree, and that, by his recommendation, he will contribute to diffuse the knowledge of the author, and facilitate a favorable reception to future performances, is a benefit far beyond the expectations, though certainly the object of the fondest wishes of
>
> Charles Brockden Brown[41]

This appeal to the Vice President must have seemed to Caritat and Brown a stroke of merchandising genius. Jefferson himself was a man of considerable cultivation and a prominent author, and the period of his ascendancy was filled with the eager expectation of a flowering of democratic culture; surely he would be interested in promoting that flowering by providing a puff for Brown's novel.

Jefferson's reply was long in coming. His letter of January 15, 1800, is courteous, noncommittal, and (in terms of Brown's aims in *Wieland*) hopelessly old-fashioned in its conventional contrast of history and fiction. Jefferson admitted that he had not had time to read *Wieland*, but

> I shall read it, and I doubt not with great pleasure, some of the most agreeable moments of my life have been spent in reading books of imagination, which have this advantage over history that the incidents of the former may be dressed in the most interesting form, while those of the latter must be confined to fact: they cannot therefore present virtue in the best and vice in the worst forms possible, as the former may.[42]

The extent of Brown's failure to convert Jefferson to the pleasures of novel reading may be measured from a letter the former President wrote to Nathaniel Burwell, March 14, 1818, in which he rehearsed the most common of objections to fiction. Of the "inordinate passion prevalent for novels," Jefferson wrote,

> When this poison infects the mind, it destroys its tone and revolts it against wholesome reading. Reason and fact, plain and unadorned, are rejected. Nothing can engage attention unless dressed in all the figments of fancy, and nothing so bedecked comes amiss. The result is a bloated imagination, sickly judgment and disgust towards all the real business of life.[43]

Caritat's second effort to help Brown reach a wider audience was more realistic, if ultimately no more successful. The subservience of American reviewers to British critical opinion was already well established, and Caritat decided to find an English publisher for Brown's work in the hope that favorable British reviews would stimulate American interest. In April 1800 Brown wrote to his brother James about the disappointment of his ambitions: "the utmost that any American can look for, in his native country, is to be re-imbursed his unavoidable expences"; but he added that "The salelibility [sic] of my works will much depend upon their popularity in England, whither Caritat has carried a considerable number of Wieland, Ormond and Mervyn."[44]

Unfortunately for Brown, Caritat's contact in England was William Lane, a former poultry butcher who had founded the Minerva Press and specialized in sensational novels of seduction and Gothic adventure:

> The form was not a gold mine for the authors—mostly women working in anonymous secrecy—who were paid a flat fee averaging five to twenty guineas per book. As a form which did not have, or which at least had lost, literary status, it attracted few professional-minded male writers to whom prestige was important.[45]

Lane apparently found *Ormond,* with its attenuated treatment of seduction, the likeliest candidate for appeal to the Minerva audience, but its reprinting proved to be an ill-conceived venture. Brown's fiction could hardly hope to compete on its own terms

with ordinary Minerva fare, yet the bare fact of its publisher determined the tone of the August 1800 criticism in *The Anti-Jacobin
Review:* "Are these the deductions of a mind imbued with the
powers of ratiocination?—No! They are effusions of a pragmatic
enthusiast! a mad-headed metaphysician!" The review concluded
with an attack on every aspect of the novel:

> We shall only add, that, *if* a want of perspicuity, *if* a want of elegance
> in style, *if* a want of imagination, *if* a want of incident, *if* a want of
> plot and connection, and, finally, *if* a want of *common sense,* be
> excellencies in a novel, the author of *Ormond, Wieland, Arthur
> Mervyn,* &c. &c. has a fair claim to the laurel of pre-eminence in
> "the temple of Minerva."[46]

That Caritat's British adventure rather retarded than forwarded
Brown's success is confirmed by another British reviewer reassessing Brown's novels in 1820: "it was the fate of those works, when
first reprinted in this country, to issue from one of the common
reservoirs of sentimental trash, and, consequently, (as we imagine)
to share in the general contempt attached to those poor productions, which, like the redundant and needy members of a great
house, have nothing but sounding titles to sustain them."[47] Whatever chance there may have been for favorable British response to
Brown's fiction was effectively negated by the very means Caritat
chose to pursue it.

Brown's third attempt to promote himself resulted
from his alternative career as a magazine writer. In 1799 his
friends in New York helped Brown to begin the *Monthly Magazine
and American Review,* which ran for three volumes, April 1799 to
December 1800. Its successor was *The American Review, and Literary Journal* (1801–1802).[48] In 1801 and 1802 a two-part review of
Wieland appeared in *The American Review.* Scholars have treated it
as another anonymous review,[49] but it is surely, in whole or in
large part, the work of Brown himself. The review is an expansion
of concerns already expressed in Brown's other writings, concerns
to which he frequently returned in later years; it identifies exactly
and quotes from the sources for ventriloquism, spontaneous combustion, and *Wieland's* delusion; it is written in a style which is

unmistakably Brown's; it is an unsigned review in a periodical that Brown may have helped to edit, and he was certainly responsible for book reviews and literary matters for *The American Review.* For these reasons, the review must be read as an exercise in self-criticism and as an attempt to understand the failure of *Wieland* as well as a last effort to arouse public interest in a novel which was by then almost four years old.

The review is prefaced by a consideration of the cultural position of the novel as genre. Its ancestry in the classical and medieval romance has given the novel a dubious reputation, and the review begins with a little *exemplum:* "A Greek Bishop is said to have been the first *romance* writer. His work was condemned by an ecclesiastical synod, as dangerous to the morals of youth; and the author, rather than resign or repress his book, relinquished his bishoprick. This was a proof either of licentiousness in the prelate, or of unreasonable prejudice in his brethen."[50] The moral dangers inherent in the novel form are balanced by the potential for moral instruction:

> No species of composition is more universally read, since none so powerfully excites curiosity and sympathy, the active principles of every human being. Truths inculcated in the more solemn forms of instruction make slighter impressions, and have less influence on the great mass of mankind, than when practically illustrated by examples which come home to the apprehension and feelings of every class of men, and in which every reader, in some degree, finds the sentiments of his own heart and the incidents of his own life, reflected before him. It is not surprising, therefore, that men of deep insight into the springs of human action, as well as rigid moralists, have approved and practiced this mode of teaching virtue. (1:333)

The review goes on to locate the appeal of the novel in "the love of *novelty*": "The bulk of mankind, restless and impatient, seek, in the variety and change of real or imaginary objects, relief from the tedious uniformity of common life." The reader opens his book seeking amusement, but permanent effects were wrought by a text, and a serious writer can use fiction to achieve moral ends: "why should the benefactors of the human race, those who seek to inform, instruct and direct the conduct of men, regard this class of writers with unmingled contempt, and wholly neglect so obvious and popular means of inculcating the principles of morality?" (1:334).

The issues raised here are consistent with Brown's thought as far back as *The Rhapsodist;* more particularly, they are an expansion of the "Advertisement" to *Wieland* and of his letter to Jefferson. To the apology for a moral fiction the self-criticism adds Brown's motive for adopting the Gothic novel: the "great avidity" with which readers devour novels employing "the wonder-working powers of gothic machinery" has induced him to "profit by this love of the marvelous, to display and illustrate some remarkable properties in the physical and moral constitution of man." The use of ventriloquism, a "real but extraordinary faculty," constitutes a "machinery . . . more dignified and instructive than ruined castles, imaginary spectres, and the monkish fictions of modern romance." Still, questions of genre are secondary; more important are the author's "vigorous and creative fancy" and "strong talents for moral description" (1:334).

As these theoretical conceptions suggest, an essential ambivalance toward the audience for the novel runs through the self-criticism. Novel readers are envisioned as having no powers of discrimination whatever, though obviously they read some novels and not others. Their love of novelty leads them to favor gothic machinery, though such machinery is less dignified and instructive than a *real* (but extraordinary) marvel like ventriloquism. The moral benefactors of the human race may adapt the novel to didactic ends, but the public insists on indulging writers interested only in riches and fame. Such ambivalence is hardly surprising in a writer who has (by 1801) published six novels to virtually universal indifference.

Equally notable, however—especially in light of those modern critics who have argued that Brown rejected the psychological and cultural implications of his own fiction—is that he still insists on the possibility of a moral fiction that will "enchain the attention and ravish the souls" of its readers, the aim he expressed in the advertisement for *Sky-Walk.* Thus the review introduces the plot summary of *Wieland* with this sentence: "The principal incidents, however incredible and shocking, are founded on well-authenticated facts, and are sublime and tragical in the highest degree" (1:335). This effectively summarizes the means and goals of Brown's fiction.

The plot summary (complete with extracts) that follows is notable only for the anxiety to establish the factual sources that ground the plot. If the gothic machinery of *Wieland* is to be dignified and instructive, the "one parallel fact" furnished by history must be adduced. Consequently, the reader is supplied with the source for Wieland's homicidal delusion (*New-York Weekly Magazine*, 2:20–28), spontaneous combustion (the *Literary Magazine*, 4:336) and *biloquium,* or ventriloquism (the review reprints verbatim Brown's note in *Wieland,* p. 198n). For the most part this source work is a more explicit version of the hints Brown included in *Wieland* itself. For example, a note in the novel refers the reader to an article in the *Journal de Medicine* for a case of spontaneous combustion without admitting that a far more accessible source exists in English; the review cites and quotes the English language article, demystifying to some extent the authority for that particular marvel. In his attempts to ground his fiction at the margin of the real and the fabulous, Brown evidently discovered that veiled hints are not enough to reach most readers; everything must be made quite plain.

Finally, the self-criticism offers general assessments of *Wieland.* The style is "clear, forcible and correct" (this may be the only kind remark about his style in the history of Brown criticism). The incidents arouse terror and distress; in fact, "Persons of lively sensibility and active imaginations may, probably, think that some of the scenes are too shocking and painful to be endured even in fiction" (2:36). As for the novel's lack of popularity, the answer may lie in the psychological dissection which is Brown's *forte:*

> The soliloquies of some of the characters are unreasonably long, and the attention is wearied in listening to the conjectures, the reasonings, the hopes and fears which are successively formed and rejected, at a moment when expectation is already strained to its highest pitch. These intellectual conflicts and processes of the

imagination show fertility of conception, and the art of the narrator; but this art is too often exercised in suspending the course of the action so as to render the reader restless and impatient. The generality of readers love rather to be borne along by a rapid narrative, and to be roused to attention by the quick succession of new and unexpected incidents. (2:36–37)

In the end there is still the question of the moral instruction which must, according to the definition prefacing the review, motivate the novelist. What is the moral of *Wieland*? It seems impossible to generalize. "Against the freaks of a *ventriloquist*, or the illusions of a madman, no rules can be prescribed for our protection." The example of Wieland may warn us against "the folly of the presumptuous desire which seeks for gratifications inconsistent with the laws of existence and the ordinary course of nature," but then again it may not. The self-criticism's conclusion is remarkably equivocal:

From the exhibition, however, of an infatuated being, deluded by the suggestions of a disturbed intellect, into the commission of acts the most unnatural and horrid, it is doubtful whether any real good is to be derived. But whether benefit or harm, or how much of either is to be received from tales of this kind, we are not prepared to decide, and they are questions not easily solved. The good or ill effect of a book, in most cases, depends on the previous disposition and character of the reader. (2:38)

This conclusion, following on the optimistic arguments of the introductory section of the review, suggests a profound perplexity on Brown's part, as if the more he considered the effect of a work on its reader, the less he understood about it. Part of his difficulty was the lack of a critical vocabulary for talking about the way *Wieland* probes psychic states. There was no way for Brown to discuss the therapeutic effect of writing that Clara experiences and no means for suggesting how such an effect could be transferred to the reader; it did not fall within the scope of eighteenth-century literary theory, since it neither instructed nor delighted the reader in any tangible way. Brown could merely cite his intention to enchain the reader's attention, but without an end in view such enchaining seemed arbitrary, if not pernicious.

This admission was Brown's explanation in 1801 for the poor reception of *Wieland*. Even his candor, however, could not stimulate public interest in the novel, and it continued to sell very slowly. In 1799 Mathew Carey of Philadelphia, the largest book distributor in the country, ordered twenty-eight copies of *Wieland* and forty-two copies of *Ormond* (which is set in Philadelphia and thus had more local appeal). He did not need to reorder until 1803.[51]

V

In 1806 Brown considered the problem of authorship in America once more. By then his novels were well behind him, safely immured in obscurity, and his attitude toward the business of publishing was thoroughly professional. His explanation of the lack of original writing in America ignored all the usual references to immaturity or cultural dependence; he focused on market forces:

> In investigating the state of book-making, in any country, and the causes that encourage or depress it, we are apt in general to refine too much, and to seek the causes of appearances, rather in the constitutional genius of the people, than in the common and obvious circumstances on which the fruits of literary genius and industry, like all other commodities, depend for their abundance and scarcity. Authors will, in fact, be always found, and books be written, where there is a pecuniary recompence for authors, and a ready sale for books, but where any circumstance denies them this reward, or reduces the sale of books, there will necessarily be few authors.[52]

Gone are the appeals to patriotism, the theories about the reader's love of novelty, and the writer's capacity to enchain and ravish. Remaining is a cold vision of economics—the dismal science—and a kind of compassion for the American bookseller, who must say to the American writer, here have I a choice of books from England, the popularity of which is fixed and certain, and which will cost me nothing but the mere expences of publication; whereas, from you, I must purchase the privilege of printing what I may, after all, be unable to dispose of, and which therefore may saddle me with the double loss of the original price and the subsequent expences.[53]

The bookseller is a reasonable man, and no reasonable man will expect him to abandon his caution. The project for an American novel has become a matter of supply and demand.

Brown's career illustrates dramatically the dilemma of the American writer before 1820. Born with a peculiar talent, nurturing lofty ambitions, rejecting a secure legal career to hazard his fortune, possessing helpful and influential friends and an almost limitless energy, Brown nevertheless failed to find an audience for his fiction. His publisher, who had the merchandising genius to establish a circulating library and a bookshop during a time of economic depression and epidemic disease, could not find a buying public for him. Contributing to Brown's failure were six primary factors. First, his attitude toward the law and lawyers offended those who controlled the reviewing press and could have created public interest in his work. Second, the conditions in which he produced and published his novels guaranteed errors and inconsistencies in the texts. Third, the lack of adequate critical vocabulary prevented him from explaining the intentions of his work, intentions which lay far beyond the horizon of expectations of the general reader of 1798. Fourth, the subservience of American reviewers to British critical opinion made it almost impossible to get an American reviewer to venture an opinion on a novel until he had read the British journals. Fifth, Caritat's association with the Minerva press scuttled any potential serious reception for Brown in England. Finally, as William Charvat has pointed out, the economics of a circulating library and the economics of publishing proved to be very different things:

Fiction had low cultural status but a rapidly growing public, especially among women. Most of these women, however, were novel renters, not buyers; and what the novel gained from them, it lost in the many homes where the novel was refused a place on the family book shelves.[54]

Brown's failure was not the result of internal conflicts, psychological tensions, or even a specifically cultural ambiguity in eighteenth-century thought. Rather, his ambitions foundered on social and economic circumstances in the newly independent nation, and on his own inability to imagine an audience other than the idly curious. Only when a way was found to circumvent these circumstances could an audience be found for an indigenous American novel.

CHAPTER THREE

"An American Novel Professedly"

In *Notions of the Americans* Cooper saluted Brown: "One of their [i.e. Americans'] authors of romance, who curbed his talents by as few allusions as possible to actual society, is distinguised for power and comprehensiveness of thought. I remember to have read one of his books (Wieland) when a boy, and I take it to be a never-failing evidence of genius, that, amid a thousand similar pictures which have succeeded, the images it has left, still stand distinct and prominent in my recollection."[1]

At the outset of his own career, Cooper had Brown's failure very much in mind. It would be too much to say that he learned anything concrete from that failure, but it set a gloomy precedent that the ensuing two decades had done little to dispel. It was clear that ambition and genius could not guarantee success in the American market, but it was not at all clear what would.

Almost by accident, Cooper became a novelist, writing for the amusement of first his wife and then an enlarging circle of friends. The private audience urged him to publish; after his first attempt, they urged him to write an *American* book, and so history was made. If this naive traditional account omits everything of importance about the beginning of Cooper's career, it does offer a clue to the essential point of Cooper's early success, for his private audience was a tangible quantity, a specific group of readers whose tastes he strove to satisfy and to cultivate, and Cooper's success was based on his sensitivity to the problem of cultivating an audience. *Precaution* aimed at an audience accustomed to the works of Amelia Opie, Hannah More, and William Wilberforce. The only certifiably "American" quality to the work is a vein of suppressed violence which attends the hero's attempt to create himself anew, without father or property, in order to win the hand of the fastidious heroine. *The Spy,* an "American novel professedly," employs the same set of characters, the same central plot, and the same high moral tone as *Precaution,* but the earlier novel's latent violence manifests itself in the Revolutionary War setting of *The Spy.* Cooper worked to expand his original audience's horizon of expectations while attracting new readers by adopting the historical romance, transferring his setting from England to America, and adding ethnic and regional characters. In addition, Cooper acted as his own publisher for his first novels, and gradually he learned enough about the trade to realize substantial profits.

I

The beginning of Cooper's career as a novelist is justly famous, but the bits of information we have do not easily assemble into a coherent picture. Susan Fenimore Cooper herself told the story three times with varying emphases.[2] Her second account is the best known:

> A new novel had been brought from England in the last *monthly packet;* it was, I think, one of Mrs. Opie's, or one of that school. My mother was not well; she was lying on the sofa, and he was reading this newly imported novel to her; it must have been very trashy; after a chapter or two he threw it aside, exclaiming, "*I could write you a better book than that myself!*" Our mother laughed at the idea, as the height of absurdity—he who disliked writing even a letter, that he should write a book!! He persisted in his declaration,

however, and almost immediately wrote the first pages of a tale, not yet named, the scene laid in England, as a matter of course.[3]

The story is more tantilizing than informative. Maurice Clavel points to three apparent paradoxes that it generates: that a gentleman farmer who "avait horreur de tenir une plume" and who at age thirty had never written anything should become the most prolific of American novelists; that the novelist of the forest and sea should have begun with "un roman de société à intention moralisante"; and that an American who had only been in London for a few days' leave from his ship should have written a novel that was taken in England for the work of an Englishman.[4] A fourth paradox is that a man who had been expelled from Yale College, had been sent to sail before the mast by his displeased father, and had spent the subsequent ten years of his married life in Westchester County and at a country "seat" on Lake Otsego should have had any adequate concept of an audience for whom he was writing; a fifth is that, having written, he should have found a publisher for his work at a time when the American publishing industry was chaotic at best.

The resolution of most of those paradoxes lies in the background that Cooper brought to his writing. He was better educated than the expulsion from Yale might suggest. In 1801 he boarded with the Reverend Thomas Ellison in Albany. There he was required to memorize long assignments in Virgil, and his roomate, William Jay, recalled that he and Cooper used to quote from memory whole dialogues from the *Eclogues*.[5] His unruliness at Yale stemmed from his relative youth (he was twelve at enrollment) and from boredom (he was far better prepared in Latin than his classmates). After blowing up another student's door with gunpowder, Cooper was expelled. He spent the next year in Cooperstown with a private tutor, the Reverend William Neill, who recalled that the boy "cordially disliked hard study . . . [and] was extravagantly fond of reading novels and amusing tales."[6]

By 1820 Cooper had gone far toward establishing himself as a public man. He was active in the Otsego Bible Society, was one of the founders of the American Bible Society (in 1816), and was a founder and the first corresponding secretary of the Otsego

County Agricultural Society (1817). More importantly, he had pre-
served his taste for the strange mixture of reading represented by
Virgil and "novels and amusing tales." Susan Fenimore Cooper has
described his frequent family readings: on the one hand, Shakespeare, Pope, Thomson, and Gray; on the other, Wilberforce,
Hannah More, Byron, Edgeworth, Scott, and Opie (see chapter 1
above).

   Thus Cooper had unusual resources to draw on when
his wife's challenge came. He may indeed have had a horror of the
pen, but he was certainly not unacquainted with it. Mrs. Cooper's
challenge was to write a better novel than "one of Mrs. Opie's or
one of that school," and his daughter says that "he aimed at a close
imitation of the Opie School of English novels."[7] Though he had
no first-hand knowledge of English society, he knew it well
through his wide reading.

   Our fourth paradox is resolved in the same way.
Cooper's daughter reports that he "resolved to imitate the tone and
character of an English tale of the ordinary type."[8] In so doing,
Cooper inherited a very definite *implied reader.* The implied reader
is, in Wolfgang Iser's definition, "a network of response-inviting
structures, which impel the reader to grasp the text": "the concept
of the implied reader is a transcendental model which makes it
possible for the structured effects of literary texts to be described."[9] Walter J. Ong has described the same concept less tran-
scendentally; Ong argues that the concept of an audience is a
convenient fiction that the author nurtures, consciously and unconsciously, in the supremely lonely business of writing a book:

> How does the writer give body to the audience for whom he writes?
> It would be fatuous to think that the writer addressing a so-called
> general audience tries to imagine his readers individually. A well-
> known novelist friend of mine only laughed when I asked him if, as
> he was writing a novel, he imagined his real readers—the woman
> on the subway deep in her book, the student in his room, the
> businessman on vacation, the scholar in his study. There is no need
> for a novelist to feel his "audience" this way at all.[10]

Instead the writer imitates a voice from an earlier book, hoping
that with the voice will come the audience for that book:

If the writer succeeds in writing, it is generally because he can fictionalize in his imagination an audience he has learned to know not from daily life but from earlier writers who were fictionalizing in their imaginations audiences they had learned to know in still earlier writers, and so on back to the dawn of written narrative. If and when he becomes truly adept, an "original writer," he can do more than project the earlier audience, he can alter it.[11]

Just as an author must construct, clearly or vaguely, an implied reader, an audience cast into some sort of role (e.g., the "reflective sharers of experience" who listen to Conrad's Marlowe), so the reader has to play the role cast for him. Ong analyzes the opening paragraph of Hemingway's *A Farewell to Arms* and shows that phrases like "the late summer of *that* year" and "across *the* river and *the* plain to *the* mountains" engage the reader in the role of "tight-lipped empathy based on shared experience" despite the fact that none of Hemingway's readers knows that year, the river, the plain, or the mountains.[12]

When Cooper determined to adopt "the tone and character of an English tale of the ordinary type," he was as well adopting an implied reader. Cooper himself seems to have been perfectly clear on this point. Before attempting to publish *Precaution* he read it to a gathering of friends and family at the Jay residence in Bedford:

> There was a Miss McDonald, a friend of the Jays staying with them at the time; she declared the book quite interesting, but it was not new; "I am sure I have read it before," she declared—this the author considered as a complimentary remark, as he had aimed at close imitation of the Opie School of English novel.[13]

What higher praise could Cooper ask than the sense that "I have read it before"? It is the ultimate validation of his attunement to his chosen audience.

From the perspective of its orientation to its audience, *Precaution* deserves some reconsideration. It has long been acknowledged that, whatever the book he flung down in disgust may have been, the model Cooper chose to imitate in his first novel was Jane Austen's *Persuasion*.[14] Characters, incidents, and the whole development of the plot of *Persuasion* reappear in *Precaution;* the very titles suggest a close relationship. Both the similarities and the differences between the two novels are important for an understanding of the beginning of Cooper's career.

The central family of *Precaution* is lifted intact from Austen's novel. Cooper presents an English baronet (Sir Edward Moseley), his wife, and their three daughters (Clara, Jane, and Emily). The narrative concerns the problem of marriage for the three daughters. Clara, the oldest and least imaginative of the three, marries safely early in the plot. Jane, influenced by her complacent mother, is ambitious for rank and wealth; she becomes engaged to a Colonel Jarvis but is later jilted by him and ends in abashed spinsterhood. Emily, the youngest, has been brought up completely by her father's sister, Mrs. Wilson, and so is replete with the title quality, "precaution." Emily falls in love with a George Denbigh, suppresses that love when it becomes clear that Denbigh is not who he claims to be, and at last marries him when his true identity is at long last revealed (he is the Earl of Pendennyss). In all these characters and circumstances there are echoes of Austen's Sir Walter Elliot, his daughters, Elizabeth, Anne, and Mary, and Anne's friend and counselor, Lady Russell. More important for Cooper than these echoes, however, is that the Moseley family will be carried over to *The Spy, The Pioneers, Home as Found,* and *The Deerslayer.* In *The Spy* the (largely superfluous) mother and oldest sister have been eliminated, but the other characters remain. Sarah Wharton is taken with British rank and wealth, ignores the advice of her aunt, and falls in love with Colonel Wellmere, who proves to be a bigamist. Frances Wharton follows her aunt's advice and, after the temporary misunderstanding caused by the appearance of Isabella Singleton, marries Peyton Dunwoodie. Mr. Wharton, with his "natural imbecility of character," is an avatar of Sir Edward Moseley:

> Nature had not qualified Sir Edward for great or continued exertions, and the prudent decision he had taken to retrieve his fortunes was perhaps an act of as much forecast and vigor as his talents or energy would afford; it was the step most obviously for his own interests, and the one that was safest both in its execution

and consequences, and as such it had been adopted: but, had it required a single particle more of enterprise or calculation, it would have been beyond his powers, and the heir might have yet labored under the difficulties which distressed his more brilliant but less prudent parent.[15]

Yet in adopting Austen's characters and plot, Cooper was not aiming at her audience. The first paragraph of *Persuasion* defines the implied reader very clearly:

Sir Walter Elliot, of Kellynch-hall in Somersetshire, was a man who, for his own amusements, never took up any book but the Baronetage; there he found occupation for an idle hour, and consolation in a distressed one; there his faculties were roused into admiration and respect, by contemplating the limited remnant of the earliest patents; there any unwelcome sensations, arising from domestic affairs, changed naturally into pity and contempt, as he turned over the almost endless creations of the last century—and there, if every other leaf were powerless, he could read his own history with an interest that never failed—[16]

The deft irony of this paragraph defines Sir Walter's character, but it does so only insofar as the reader assents to the role Austen projects. We must share a rather lofty amusement at a man for whom the Baronetage has replaced the Bible; we must disapprove of Sir Walter's inability to cope with domestic affairs and laugh at the fastidiousness of "unwelcome sensations"; we must see and condemn the narcissistic infatuation with "his own history." The reader's sense of heightened perceptions and ironic detachment are essential to Austen's fiction.

Cooper intended something quite different. After reading several works by Mrs. Opie, Hastings concluded that "*Precaution* is in no sense any imitation of any of her tales,"[17] but Hastings was looking only at characters and plot. When Cooper proclaimed that he "aimed at a close imitation of the Opie School of English novels," he meant it. Mrs. Opie's fiction had an established audience,[18] and her tales were aggressively moral:

Sometimes she shows the calamities resulting from lying, from temper, from improper education, and again the happy results of doing one's duty, controlling one's temper, and honouring one's parents. It is seldom that Mrs. Opie leaves her readers to draw the moral themselves. . . . Usually there are numerous signposts.[19]

Her tales typically involve the gentry or nobility, avoid extended descriptions of indoor or outdoor settings, pivot on some current debate in social or political ideas, and fairly wallow in the eighteenth-century cult of "sensibility."

All these qualities prevail in *Precaution*. Even where Cooper has apparently lifted an episode wholesale from *Persuasion*, he transforms it into an Opie mode. In *Persuasion* Anne Elliot discusses poetry with Captain Benwick, a young man whose fiancée has died and who has immersed himself in the poetry of Byron and Scott. Austen treats the scene with her usual irony; the young people debate the poet's standing, "trying to ascertain whether *Marmion* or *The Lady of the Lake* were to be preferred, and how ranked the *Giaour* and *The Bride of Abydos;* and moreover, how the *Giaour* was to be pronounced." Anne objects that poetry is "seldom safely enjoyed by those who enjoyed it completely; and that the strong feelings which alone could estimate it truly, were the very feelings which ought to taste it but sparingly." She, "feeling in herself the right of seniority of mind," recommends that Benwick undertake "a larger allowance of prose in his daily study" to provide him with the "strongest examples of moral and religious endurances." Benwick obediently writes down the titles she recommends, but Anne leaves amused by her own preaching and reflects that "like many other great moralists and preachers, she had been eloquent on a point in which her own conduct would ill bear examination."[20] Austen's attitude toward Scott and Byron may remain in doubt, but her amusement at Anne's moralizing does not.

Cooper's Emily Moseley is not in the least amusing; she would never moralize on a point where she was herself weak. "It might be said Emily Moseley had never read a book that contained a sentiment or inculcated an opinion improper for her sex or dangerous to her morals" (*Precaution*, p. 137); her intentions in reading are extremely chaste: "Emily seldom opened a book, unless in search of information; or if it were in indulgence of a less commendable spirit, it was an indulgence chastened by a taste and judgment that lessened the danger [of "the irretrievable injury to be sustained from ungoverned liberty" in reading], if it did not entirely remove it" (*Precaution*, p. 217). Emily's sister Jane, lacking their aunt's careful guidance in reading, enjoys the poetry of Thomas Moore until an evening when a woman she detests praises it. Then she throws Moore's poetry into the fire:

> "Oh!" cried Jane, "I can't abide the book, since that vulgar Miss Jarvis speaks of it with so much interest. I really believe Aunt Wilson is right in not suffering Emily to read such things." And Jane, who had often devoured the treacherous lines with ardor, shrank with fastidious delicacy from the indulgence of a perverted taste, when it became exposed, coupled with the vulgarity of unblushing audacity. (*Precaution*, p. 87)

This is remarkably strong language for a novelist who seems to have admired Moore's poetry enough to use it often for epigraphs to his later works, but it embodies the attitude toward poetry that Mrs. Opie's audience expected. In *Temper, or Domestic Scenes* (1812) her heroine, Emma, reflects on poetry and adultery after seeing the tomb of Abelard and Eloisa:

> When Mr. Egerton first read aloud to me the poem whence Mr. Varley quoted those fine lines, I was charmed by the beauty of the verse, and interested for the sorrow that it expressed. But when I found that it was the sorrow of unlawful love, and not of a virtuous wife separated by force from a virtuous and beloved husband, that the writer too was a woman not ashamed of her error, but glorying in it, and preferring the title of mistress to that of wife, while the poet had only given more power and notoriety to her own profligate prose by clothing it in the most seducing poetical language, I lost the deep interest I originally felt for the eloquent nun, and can, I confess to you, gaze on this tomb with as much indifference nearly as on that of the mistress of Henry the Second.[21]

The seductive power of beautiful language must always be resisted in Mrs. Opie's novels of purpose, and Cooper assumed the same moral posture in *Precaution*.

In addition to the high moral tone of the Opie school, Cooper also adopted the characteristic theme of the novel of purpose. All of Mrs. Opie's tales illustrate the effects of proper or improper education on young women. The essential business of the Opie school is the dissemination of Lockean principles of education. In the typical Opie tale an ineffectual father, stripped of the authority of patriarchal institutions, struggles to inculcate in his daughters some moral quality or idea—truthfulness, temperance, obedience—that will insulate them from the seductive evils of the social world. His success or failure depends on the consistency and rationality of his efforts rather than on his authority as a parent. Often an aunt will take one daughter in hand and raise her in a manner that creates the desired principle, while the father impotently struggles with the other daughters. The novel of purpose isolates and formalizes one of the central anxieties of eighteenth-century British culture: the apparent threat to traditional social institutions represented by the erosion of parental authority. In *Precaution* Cooper presents an ineffectual father, a superficial mother, and an exemplary aunt. The mother's ambitions for rank and wealth leave one daughter susceptible to seduction; the aunt's good sense arms the youngest daughter with "precaution." With its family as a microcosm of the social body, *Precaution* belongs to the efforts to redefine Protestant culture in the wake of the European revolutions that began in 1640 and to the rise of individualism and capitalism that transformed England into a modern class society.[22]

Cooper's success at adopting the sententious moralizing of the Opie school has had a predictable side effect: hardly anyone who takes fiction seriously has been able to endure reading *Precaution*. William Cullen Bryant, eulogizing Cooper in 1852, confessed, "I have merely dipped into this work." In careful deference for the late writer, Bryant declared himself "not unwilling to believe what is said of it, that it contained a promise of the powers which its author afterward put forth." With understandable pride, Hastings records his decision "to join that noble band, the chosen few, who have actually read *Precaution*."[23] The reader who approaches it as Cooper's first work will find little to engage him.

Approached in the context of the Opie school, however, *Precaution* yields some surprises. There are traces of a suppressed violence that is foreign to the frail sensibilities of the domestic novel. On three occasions an alien world of mortality and madness intrudes on the genteel world of the Opie school. These intrusions are important both as indications of what Cooper's imagination transformed from the Opie novel and as precursors of Cooper's subsequent development of an indigenous American fiction.

The three episodes all involve George Denbigh, the incognito Earl of Pendennyss. On one level each serves as a mechanism for the exposition of Denbigh's character; on another, each is an event in the metamorphosis of George Denbigh, whose background is a cypher, into the Earl of Pendennyss, whose character satisfies all the requirements of Emily Moseley's precaution.

The first episode introduces Denbigh to the novel. The parish rector's son, himself newly ordained, is delivering his first sermon in his father's church. He speaks on "the hope, the resignation, the felicity of a Christian's death-bed"; the congregation is entranced by his eloquence until they are startled by "a sudden and deep-drawn sigh" that fixes their attention on Denbigh and his father: "The younger stranger sat motionless as a statue, holding in his arms the body of his parent, who had fallen that moment a corpse by his side" (*Precaution,* p. 82). The ghoulish irony of the death takes first place in the village gossip and cloaks Denbigh in mystery. He is the first in a long line of orphaned sons in Cooper's fiction—sons who knowingly or unknowingly set about the task of recovering "authority and genealogy"[24] for themselves. Denbigh enters the world of *Precaution* as a devoted son, yet fatherless; with a name, yet without an identity.

The second episode is Cooper's version of the "accident" that decisively affects the course of love. In *Persuasion* Louisa Musgrove falls and hits her head; she has to stay at Lyme for two months of recuperation, during which her attraction to Captain Wentworth fades and she becomes engaged to Captain Benwick. As a result, Anne Elliot's love for Captain Wentworth is free to revive. Cooper's accident is far more melodramatic. John, Emily's brother, points a gun he thinks unloaded at her and pretends to shoot her:

"Hold!" cried Denbigh, in a voice of horror, as he sprang between John and his sister. Both were too late; the piece was discharged.

> Denbigh, turning to Emily, and smiling mournfully, gazed for a
> moment at her with an expression of tenderness, of pleasure, of
> sorrow, so blended that she retained the recollection of it for life,
> and fell at her feet. (*Precaution*, p. 183)

Denbigh becomes delirious when fever sets in; he repeatedly
speaks Emily's name, but he also speaks of "his poor deserted
Marian," begs her forgiveness and promises never to leave her
again. In the succeeding month of his convalescence, Emily fails
in love with Denbigh, but the mystery of poor deserted Marian
prevents her from surrendering to her feelings. At the end of the
month Sir Edward Moseley is distressed by Denbigh's pending
departure, and he proposes to adopt the fatherless son:

> "Mr. Denbigh, I could wish to make this house your home; Dr. Ives
> may have known you longer, and may have the claim of relationship
> on you, but I am certain he cannot love you better, and are not the
> ties of gratitude as binding as those of blood?" (*Precaution*, p. 196)

Cooper would repeat the accident of the playful wound
in a simpler yet even stranger form in *The Pioneers*.[25] In *Precau-*
tion the episode serves to further the love plot, but the aggression
implicit in Denbigh's wounding and the arbitrary offer of adoption
are remarkable elements. They are, of course, soundings of Denbigh's unknown character: will he shrink from the gun, as Captain
Jarvis did? Will he accept Sir Edward's proposal in order to stay
illegitimately close to Emily? But within the imaginative development of the novel these are more than tests: they are opportunities
for Denbigh to create his character in the present, to invent his
own authority against his featureless past. Denbigh's success
is highlighted by the parallel career of Colonel Egerton, Jane
Moseley's suitor, who wears the gaudy trappings of authority but
proves to be a seducer, a gambler, and a would-be rapist. Egerton
sprains his ankle at the Jarvis' gate and stays with them a few days
"under the care of the young ladies" (*Precaution*, p. 58). Later, one
day after proposing to Jane Moseley, he elopes with Mary Jarvis
when she unexpectedly comes into an inheritance; that is, he
succumbs to the temptation that Denbigh resists.

The third episode concerns Denbigh's father, mother,
and father's brother. His father (also named George) and his fa-

ther's brother, Francis, had both loved and courted Marian, Lady Pendennyss. George was handsome and lively; Francis was scarred by smallpox and had a melancholy disposition. Marian could not choose between them until Francis was effectively disinherited. She promptly encouraged George, and they were married. The outcome of this miniature drama is a striking scene in which George and Marian seek shelter from a storm at a farm house. During a lull they hear a male voice singing a ballad:

> Oh! I have lived in endless pain,
> And I have lived, alas! in vain,
>   For none regard my woe—
> No father's care conveyed the truth,
> No mother's fondness blessed by youth,
>   Ah! joys too great to know—
>
> And Marian's love and Marian's pride
> Have crushed the heart that would have died
>   To save my Marian's tears—
> A brother's hand has struck the blow,
> Oh! may that brother never know
>   Such madly sorrowing years!
> (*Precaution*, pp. 436–37)

George recognizes the voice of Francis, who has been wandering around the Lake Country for years "with an eye roving in madness." George instantly realizes what he has done to his brother, Marian collapses in guilt, and Francis bursts a blood vessel and dies. Marian takes to her bed, and, though she lives on for seventeen years after the death of Francis, she never leaves her room again. The whole story is revealed to her son in a letter Marian writes him as she is dying. She warns him against self-love, the blandishments of flatterers, and the vice of coquetry, "a kind of mental prostitution" (*Precaution*, pp. 439–40). The tale inspires in Denbigh a "jealous dread of his own probable lot in the chances of matrimony," the dread that has induced him to play the minor imposture that has troubled Emily.

Here again Cooper invents a theme to which he will return in later novels: the two brothers who love one woman recur

not only in, for example, the Effinghams of *Home as Found* but
(slightly modified) in *The Pioneers* and *The Pathfinder*. Always the
more sensitive, more admirable, less comely man loses; often he
goes mad and becomes a poet or a recluse or a solitary hunter. In
Precaution the tale provides Denbigh with a thoroughly mixed
genealogy. Through his mother's letter he inherits her guilt and
his uncle's sensitivity and melancholy as well as his father's complacent good sense. We are supposed to realize that the George
Denbigh we have known has been created specifically to *contain*
the forces that left his uncle raving and his mother bedridden.
Again, Colonel Egerton is a foil to Denbigh; his attempt to rape a
woman whom he encounters in Spain, his gambling and his dis-
solute life result from forces that are concealed but not contained
by his finery and manners.

      The episodes of violence in *Precaution* are more em-
phatic than those of abandoning seducers or intemperate liars in
Mrs. Opie's tales, but the true significance of Cooper's imaginative
use of violence lies elsewhere. For Mrs. Opie, tragedy is a consequence of inadequate parental guidance. Her characters suffer as
the result of poor training, and the message is truly precautionary.
For Cooper, as we have seen, violence is a mode of creating and
defining character. The distinctive quality of Cooper's use of violence becomes clearer if we realize that his purpose is to subject
Denbigh to a series of radical experiences at the extreme limit of
his culture—not, as we might expect in a British novel, to test
Denbigh's socialization, but rather to give Denbigh the opportunity to create an individuality of which he has been shorn by the
circumstances of his entry into the world of the novel. As Richard
Slotkin has argued, "regeneration through violence" is a funda-
mentally American myth of initiation, "the myth of regeneration
through the violence of the hunt," which is the heart of the American literary tradition.[26] Because Denbigh is in fact the Earl of
Pendennyss, all of Emily Moseley's precaution is wasted, and the
novel is not really "about" the consequences of improper training.
Instead, it is about Denbigh's ability to create himself in the violent transitions to which his author subjects him. The suppressed
violence in the novel is the American undercurrent to the British

form, the "immortal serpent," as D. H. Lawrence calls it, "who writhes and writhes like a snake that is long in sloughing"; it is the quality that leads Lawrence to his famous formulation of the figure of Deerslayer: "The essential American soul is hard, isolate, stoic, and a killer."[27]

But in *Precaution* it remains an undercurrent, scarcely disturbing the calm surface of the Opie tone. His intention of capturing the audience of Mrs. Opie's tales governed the writing of the novel, and Cooper had a member of that audience at hand: his wife. "He usually wrote in the drawing-room, and after finishing a chapter always brought my Mother in to hear it," reports Susan. Mrs. Cooper urged him to print the book, but Cooper was uncertain: "my Father had some doubts on the subject, and at last it was decided that if his friends the Jays listened with interest to the reading, the printing should take place."[28] After Miss McDonald's conviction that she had read the book before, Cooper's course was clear.

However, he knew nothing about publishing. On May 31, 1820, having completed thirty-two of *Precaution*'s forty-nine chapters, he wrote a letter labeled "*Most-Strictly confidential*" to Andrew Thompson Goodrich. Goodrich had a bookstore and variety store at 124 Broadway, across from the City Hotel, where Cooper stayed when in New York. He hoped that Goodrich could supply him with all the necessary information for publishing his manuscript.

I commenced the writing of a moral tale—finding it swell to a rather unwieldy size—I destroy'd the manuscript and chang'd it to a novel—the persuasions of my wife and the opinion of my Friend Mr. Wm. Jay—have induced me to think of publishing it—it is not yet completed and the object of this letter is to obtain some mechanical information that may regulate the size of my volumes—I am now writing the eighth Chapter of the second volume—the first contains twenty five Chapters—in the whole volume (i.e. the first) one hundred and twelve closely written pages of about eight Hundred words each—this I compute will make an ordinary volume, such as Ivanhoe, which I took for a guide—of two Hundred and Fifty pages of *matter*—my present plan is to complete the second volume of the same size—What I want to know follows—

Would two Hundred and twenty four pages of manuscript, of eight Hundred words each, and a fair proportion of
conversation make two common sized volumes?

What would be the expense of printing an edition of a
thousand copies—in the style of the Philadelphia edition of
Ivanhoe?—including *commissions* as I must be in the dark—the
novel being *English*.

What would be the probable sales and at what prices of a
respectable moral work of the kind and commissions of sales? What
are printers terms? (*L/J*, 1:42)

The letter reveals much. First, in changing the *tale*
into a *novel*, Cooper had to conform to current practice: in England, novels were printed in three volumes; in the United States, in
two. This format was the norm between 1820 and 1844; in 1841
Catherine Sedgwick remarked that it had never occurred to her
that there could be more or fewer than two volumes in a novel. "In
England, the printing of small novels in two separate volumes, and
longer ones in three, was a product of bookseller collusion to keep
the prices of books high."[29] Such collusion was impossible in
America, but so pervasive was British influence in literary matters
that the word "novel" came to mean a two-volume work, and
Cooper never varied from this norm except by dividing *Afloat and
Ashore* into two two-volume novels. The length of Cooper's works
now seems prohibitive beside the economy of *The Scarlet Letter*,
but it was a part of Cooper's task to fill the two volumes no matter
what his tale.

Second, in appearance if not in matter, Cooper's novel
was already influenced by Scott. Of all the books he might have
chosen as a physical model for his own, he settled on *Ivanhoe*. The
importance of appearance is suggested in a later letter to Goodrich
(June 12, 1820): "I should wish good paper—and a full clear type as
the book [h]as to[o] many imperfections in its matter to disregard
the manner . . ." (*L/J*, 1:43–44).

Third, the financial arrangements were of pressing
concern to Cooper. Cooper's father had left an enormous estate,
but the depression following the War of 1812 had rendered his
lands unsaleable, there were still unsettled claims against the es-

tate, and each of Cooper's four older brothers had died. Cooper undertook not only the management of the estate but the financial responsibilities of his brothers as well; he speculated heavily in land deals of various kinds and in a whaling vessel, but he succeeded only in enlarging his own debt. By 1820 Cooper needed money badly, and publishing was a risk he was willing to venture.

The risk was to be entirely his. He wrote Goodrich that "I wish to use your agency in printing and selling under such terms as we may agree upon—I do not desire to saddle you with my productions at any risk" (*L/J*, 1:42–43). Goodrich could protect Cooper's anonymity and supply technical expertise, but Cooper was in effect his own publisher. He paid the printer, paid Goodrich a commission for handling and publishing and selling, and kept the profits, if any, for himself.

Cooper's desire to publish anonymously had many sources. Some of them are suggested in letters to Goodrich immediately after the printing of *Precaution* was complete. Cooper enjoyed the game of having people guess at the book's author, and he plied Goodrich with suggestions. He would

> not avow it—cannot some use be made of that to induce people to *unsuspect* me of this—I do not believe my being known as the author will hurt the sale of Precaution, but I believe it will hurt its reputation on the whole I am much more sanguine of its success in England than in this country and much more in Boston and Philadelphia than in New-York—(*L/J*, 1:64)

On another occasion he wrote, "If *I* am supposed the author the book will fail in New-York—if Washington Irvine [sic] was thought the writer it would be thought *good*—" (*L/J*, 1:66). Cooper demanded that Goodrich forward any gossip he had gathered: "who has enquired for the Book? And who have mentioned my name? Who else is mentioned as the probable author—" (*L/J*, 1:65). One reason for anonymity was the hope of stirring the kind of public interest in the author's identity that had attended Scott's anonymous novels, and Cooper did as much as he could to encourage that interest.

A second reason is suggested by Cooper's first letter to Goodrich: the hope that the novel would be taken for an English product. Such a course was merely prudent in the Anglophile book market of 1820, and it was consistent with his desire for the established audience for a moral novel. The same concern influenced his thinking about possible reviewers for the book:

> Any one who reviews such a work [should] be a *christian*. . . . I would rather Mr. [William] Jay reviewed than any one else—I read the book to him and to Mr. Aitchison—the latter the best scholar and critic—both *flattered* me I suppose of *course*—but Mr. Jay the most—not that he *said* more than *the other*—but *what* he *said* was more to my *taste*—he *understood me*—one is a christian and the other a Deist— (*L/J,* 1:66)

For the same reason Cooper expected a better reception in England than in America, and in Boston and Philadelphia than in New York.

On June 12, 1820, Cooper wrote Goodrich that he had completed *Precaution* (seventeen chapters in twelve days!); he inquired about paper and type and asked Goodrich how to proceed in obtaining copyright. On June 28 he sent Goodrich the first three chapters of his manuscript. Then began a comedy of errors that ran on until October. Cooper, living at Angevine (his small farm at Scarsdale) entrusted letters and manuscript to a stagecoach driver; proof returned to him in the same way. This procedure itself created anxiety whenever there was any sort of delay: "I wrote you by Davis, the Stage Driver—sending . . . the three first Chapters of 'Precaution'—and have not heard of their safe arrival, Davis leaving them, in charge of your neighbor *Allen*—" (*L/J,* 1:45). Meanwhile, Cooper had other affairs on his mind. The June 28 letter announced that "I have commenced another tale to be called the 'Spy' scene in West-Chester County, and time of the revolutionary war—" (*L/J,* 1:44), and the more he wrote of the new book, the less interested he was in the old one: on July 8 he wrote, "[Precaution] is so—very—very—inferior to the 'Spy' that I have lost most of my expectations of its success—" (*L/J,* 1:48). His whaling ship, the *Union,* arrived at Sag Harbor and Cooper had to turn over to his wife the task of reading proof. In September he expected to be called to the New York State Militia rendezvous, though at the last minute the maneuvers were cancelled.

Throughout the summer and fall Cooper pressed Goodrich to hurry the printing and berated him for the results. Occupied with the writing of *The Spy,* Cooper did not bother to make a fair copy of his manuscript and relied on the printers to make paragraph divisions, convert his habitual long dash into more orthodox punctuation, and tidy up a host of other errors in spelling and usage. He was disappointed to learn that printers make new errors much more readily than they correct old ones. The tone of his letters to Goodrich became increasingly hostile. Returning the first proofsheets, he wrote that the printers "mistake many words" (*L/J,* 1:49). By mid-July he was expressing his awe that "they make not *very many* but such as they are *tremendous mistakes*" (*L/J,* 1:50). The situation deteriorated until, by early September, Cooper was threatening to sue Goodrich: "Things between us, are coming to a crisis that I regret extremely on more accounts than one—But my resolution is taken—I know my rights and will never yield them" (*L/J,* 1:58). Goodrich's proposal that an errata sheet be included with each volume proved acceptable to Cooper, and the book appeared at last on November 10, 1820.

Publication "brought Cooper immediately into the New York literary circle which frequented Charles Wiley's book-shop at 3 Wall Street" (*L/J,* 1:24). It also renewed Cooper's acquaintance with Colonel Charles K. Gardner. Cooper and Gardner had been brother officers in the Navy at Oswego in 1808 and 1809, and Gardner had recently founded a "patriotically inspired" quarterly, *The Literary and Scientific Repository and Critical Review.* The *Repository* carried the first extensive comment on Cooper's fiction in an article that compared *Precaution* with another new work, *Melmoth the Wanderer.* The review's nationalistic bias is apparent from the outset: "We have now before us the last English, and the last American novel; and, startling as it may appear to some of our readers, who are inclined to think nothing praiseworthy that is native, we mean to examine their merits comparatively." After a discussion of *Melmoth* ("these chimeras dire—these feverish imaginations"), the review turns to "the solidity and healthful spirit of Precaution." Almost everything about *Precaution* proves praiseworthy; it is a "didactic novel," but one of subtlety: "Religious principle, without being rendered obtrusive, is assigned the rank it should ever hold in human affairs; and throughout the work, the reader is unconsciously led to acknowledge that 'wisdom's ways are ways of pleasantness.'" The characters are varied and engaging; the dialogues, graceful; the style, "remarkably easy and flowing." In fact, the only flaw in all of *Precaution* is that it isn't long enough: "The author has committed an error—not very common to modern novelists, who lengthen their threadbare stories till their interest is entirely exhausted: the incidents and characters are rather crowded, and might easily have supplied ample matter for another volume."[30] The review concludes by praising the "healthy and proper tone" of *Precaution,* contrasting it with the unhealthy agitation of *Melmoth:*

> We closed Precaution with sentiments of gratitude towards the author. The last scene is admirable; it glows with the best feeling,— and while we finished Melmouth with something of the sensation of waking from an incoherent and feverish dream, we rose from Precaution with those pleasurable thoughts, which the contemplation of a groupe of deserving and happy fellow beings cannot fail to excite. The one causes us to turn sickened with life and living things; the other leaves us calm and satisfied.[31]

Whoever the author of this anonymous review, he was obviously the "christian" Cooper had desired, and he took *Precaution* precisely in the spirit with which it was written. At the same time he ignored the polite fiction that this was an English book; that fiction served Cooper when he was imagining an audience for his work, but it had to give way before the larger purpose of promoting the integrity of American fiction vis-à-vis British. Even Cooper's first novel entered into the national debate. To be sure, the terms of that debate are not promising; the American novel under review is more English than the English. Still, Cooper had made contact with a patriotic literary circle, and later that year he would be convinced to publish *The Spy.*

In February 1821 *Precaution* was printed in England by Henry Colburn. Cooper could not, of course, obtain copyright for it; in 1838 he recalled that "Precaution was disposed of to Mr.

Colburn, by means of the American Publisher, and without my agency, the transfer being made by my consent, however—I presume no assignment was ever made by any body" (*L/J*, 3:306). English reviews, lacking patriotic incentives, found it an entertaining but somewhat labored effort. *The New Monthly Magazine's* critic remarked, somewhat ironically, that the novel "has a moral tendency" and pointed out that the author was guilty of the same error as his character Mrs. Wilson: "She laboured under the disadvantage of what John called a didactic manner, and which, although she had not the ability, or rather taste, to amend, she had yet the sense to discern." The review praised the novel's characters and concluded, "the author displays talents for novelwriting which will undoubtedly secure him the approbation of the public, if, in his future works, he can divest himself of a certain formality of style, which perhaps is, in the present instance, occasioned by too great an anxiety, that none of his 'usefulness' shall be lost for want of being set forth with, what he may conceive, becoming sententiousness of diction."[32] The reviewer for *The Gentleman's Magazine,* though somewhat confused by "the multiplicity of characters to which we are introduced," nevertheless praised *Precaution:* "as a Work of entertainment it claims a distinguished place amid this species of publications."[33]

Despite the boost from Gardner's magazine, *Precaution* sold poorly in the United States, and Cooper had to remainder much of the American edition of one thousand copies to Harpers. In England, on the other hand, it had twice the sale of *The Spy,* and by 1851 it had gone through five British editions.[34] Unfortunately, Cooper gathered no income from British publication. As a profit-making venture, *Precaution* was a total loss. Aesthetically, too, it is hard to argue with Robert Spiller's judgment: "Seldom has there been a less promising first novel."[35]

In other respects, however, *Precaution* was extremely valuable for Cooper. It convinced him that he could develop and sustain a tone appropriate to his chosen audience and that he could produce a work that would be deemed superior to most representatives of its type; it gave him valuable experience in the craft of writing and in the mysteries of publishing; it supplied him

with a central stock of characters and conflicts that he could employ as the skeleton in the fleshing out of his American works. In
deciding to write as an Englishman in an English form, Cooper
materially reduced the burdens most would-be American writers
had had to bear. The "novel of purpose" was admirably suited to the
critical requirements of Common Sense philosophy, and in dealing
with English characters Cooper had at least postponed the problem of matching a form to his American materials. Finally, the
happy coincidence of his previous acquaintance with Gardner insured Cooper of indulgent treatment by a patriotic journal which
might otherwise have been disposed to spurn a mock-English
novel. While *Precaution* was neither a great book nor a great success, it was an auspicious beginning for Cooper's career.

II

In his preface to the 1849 edition of *The Spy* (the fifth
preface he wrote for this work), Cooper refers to the foreign setting
of *Precaution:*

> When this tale was published, it became a matter of reproach
> among the author's friends, that he, an American in heart as in
> birth, should give the world a work which aided perhaps, in some
> slight degree, to feed the imaginations of the young and unprac-
> tised among his own countrymen, by pictures drawn from a state of
> society so different from that to which he belonged. The writer,
> while he knew how much of what he had done was purely acciden-
> tal, felt the reproach to be one that, in a measure, was just. As the
> only atonement in his power, he determined to inflict a second
> book, whose subject should admit of no cavil, not only on the
> world, but on himself. He chose patriotism for his theme.[36]

This account is obviously inaccurate, since Cooper began writing
The Spy long before *Precaution* was published. Still, the substance
of it is surely accurate. Novelists had long been taken to task for
filling the minds of the young with impossible yearnings for social
elevation or romantic adventures, and while Cooper had carefully

structured *Precaution* as a moral novel, he had indeed cast his hero as a disguised Earl and transported his lovers to a British castle. These considerations supplied the initial impetus for writing an American tale.

Having begun, Cooper encountered difficulties. He found that, in the absence of models like Austen and Opie, he wrote much more slowly than he had expected. On June 28, 1820, he told Goodrich, "The task of making American Manners and American scenes interesting to an American reader is an arduous one—I am unable to say whether I shall succeed or not—" (*L/J,* 1:44). Two weeks later he again wrote Goodrich concerning his slow progress: "The 'Spy' goes on slowly and will not be finished until late in the fall—I take more pains with it—as it is to be an American novel professedly" (*L/J,* 1:49).

The Spy, however, was not finished that fall. Cooper had laid aside his manuscript as "too great a financial risk" (*L/J,* 1:24–25). In its place he undertook another British imitation. In 1820 Goodrich, Charles Wiley, and William P. Gilley had jointly published Mrs. Opie's *Tales of the Heart,* and it apparently was profitable enough to induce Cooper to try something similar. The project was announced in Gardner's *Repository* as "*American Tales,* by a Lady, viz. Imagination—Heart—Matter—Manner— Matter and Manner."[37] Only "Imagination" and "Heart" were actually written, and they probably never would have been published if Wiley, Cooper's publishing agent from 1821 to 1825, hadn't been in severe financial difficulties and persuaded Cooper to let him try them. Over the same period Cooper reinforced his new role as man of letters by reviewing four books for the *Repository.* These reviews (no mere notices) reveal Cooper's customary energy: eighteen pages on a *Naval History of the United States,* twenty-one pages on *An Examination of the New Tariff,* thirty-one pages on Parry's *Journal of a Voyage of Discovery.*[38]

In mid-1821 Cooper again took up *The Spy;* according to his 1849 preface, the first volume of the work had already been printed and the second volume was set up as Cooper wrote. Eventually Wiley, who was perpetually on the brink of financial ruin,

intimated that the work might grow to a length that would con-
sume the profits. To set his mind at rest, the last chapter was
actually written, printed and paged, several weeks before the chapters which precede it were even thought of. This circumstance,
while it cannot excuse, may serve to explain the manner in which
the actors are hurried off the scene. (*Spy,* p. xi)

Like Brown, Cooper worked under considerable pressure from his
printer, and it is clear that from his perspective in 1849 he regrets
the botching of his work.

Cooper's uncertainty about his venture into "an American novel professedly" is indicated in its slow course to publication, and all his doubts surface in the preface he wrote for the first
edition. There, with a kind of desperate jocularity, he wrestles with
the concept of an American novel and its potential audience.[39]
"There are several reasons why an American, who writes a novel,
should choose his own country for the scene of his story—and
there are more against it."[40] Cooper notes that "the ground is
untrodden" except by one other author. Though that author is
unnamed, it is evident that Cooper means Charles Brockden
Brown. No sooner does Brown come to mind than Cooper di-
gresses to the neglect Brown suffered;

as yet but one pen of any celebrity has been employed among us in
this kind of writing; and as the author is dead, and beyond hopes
and fears of literary rewards and punishments, his countrymen are
beginning to discover his merit—but we forget, the latter part of
this sentence should have been among the—contras.

The effect of this immediate adversion to Brown is strange enough,
but in fact the whole preface is haunted by what Brown achieved in
his novels and did not achieve with his audience. Any American
novelist, Cooper suggests, would have to *compete* with Brown: "a
new candidate for literary honours of this kind, would be compared with that one, and unfortunately he is not the rival that
every man would select." On the other hand, Cooper fears that
when critics call for works that display "American manners," what
they mean is "Indian manners":

we are apprehensive that the same palate which can relish the cave scene in Edgar Huntly, because it contains an American, a savage, a wild cat, and a tomahawk, in a conjunction that never did, nor ever will occur—will revolt at descriptions here, that portray love as anything but a brutal passion—patriotism as more than money-making—or men and women without wool.

Here Brown's career seems to have contradictory meanings for Cooper. Brown failed to find an audience for his works, and he created an audience that will expect all future American writers to repeat his effects; he is a formidable rival, and he wrote impossibly romanticized fictions. Ultimately the figure of Brown betrays not "the anxiety of influence" but rather Cooper's anxiety about his own performance, a mingled pride and shame.

    Cooper lists the advantages an American novelist enjoys and then negates each one: the ground is virtually untrodden, but one must compete with Brown; patriotic feeling will insure sales, but patriotism after all *does* often come down to mere money-making; an American should be able to describe American scenes and characters well from his intimate knowledge of them, but American readers are equally familiar with them and "the very familiarity will breed contempt; besides, if we make any mistakes every body will know it." Cooper concludes this portion of his preface by suggesting that the moon would make an ideal setting for a novel, since there one could escape all national quibbles.

    Having gotten this far in his consideration of the possibility of an American novel, Cooper abruptly begins to address "still another class of critics, whose smiles we most covet, and whose frowns we most expect to encounter—we mean our own fair" (i.e., American women). The simultaneously coy and bullying tone of this portion of the preface is even odder than that of the earlier portion. It is evident that Cooper thinks the majority of novel readers are women and that he fears they will be disappointed by *The Spy*. By the time he published *The Pilot* in 1823, Cooper was ready to abandon women readers altogether ("*The Pilot* would scarcely be a favorite with females"), but in 1821 he was not prepared for so bold a step: "The truth is, that a woman is a bundle of sensibilities, and these are qualities which exist chiefly in the fancy. Certain moated castles, draw-bridges, and [a kind] of classic nature, are much required by these imaginative beings." The traditional objection that the cultivation of such sensibilities breeds social discontent is made painfully explicit as Cooper veers off into a portrayal of the seduction of American women by foreign adventurers:

> The artificial distinctions of life also have their peculiar charms with the softer sex, and there are many of them who think the greatest recommendation a man can have to their notice, is the ability to raise themselves in the scale of genteel preferment; very many are the French valets, Dutch barbers, and English tailors, who have received their patents of nobility from the credulity of the American fair; and occasionally we see a few of them, whirling in the vortex left by the transit of one of these aristocratic meteors, across the plane of our confederation.

On the surface Cooper promises not to seduce his reader and implies an open, "manly" intercourse instead; but his hectoring tone is almost brutal, and he reveals no sympathy for those whose own pretensions make seduction possible. The whole passage displays a remarkable ambivalence toward the audience he presumably is courting. He enjoins "the American fair" to be content with the moatless confines of the Wharton cottage, and he finishes with an insulting salute to women:

> We repeat we mean nothing disrespectful to the fair—we love them next to ourselves—our book—our money—and a few other articles. We know them to be good-natured, good-hearted—ay, and good-looking hussies enough: and heartily wish, for the sake of one of them, we were a lord, and had a castle in the bargain.

The preface concludes with the claim that "a goodly portion" of *The Spy* is true and that "every passion recorded in the volumes before the reader, has and does exist." With another little flourish, Cooper leaves the reader: "we send our compliments to all who read our pages—and love to those who buy them."

In the disjunctures, contradictions, and aggressions of the 1821 preface we can see a microcosm of the eighteen months

Cooper spent working on the book. Hesitation and ambivalence are everywhere apparent; Cooper liked *The Spy* very much, but he feared the public reaction. In effect, the preface is an elaborate defense against the onslaught of negative response that Cooper fully expected. After the novel had succeeded, Cooper withdrew the 1821 preface and substituted a more detached preface in which he argues that "common sense" is the characteristic mentality of the American people.

The first difficulty confronting Cooper in planning an American novel was that of form, and he turned to a model he knew to be successful. As George Dekker notes, "*The Spy* is subtitled 'A Tale of the Neutral Ground'; and as 'neutral ground' is a phrase that crops up frequently in the Waverley Novels, Cooper's subtitle can probably be taken as an announcement that he is following in the footsteps of Sir Walter Scott." However, as Dekker points out, Cooper's neutral ground is quite different from Scott's: "To Scott the phrase means 'common ground'; to Cooper it means 'No-Man's-Land.' Thus what is frankly an imitation of a Scott novel often often seems to be, as well, a sharp critique of Scott's soft centre."[41] Cooper's treatment of landscape and character are in fact quite different from Scott's. In examining that difference more closely, we can appreciate what Cooper accomplished in making "American Manners and American scenes interesting to an American reader." By a careful alteration of the generic norms of historical romance, Cooper led his reader into the American novel.

Scott had defined "neutral ground" in the "Dedicatory Epistle" to *Ivanhoe,* the book whose physical appearance Cooper had wanted to imitate in his first novel. The "Epistle" discusses the romancer's need to compromise between devotion to historical accuracy and the requirements of the modern reader. Scott had edited Joseph Strutt's posthumously published novel, *Queen-Hoo-Hall;* when the novel failed, Scott attributed the lack of reader interest to its wealth of historical detail, which could only appeal to an antiquarian. He concluded that the language and manners of the historical romance would have to consist of those elements which the past and the present held in common:

The late ingenious Mr. Strutt, in his romance of Queen-Hoo-Hall, acted upon another principle; and in distinguishing between what was ancient and modern, forgot, as it appears to me, that extensive neutral ground, the large proportion, that is, of manners and sentiments which are common to us and our ancestors, having been handed down unaltered from them to us, or which, arising out of the principles of our common nature, must have existed alike in either state of society.[42]

For Scott the neutral ground is first of all a conception rooted in the historical imagination, and it is closely connected to those devices Scott developed for mediating between the modern reader and remote language and manners: the "wavering" hero and the perspectivist treatment of history and character.[43] The wavering hero represents the reader in his vague knowledge of an imaginative interest in the past. Waverley, whose name reflects his function, is the outstanding example: "His initial feeling of unfamiliarity with and secret embarrassment at Scottish customs—which is only to be conquered through his gradual understanding of them—automatically establishes a link between his own and the reader's reactions."[44] Through the play of his imagination, Waverley invests traditional lore with human passions and actions and brings the past to life. In the process, historical reality becomes the focal point of the novel, and the traditional hero recedes into the background. Similarly, historical tableaux and historical characters are presented by a technique that Iser calls "fanning out." The reader is given partial portraits of a scene or person from several perspectives, as when Waverley meets Gilfillan: first the narrator describes Gilfillan in detail (an objective rendering); then Waverley's reaction is added (an imaginative response which links Gilfillan with "the Roundheads of yore"). "The way is laid open for the imagination [of the reader] to penetrate the diversification and to bind the various aspects together in a unified picture."[45]

Cooper's task was very different, as his 1821 preface to the first edition of *The Spy* suggests. The problem was not the reader's unfamiliarity with the language and manners of "sixty years since"; on the contrary, Cooper was keenly aware of the danger that history held too few surprises to engage his reader's interest. The rich stock of traditions and customs that Scott could employ as catalysts for the historical imagination were altogether ⁒ lacking in America, as Cooper later observed in *Notions of the Americans:*

> There are no annals for the historian, no follies (beyond the most vulgar and commonplace) for the satirist; no manners for the dramatist; no obscure fictions for the writer of romance; no gross and hardy offences against decorum for the moralist; nor any of the rich artificial auxiliaries of poetry. The weakest hand can extract a spark from the flint, but it would baffle the strength of a giant to attempt kindling a flame with a pudding-stone.[46]

In the absence of those elements that are the heart of Scott's historical romance, Cooper "chose patriotism as his theme" (*Spy*, p. x). As James Franklin Beard has shown, that choice involved Cooper in an exploration of America's "Revolutionary Mythos": "that elusive but distinctively coherent cluster of ideas, values, and attitudes (more a *Weltanschauung* than an ideology) that enabled reflective citizens of the early Republic to comprehend the awesome circumstances that brought them to their independence and guided their thinking about themselves into the nineteenth century."[47] As an example of the effect of the Revolutionary Mythos, Beard cites a passage in *Notions of the Americans* in which the Bachelor visits Mount Vernon. He finds himself alone in an office:

> I shall never forget the sensation that I felt, as my eye gazed on the first object it encountered. It was an article of no more dignity than a leathern fire-bucket; but the words "Geo. Washington" were legibly written on it in white paint. I know not how it was, but the organ never altered its look until the name stood before my vision distinct, insulated, and almost endowed with the attributes of the human form.[48]

In *The Spy* Cooper used the Revolutionary mythos in place of Scott's Scottish traditions. Because *The Spy* was intended to reach an American audience, Cooper could assume that his readers shared with him the awe invoked by the mere presence of Washington's name, and he could dispense with the mediating figure of the wavering hero.[49] Because the Revolutionary mythos found its clearest expression in those documents which brought America into being (the Declaration of Independence, *The Federalist,* the Constitution and the Bill of Rights), Cooper replaced Scott's perspectivist presentation of historical tableaux and characters with formal debates around the Wharton dinner table. The figure of Washington was presented with a quasireligious aura,[50] yet even that was not enough to satisfy Cooper's patriotic critics, some of whom complained of Harper "as an impious attempt to describe a character that would baffle the powers of Shakespeare" and implied that Washington "was never known to eat, drink, or sleep during the whole war."[51]

The opening of the novel demonstrates the economy of means by which Cooper converted his imitation British materials from *Precaution* into the substance of an American novel. Landscape and atmosphere become important for the first time in his writing as Harper/Washington seeks shelter from a gathering storm:

> The easterly wind, with its chilling dampness and increasing violence, gave unerring notice of the approach of a storm, which as usual might be expected to continue for several days: and the experienced eye of the traveller was turned in vain, through the darkness of the evening, in quest of some convenient shelter, in which, for the term of his confinement by the rain that already began to mix with the atmosphere in a thick mist, he might obtain such accommodations as his purposes required. (*Spy,* p. 11)

The storm is a convenient way to get Washington to the Wharton house and to set in motion the plot, but it also serves as an emblem of the Revolutionary War, of which Washington is also the victim. The emblem is more specific later, as Washington contemplates the Westchester countryside after the clearing of the storm:

> The air was mild, balmy, and refreshing; in the east, clouds, which might be likened to the retreating masses of a discomfited army, hung around the horizon in awful and increasing darkness. At a little elevation above the cottage, the thin vapour was still rushing toward the east with amazing velocity; while in the west the sun

had broken forth and shed his parting radiance on the scene below, aided by the fullest richness of a clear atmosphere and a freshened herbage. Such moments belong only to the climate of America, and are enjoyed in a degree proportioned to the suddenness of the contrast, and the pleasure we experience in escaping from the turbulence of the elements to the quiet of a peaceful evening, and an air still as the softest mornings in June.

"What a magnificent scene!" said Harper, in a low tone; "how grand! how awfully sublime!—may such a quiet speedily await the struggle in which my country is engaged, and such a glorious evening follow the day of her adversity!" (*Spy,* p. 58)

Landscape is an agent of the Revolutionary Mythos in *The Spy;* it adumbrates the anxiety of war and the hope for peace. It is the "neutral ground" where the armies clash by day and the Cow-boys and Skinners roam by night. As such, landscape is the externalized manifestation of the latent violence in *Precaution:* the residual Americanness of the earlier novel becomes America itself in the successor.

At the center of this initial landscape stands the Wharton house:

The house was of stone, long, low, and with a small wing at each extremity. A piazza, extending along the front, with neatly turned pillars of wood, together with the good order and preservation of the fences and out-buildings, gave the place an air altogether superior to the common farm-houses of the country. (*Spy,* p. 15)

The Wharton house contrasts with the "very humble exterior" of Harvey Birch's dwelling. Although the secret of Mr. Wharton's Tory leanings is long withheld from us, the house itself, with its superior appearance, "extremely neat parlour," Madeira-drinking host, and formal dinners, is a repository of British values, and within its walls the genteel minor plot of *The Spy* will be played. The very name of Wharton's estate, "The Locusts" (*Spy,* p. 29), suggests that Wharton's wealth and comfort are a kind of plague on the new nation.

The Wharton house in the middle of the neutral ground is a synechdoche for life in America during the Revolution: British troops huddle behind their pickets in New York and foray

into Westchester; American troops camp at Four Corners and sally
forth to engage the British. Much has been written on Cooper's use
of landscape in his American novels,[52] but little notice has been
given to the tendency of those landscapes to become threatening
expanses from which characters must defend themselves. The
Wharton house is the first in a long line of fortresses in Cooper's
fiction; the romantic moated castle of the British sentimental tradition becomes the realistic stronghold of a new American tradition. There is a spectrum of such fortresses in *The Spy;* it ranges
from the Wharton's elegant house to Harvey Birch's cave-like hut
in the Hudson Highlands. To venture from one fortress to another
is to enter a world of real and imaginary danger. Lawton and Dr.
Sitgreaves ride from Four Corners to the Locusts and receive a
warning from the invisible Harvey Birch that they are risking their
lives; Caesar flees the ghost of Johnny Birch; Harvey Birch, whose
calling demands that he continually subject himself to the dangers
of the landscape, is captured repeatedly. The true denizens of the
landscape, the Skinners, occasionally overcome a fortress, remove
anything of value, and put it to the torch. After they loot The
Locusts, we are told that "The walls of the cottage were all that was
left of the building; and these, blackened by smoke, and stripped
of their piazzas and ornaments, were but dreary memorials of
the content and security that had so lately reigned within" (*Spy,*
p. 307). Harvey Birch's Highlands hut, composed of logs, bark,
mud, and leaves, contains almost nothing from the civilized world
except a glass window, and when he learns that light reflecting
from the glass has betrayed the hut's location to Frances, he
smashes the window:

> "'Tis but little luxury or comfort that I know," he said, "but even
> that little cannot be enjoyed in safety! . . . I am hunted through
> these hills like a beast of the forest; but whenever, tired with my
> toils, I can reach this spot, poor and dreary as it is, I can spend my
> solitary nights in safety." (*Spy,* p. 410)

All possessions, comforts, and wealth must be sacrificed to the
exigencies of survival in the violent American landscape. The characters who have been able to make this sacrifice—Birch and

Harper—are the seminal forces of the Revolution. They possess patriotism, the integrity of their cause. Those who are incapable of such sacrifice lose everything, including their integrity.

Cooper effected the Americanization of scene by a simple reversal. The latent violence of *Precaution* was contained by the formal class structures of British society. In *The Spy* the structures of society are contained by the landscape of violence. Cooper achieved the Americanization of his characters by a variety of means. Some characters are essentially unchanged from *Precaution;* some are derived by an isolation of personality traits; some are invented altogether. In every case Cooper's proclaimed theme, patriotism, controls the rendering of character.

We have already seen that the central cast of characters, the Wharton family, is a repetition of the Moseley family. With a few minor adjustments, Cooper brilliantly integrated his British characters into his theme of patriotism. In the first place, as Cooper pointed out in his 1849 preface, "The dispute between England and the United States of America, though not strictly a family quarrel, had many of the features of a civil war" (*Spy,* p. vi). His central family, then, could represent the larger conflict. Rather than summarizing the course of the Revolutionary War or entering circumstantially into its political, social, and economic origins, Cooper could ground his presentation of the war in the personal reasoning and passions of individuals.[53] The mildly comic English baronet becomes a Tory sympathizer who attempts to conceal his true interests behind the appearance of neutrality. Wharton wants merely to preserve his property from "my kind neighbors . . . who hoped, by getting my estate confiscated, to purchase good farms, at low prices" (*Spy,* p. 35). In a revolution, however, as in any family crisis, such vacillation has terrible consequences. In the microcosm of his family, Mr. Wharton's "natural imbecility of character" (*Spy,* p. 26) contributes to the disastrous engagement of his elder daughter, Sarah, to the flashy Colonel Wellmere; in the macrocosm of the war, it leads to the burning of The Locusts by the Skinners. The combination of Sarah's aborted wedding and the Skinners' attack reduces Wharton to his essential condition: "Mr. Wharton sat in a state of perfect imbecility, listen-

ing to, but not profiting by, the unmeaning words of comfort that
fell from the lips of the clergyman" (*Spy,* p. 296). In this state he is
borne away by an ironic emblem of his character: a clumsy car-
riage, faded and tarnished, with a coat of arms on its door: "The
lion couchant of the Wharton arms was reposing on the reviving
splendour of a blazonry that told the armorial bearings of a prince
of the church; and the mitre, that already began to shine through
its American mask, was a symbol of the rank of its original owner"
(*Spy,* p. 311). This mottled picture is all that remains of Sir Edward
Moseley's rank in *Precaution.*

Sarah is avowedly pro-British. As the elder daughter,
she has been subject for some time to the flattery of the British
soldiers who had frequented the Wharton house in New York City.
"It was much the fashion then for the British officers to speak
slightingly of their enemies; and Sarah took all the idle vapouring
of her danglers to be truths" (*Spy,* p. 30). The words "fashion,"
"idle vapourings," and "danglers" fix the moral status of both the
British officers and Sarah. It is this consistent under-estimating of
American will and ability that will cost the British their colonies,
in Cooper's judgment;[54] by sharing it, Sarah exposes herself as
susceptible to superficial appearances and vain boasting.

Sarah's engagement to Wellmire is a brilliant metonymy for America's colonial connection to Great Britain: the
colorful Englishman courts the unsuspecting daughter of America
despite his wife at home. British occupation, like bigamy, is a
violation of natural law—that natural law which is the basis for the
Revolutionary mythos. It is no accident that, while waiting for
Caesar to fetch the wedding ring, Dr. Sitgreaves should begin meditating on the "natural" status of monogamy:

> Marriage, madam, is pronounced to be honourable in the sight of
> God and man: and it may be said to be reduced, in the present age,
> to the laws of nature and reason. The ancients, in sanctioning
> polygamy, lost sight of the provisions of nature, and condemned
> thousands to misery, but with the increase of science have grown
> the wise ordinances of society, which ordain that man should be the
> husband of one woman. (*Spy,* p. 289)

Frances, to whom these remarks are addressed, answers, "as if fearful of touching on forbidden subjects," that she had thought the teachings of the Christian religion were the basis of monogamy. Sitgreaves replies:

> True, madam, it is somewhere provided in the prescriptions of the apostles, that the sexes should henceforth be on an equality in this particular. But in what degree could polygamy affect the holiness of life? It was probably a wise arrangement of Paul, who was much of a scholar, and probably had frequent conferences, on this important subject, with Luke, whom we all know to have been bred to the practice of medicine— (*Spy,* p. 290)

Sitgreaves' comic banter raises an issue of great importance: it is not revealed religion, but rational deductions of natural law that provide the basis for monogamy, whether in marriages or among nations. Revelation or enthusiasm are too often merely the glozing of selfish motives, as the Skinners amply demonstrate through their parroting of Revolutionary rhetoric. Sarah has been seduced, both politically and emotionally, by Wellmere, just as the "American fair" of the 1821 preface have been seduced by the pretensions of European adventurers.

The political implications of Wellmere's crime are further developed when Lawton asks him what the punishment is for bigamy:

> "Death!—as such an offence merits," he said.
> "Death and dissection," continued the operator [i.e. Sitgreaves]: "it is seldom that the law loses sight of eventual utility in a malefactor. Bigamy, in a man, is a heinous offence!" (*Spy,* p. 290)

Sitgreaves adds "dissection" in the interest of accuracy and from his professional bias, but it is as well a forecast of the dismemberment of the British empire: dissection as the penalty for British colonial policy.

The wedding of Sarah and Wellmere precipitates a crisis on many levels of the narrative. Harvey Birth, the ubiquitous servant of the Revolution, interrupts with the news that Wellmere has an English wife; the Skinners assault The Locusts and burn it to the ground; Sarah falls senseless and lapses into insanity. Sitgreaves, summoned to attend to Sarah, speaks as if her sanity were the price of American independence:

> "This is a melancholy termination to so joyful a commencement of the night, madam," he observed in a soothing manner; "but war must bring its attendant miseries; though doubtless it often supports the cause of liberty, and improves the knowledge of surgical science." (*Spy,* p. 309)

Once the ties of Sarah's mental dependence have been removed, she, like her father, has no support; the two of them represent the fate of American Tories, dispossessed and stupified by the defeat of the British.

Frances, the younger daughter, manifests first mental independence, then support for the Revolution. At first she, too, had believed the "idle vapourings" of the British officers:

> but there was occasionally a general, who was obliged to do justice to his enemy in order to obtain justice for himself; and Frances became skeptical on the subject of the inefficiency of her countrymen. Colonel Wellmere was among those who delighted most in expending his wit on the unfortunate Americans; and, in time, Frances began to listen to his eloquence with great suspicion, and sometimes with resentment. (*Spy,* p. 30)

Frances is, of course, Emily Moseley in American dress, but instead of precaution, Frances takes as her guiding principle patriotism. Two circumstances exemplify Frances' patriotism: her love for Payton Dunwoodie, and her adoption of Washington as a surrogate father. The love of a Tory daughter for a patriot hero, a theme which was to become a cliché of the Revolutionary War novel,[55] contrasts with the bigamous marriage Wellmere proposes: Dunwoodie is one-dimensional in all things, as his passionate friendship with the significantly named George Singleton suggests.[56] While the course of their true love is ruffled by misunderstanding, ultimately the marriage of Frances and Dunwoodie is never in doubt. When the aged Harvey Birch meets Wharton Dunwoodie during the War of 1812, the United States and the child of the marriage merge into one: "'Tis like our native land!' exclaimed the old man with vehemence, 'improving with time;—God has blessed both'" (*Spy,* p. 458). The Dunwoodies are the legitimate, fertile parents of the new nation.

The imbecility of her father leaves an absence at the center of Frances' family life—an absence that Washington unmistakably fills. The first time Washington (in disguise) speaks to her, he gives her a "smile of almost paternal softness" (*Spy,* p. 20), and in Harvey Birch's hideout, Washington expresses his admiration for Frances' courage:

> God has denied to me children, young lady; but if it had been his blessed will that my marriage should not have been childless, such a treasure as yourself would I have asked from his mercy. But you are my child: all who dwell in this broad land are my children, and my care; and take the blessing of one who hopes yet to meet you in happier days. (*Spy,* p. 412)

George Dekker has criticized Cooper's treatment of the Wharton sisters as excessively stereotyped "for the sake of the scheme,"[57] but the paternal image is not simply the literalization of Washington as "the father of his country." It connects to a complex pattern of paternity and familial relations in *The Spy,* and this pattern in turn is Cooper's exploration of the meaning of his original insight into the Revolution as a civil war, the portrayal of what Jay Fliegelman has called "the American revolution against patriarchal authority," a comprehensive re-orientation of American culture in the interest of justifying the rebellion against the patriarchal authority of the British monarch. Throughout the eighteenth century the relation of the colonies to the crown was conceptualized as that of children to a father, and the gathering impetus for revolution can be traced in the changes in the rhetoric of family comity beginning in the early 1760s.[58] As Fliegelman has shown, the rhetoric of patriarchal authority was transformed by the educational theory of John Locke; in the course of the eighteenth century the image of the stern, autocratic father was usurped by a new father whose authority derived from his capacity to nurture his children and to prepare them for a life of virtue. The hagiography of Washington, the childless father of his country, precipitated Washington's role as the adoptive "good father," the antithesis to the authoritarian yet curiously weak extremes of George III:

> The new understanding of greatness as goodness reflected an essential theme of the antipatriarchal revolution that would replace patriarch with benefactor, precept with example, the authority of position with the authority of character, deference and dependence with moral self-sufficiency, and static dichotomies with principles of growth: Sovereignty and power were no longer glorious in and of themselves. Rather, they were glorious, as Washington had demonstrated, only as opportunities to do good.[59]

Thus Cooper, by a series of minor adjustments, brilliantly transformed his British comedy of familial relations into a drama of revolutionary aspirations, creating a pattern of familial and political conflict, a pattern which was indisputably American and yet which would be accessible to an audience accustomed to British fiction.

Around this central core Cooper wove his theme of patriotism. His primary means for dramatizing this theme was also his most radical and enduring act in the making of an American novel: the invention of Harvey Birch. The seed was planted by John Jay, the former Chief Justice and governor and the father of Cooper's boyhood friend, William. During the Revolution Jay had been chairman of a Congressional committee charged with disrupting British activities among Tory Americans:

> In the discharge of the novel duties which now devolved to him, Mr. [Jay] had occasion to employ an agent whose services differed but little from those of a common spy. This man, as will easily be understood, belonged to a condition of life which rendered him the least reluctant to appear in so equivocal a character. He was poor, ignorant, so far as the usual instruction was concerned; but cool, shrewd, and fearless by nature. (*Spy*, p. vii)

After the war Jay succeeded in getting a Congressional appropriation to reward his spy, but when the two met, the spy refused payment:

"The country has need of all its means," he said; "as for myself, I can work, or gain a livelihood in various ways." Persuasion was useless, for patriotism was uppermost in the heart of this remarkable individual; and Mr. [Jay] departed, bearing with him the gold he had brought, and a deep respect for the man who had so long hazarded his life, unrequited, for the cause they served in common. (*Spy*, pp. viii–ix)

The point of Jay's anecdote, of course, was his pleasure at finding a man whose patriotism overcame all personal considerations. The spy's poverty and lack of education reinforce the self-denial of his refusal to take payment, and he becomes a representative of those men who, in signing the Declaration of Independence, pledged their lives, fortunes, and sacred honor to the cause of liberty. That the anecdote deeply impressed Cooper is evident from his choosing it to represent the theme of his first American work. But the story of the spy seems to have engaged him at a psychological level as well. In writing an American novel Cooper was risking a great deal. We have already seen that doubts over the potential profitability of *The Spy* had caused Cooper to set it aside for more traditional fare; in the interim his own financial affairs had continued their deterioration and were becoming desperate. Finishing and publishing *The Spy*, then, was in its way a reenactment of the spy's patriotic refusal. This identification of himself with the spy accounts for Cooper's emphasis in the 1821 preface on his intention to present "patriotism as more than money-making" and for the truculent tone of that preface. It may also account for Cooper's mysterious remark in a letter to Goodrich: "I confess I am more partial to this new work myself as being a Country-man and perhaps a younger child—" (*L/J*, 1:44). Finally, it may account for a sentence in the 1849 preface, the wording of which suggests Cooper's career as well as the spy's: "Persuasion was useless, for patriotism was uppermost in the heart of this remarkable individual."

Harvey Birch was created as a socially marginal character, in accordance with his prototype. Certainly none of the genteel characters who frequent the Wharton house would be either willing or able to act as a spy, and when Washington, with the purest of motives and without any intent to do harm, has to go under a false name, he nearly gives himself away: "a faint tinge gathered on his features" (*Spy,* p. 17) when he has to say, "Harper." It is precisely his marginality that makes Birch an effective spy. Cooper underlines this point by presenting another spy in his narrative: Caesar, the Wharton's black servant, "had established a regular system of espionage, with a view to the safety of his young master" (*Spy,* p. 57), and members of the Wharton household are given to remarking, with an indulgent chuckle, "Really, Caesar, I find I have never given you credit for half the observation that you deserve" (*Spy,* p. 281). Absolute loyalty, a kind of family patriotism, characterizes Caesar's place in the household, and his bearing is a rebuke to succeeding generations, just as Harvey Birch's is:

> The old family servant, who, born and reared in the dwelling of his master, identified himself with the welfare of those whom it was his lot to serve, is giving place in every direction to that vagrant class which has sprung up within the last thirty years, and whose members roam through the country unfettered by principles, and uninfluenced by attachments. For it is one of the curses of slavery, that its victims become incompetent to the attributes of a freeman. (*Spy,* pp. 47–48)[60]

Corollary to his social marginality is Birch's capacity to create a personality for himself, to invent himself anew at need. He is, of course, a master of the impenetrable disguise; in fact, Washington alone knows who or what he really is. More significantly, he recreates himself in moral terms in the course of the novel. At the beginning Birch's acquisitiveness is stressed. He has a pot of gold hidden under his hearthstones, and even when we have learned enough of him to regard him as a patriot, an essential dualism remains in his psyche. His eyes possess "two distinct expressions, which, in a great measure, characterised the whole man":

> When engaged in traffic, the intelligence of his face appeared lively, active, and flexible, though uncommonly acute; if the conversation turned on ordinary transactions of life, his air became abstracted and restless; but if, by chance, the revolution and the country were

the topic, his whole system seemed alerted—all his faculties were concentrated: he would listen for a great length of time, without speaking, and then would break silence by some light and jocular remark, that was too much at variance with his former manner, not to be affectation. (*Spy*, p. 41)

Birch's progress through the novel entails the gradual loss of everything associated with the avaricious side of his personality: his pot of gold, his house, his freedom of movement, his reputation as a peddler. In addition, he suffers these losses at the hands of American agents—the Skinners and Dunwoodie's troops. The effect of this process is to emphasize the choices Birch must make between self-interest and patriotism; with each such choice, he recreates himself in the form of the perfect patriot. In this respect Birch is the descendant of Denbigh. The two heroes of *The Spy*, Dunwoodie and Birch, are the product of a bifurcation of Denbigh's character into its genteel and its self-creating components. Thus, just as Denbigh's father dies at the beginning of *Precaution* and leaves him free to abandon his property and reputation, to invent himself as a propertyless gentleman, so Birch's father dies early in *The Spy* and leaves him free to serve the interests of the Revolution under our general father, Washington. Birch thus becomes what one critic has called a "renegade" archetype, his character formed "by his perpetual striving for self-definition in a fictive world in which the self can scarcely be conceived to exist outside of a stable social matrix."[61]

Still another aspect of Cooper's presentation of Birch has been pointed out by Barton Levi St. Armand.[62] St. Armand relates Birch to legendary and mythic prototypes: Birch's pack and his father's remark that "you will be a pilgrim through life" (*Spy*, p. 147) clearly suggest *Pilgrim's Progress;* his homelessness, mysterious appearances and escapes, and alienation suggest the Wandering Jew; his role as Washington's agent for the spirit of patriotism echoes Christ's role in the Trinity. For St. Armand these prototypes mean that Cooper, despite his famous distaste for New England and its religious enthusiasts, participated in the "Literary Calvinism" that was to shape the symbolic romances of Hawthorne and Melville: "Harvey Birch is suspended between two Testaments, one demanding obedience to rigid and unyielding law, the other affirming the necessity of constant and self-sacrificial love." Whether or not this is an instance of literary Calvinism, St. Armand is correct in seeing in Harvey Birch, "the domestication of an international Romantic archetype."[63] Cooper incorporated, without insisting upon, features from mythic prototypes in precisely the way that American architects and sculptors incorporated classical forms as an affirmation of a Golden Age in the New World. While Mr. Wharton's Tory sympathies are represented through his tarnished coach and through the gilded tablet that "proclaimed the virtues of his deceased parents" until Trinity Church was burned, Birch's essential Americanism is proclaimed in his relation to living legend.

The other characters in *The Spy* constitute a gallery of American types: Captain Lawton, the Virginian horseman; Dr. Sitgreaves, the philosophical pragmatist; Katy Haynes, Birch's inquisitive housekeeper; Betty Flanagan, the Irish camp follower. As yet the gallery is not very extensive, but it is the beginning of Cooper's exploration of regional types in fiction.[64] Cooper's regionalism owes something to Scott, of course, though his own comments on regional characters also mention Shakespeare and Otway, and as "types" his characters probably owe more to the traditions of the stage than to those of the novel.[65] The scene in which the American troops drink and sing, for example, is clearly a set piece. Betty Flanagan urges her liquor on the soldiers: "Try a drop of the gift. . . . Faith, 'tis but a wishy-washy sort of stuff after all" (*Spy*, p. 218). Lawton, called on for a song, delivers a burlesque *carpe diem:*

> Now push the mug, my jolly boys,
>   And live, while live we can,
> Tomorrow's sun may end your joys,
>   For brief's the hour of man.
> And he who bravely meets the foe
> His lease of life can never know.
>   Old mother Flanagan
>   Come and fill the can again;
>   For you can fill, and we can swill,
>   Good Betty Flanagan. (*Spy*, p. 219)

Major Dunwoodie sings a sentimental ballad about the contrast between the "heats of southern suns" and "Luna's milder beam," making plain his preference for Frances Wharton over Isabella Singleton. Dr. Sitgreaves sings about love as "The pain that Galen could not heal." The epigraph for this chapter of roistering, not surprisingly, is Iago's drunken song from *Othello:*

> And let me the canakin clink, clink:
> And let me the canakin clink.
> A soldier's a man;
> A life's but a span;
> Why then, let a soldier drink. (*Spy,* p. 213)

In these regional characters Cooper's readers could find something familiar and accessible. The portraits have been incorporated from various dramas, and behind the carousing of Lawton and Dunwoodie lies the carousing of Falstaff and Hal.

Regional characters would be familiar too, as representative *types*. David Levin has shown how the American Romantic historians organized their works around representative individuals (Jefferson and Washington, William the Silent, Montcalm and Wolfe):

> The representative technique applied as well to minor characters. If Daniel Boone was the representative woodsman, Benjamin Franklin—"the sublime of common sense"—represented the middle class. . . . As the Franklin of Bancroft and Parkman represents one facet of the New England character, Bancroft's Jonathan Edwards represented "the New England mind." Bancroft's and Parkman's Pontiac and Prescott's Montezuma were representative Indians.[66]

Levin attributes the historians' use of representative types to the popularity of Scott and Cooper, but the practice had been well established before either began writing novels. Its sources lie partly in the allegorical tradition represented by *Pilgrim's Progress* and *The Faerie Queene* and partly in the etiology of the Revolutionary mythos.[67] Benjamin Franklin's *Autobiography* (published in England in 1794 and in America in 1818) had established him as the prototypical middle-class pragmatist, and Parson Weems' *The Life and Memorable Actions of George Washington*

(c. 1800) mythologized Washington's life so thoroughly that we still live with the tale of young George and the cherry tree.

In presenting regional types as minor characters, then, Cooper was again using a device that would appeal to a wide audience. So sensitive was he to his audience's expectations on this point that late in his career he felt obliged to apologize for being too "realistic" in *The Pioneers:* "This rigid adhesion to truth, an indispensable requisite in history and travels, destroys the charm of fiction; for all that is necessary to be conveyed to the mind by the latter had better be done by delineation of principles, and of characters in their classes, than by too fastidious attention to originals."[68]

Cooper's treatment of characters, particularly his habit of portraying a group of genteel characters and a group of socially inferior characters with little contact between the two, has often been remarked but has rarely been understood. Coming at the problem of inventing the American novel from an imitation British work, he wanted to preserve the novelistic core while extending his subject to American themes. For Cooper, the word "novel" meant the portrayal of manners in a social field, and in fact, after *Precaution* Cooper never again used "novel" in his subtitles. (He used the general term "A Tale" eighteen times, "A Romance" twice, and "A Narrative" and "A Legend" once each, though in his prefaces he sometimes used "novel" in its more general sense.)

The resulting two-part structure was an integral part of Cooper's theory of an American novel. His most extensive explication of this theory is in *A Letter to His Countrymen* (1834), the ill-tempered farewell to fiction Cooper somewhat prematurely published after his return from Europe. *A Letter* contains a defense of *The Bravo,* a novel for which Cooper had entertained high hopes but which had suffered an unfriendly reception in the United States. Insisting on his patriotic intentions in writing a tale set in Venice, Cooper explained at length what he had undertaken: "I determined to attempt a series of tales, in which American opinion should be brought to bear on European fact." For *The Bravo* he chose to treat the conflict between the Venetian elite and the common people at whose expense the elite ruled.

The object was not to be attained by an essay, or a commentary, but by one of those popular pictures which find their way into every library; and which, whilst they have attractions for the feeblest intellects, are not often rejected by the strongest. . . . The moral was to be inferred from the events, and it was to be enforced by the common sympathies of our natures.

The selection of such a subject entailed a commitment to *theme* as the most important element of the book: "the government of Venice, strictly speaking, became the hero of the tale. Still it was necessary to have human agents." Characters and plot were created as the "machinery" of the "main design."

One of those ruthless state maxims which have been exposed by Comte Daru, in his history of Venice, furnished the leading idea of the minor plot, or the narrative. According to this maxim, the state was directed to use any fit subject, by playing on his natural affections, and by causing him to act as a spy, assassin, or other desperate agent of the government, under a promise of extending favors to some near relative who might happen to be within the grasp of the law.[69]

First comes theme (or, we infer, *major plot*), then the *minor plot*, or the narrative. The tale of Jacopo, the ill-fated Bravo, and his struggle against the elite of Venice animates the theme. Cooper's practice here was also his practice in *The Spy*, where the theme of patriotism is animated by the narrative of the Wharton family.

Richard Slotkin, discussing *The Pioneers*, argues that "Cooper was still very much under the spell of Scott and the myth of progress through conflict and Christian reconciliation which informs the historical romance." Slotkin calls the two structural devices of Cooper's novels *plot* and *saga:*

The plot . . . justifies the writing of the novel in terms of the literary conventions established in Europe and imported to the East. . . . The thematic saga, which has its origin in the quasi-fictional narrative literature of the colonies and in the Indian legends collected by Heckewelder, relates to the character development of the hunter-hero Leatherstocking and his Indian associates.[70]

Slotkin is correct about the European origins of the (minor) plot, but his focus on the Leatherstocking tales prevents him from seeing an important point about the "thematic saga." The theme was chosen *first;* the quasi-narrative literature of the colonies, the anecdote of the patriotic spy, the Indian legends, and so on, were selected as appropriate vehicles for the theme. In addition, we have seen how carefully Cooper modified the European literary conventions he inherited in order to make them cohere with his American theme.

Ultimately, what Cooper had in mind was the construction of a novel that would find its way into every library, that would have attractions for the feeblest intellects, yet would not be rejected by the strongest—a democratic novel representing the culture of the new nation. In *The Spy* Cooper was especially solicitous of an audience which knew only those European literary conventions. He courted his readers, and, for the first time in American history, an American novel became a best-seller.

In 1814 Cooper wrote to Rufus Griswold that the success of *The Spy* was "instantaneous and decided."

> It was published in the holidays, and I left town a day or two before its appearance, to join my family at a country place belonging to my wife in Westchester where the book was written. So little was anything expected from an American book, that I do not think the Spy was mentioned a dozen times among us, for the next two or three weeks. The first news from it was a notice to prepare a second edition. This was considerably within the first month of publication. An edition of 1000 copies sold, at $2 a copy, in less than four weeks; certainly notice enough, under the circumstances. Three editions were printed [in] the summer; equal in amount to six of the common editions of that day. (*L/J,* 4:342)[71]

The success of *The Spy* was surprising for several reasons. In the first place, it was an expensive book. When Scott's *Woodstock* was pirated in 1824 it sold for $1.00; the work of this unknown American cost twice as much. Again, when Carey & Lea brought out their edition of *Woodstock* they printed 6,000 copies to satisfy a well-established audience. If Cooper's figures are correct, 6,000 copies of *The Spy* were quickly sold.[72] And it continued to sell; after Carey & Lea purchased the copyright from Cooper, they reprinted *The Spy* six times between 1827 and 1838.[73]

A more complex reason for surprise at the sales figures for *The Spy* lies in the attitude Cooper took toward discounting. The common rate of discount that a publisher offered to the retail trade in 1821 was 45 percent, but Cooper, who was still acting as his own publisher, directed Charles Wiley to allow no copies of *The Spy* to be sold for a discount greater than 33⅓ percent. This slender discount rate discouraged booksellers from ordering more copies of the book than they could be certain of selling. In fact, Cooper's practice infuriated Henry Carey to the point of refusing to purchase *The Pioneers* when it was published.[74] No such resistance existed for *The Spy*, however, and Cooper's gross income from the three editions was nearly $4,000.[75]

Three factors helped to overcome the unusually expensive price for *The Spy:* current economic conditions, the nationalistic enthusiasm of Charles Wiley, and the favorable reviews the novel received. In 1821 the United States had just emerged from the severe depression that followed the War of 1812, and the great boom spurred by river and canal traffic had begun. A large portion of the public could afford to avenge themselves on the British for burning Washington, D.C., six years before by buying a more expensive American book—a book which also, as it happened, celebrated the American war for independence.[76]

One of the few publishers who had any faith in American literature was Charles Wiley, whose bookshop Cooper had begun to frequent after the appearance of *Precaution*. Wiley and his printer, C. S. Van Winkle, handled Irving's *Sketch Book*, Fitz-Green Halleck's poem *Fanny*, and Richard Henry Dana's *Idle Man* in addition to *The Literary and Scientific Repository*, and Wiley assisted in the distribution of Bryant's 1821 *Poems*. In employing Wiley as his agent, Cooper was moving to the center of the first great flowering of native literary culture.[77] The phenomenal success of the *Sketch Book* in 1819 and 1820 must have been comforting to retailers who disapproved of Cooper's low discount rate.

Finally, *The Spy* was reviewed on a scale unprecedented for an American novel. In the United States, important reviews appeared in the *Port Folio, Niles' Weekly Register,* and *The North American Review. The Spy* was the first American novel the *Review* had bothered to review in its seven-year history, and Gardiner took the opportunity to consider at length the possibilities for American fiction in addition to his detailed assessment of Cooper's novel. Verbal echoes from Cooper's 1821 preface and the priority given characters and setting in Gardiner's review indicate that Gardiner's purpose was to answer Cooper's nervous reservations about producing American fiction: "We have long been of the opinion that our native country opens to the adventurous novelwriter a wide, untrodden field, replete with new matter admirably adapted to the purposes of fiction."[78] Gardiner summarizes the common points regarding the blandness and uniformity of American life, and then he asserts "that in no one country on the face of the globe can there be found a greater variety of specific character, than is at this moment developed in these United States of America." The solution is to examine regional characters: Yankees and Virginians, New York merchants and Connecticut peddlers, Kentucky boatmen and Pennsylvania Dutch, Puritans, pioneers, and Indians:

> It would be hard indeed out of such materials, so infinitely diversified, (not to descend to the minuter distinctions which exist in each section of the country) which, similar in kind but far less various, have in other countries been wrought successfully into every form of the popular and domestic tale, at once amusing and instructive, if nothing can be fabricated on this degenerate soil.[79]

An American setting offers similar problems but has similar solutions. If there are no "gorgeous palaces and cloud capped towers" here, there is natural beauty: "You go to your mighty lakes, your vast cataracts, your stupendous mountains, and your measureless forests." Nature replaces history in the American scheme. We have no picturesque ruins teeming with romantic associations, but every peaceful edifice in the country connects to the primeval landscape: "Go back then to the day when its walls were slumbering in their native quarry, and its timbers flourishing in the living oak; when the cultivated farm was a howling wilderness, the abode of savages and outlaws, and nothing was to be seen in its borders but rapine and bloodshed."[80] This solution is Gardiner's recognition that Cooper had discovered something essentially American in his portrayal of the neutral ground as the landscape of violence.

Gardiner next proposes three specific eras of American history as "peculiarly well fitted for historical romance": the time succeeding the first settlement; the era of the Indian wars; and the Revolution. He offers characters, incidents, and themes from these eras in a veritable catalogue of potentiality, as if to bury anyone who doubts him in a mountain of detail.

All this is preamble to his discussion of *The Spy*, in which Gardiner finds a number of weaknesses. Many of them he attributes to "inexperience, and we fear we must add haste. Nothing but unpardonable haste can account for that sad huddling into confusion, towards the end, of a plot so well laid in the outset." He goes on to note inconsistencies of detail, awkward style, and grammatical errors. "We hope these indications of haste do not proceed from the pitiful ambition of feeding the compositor with sheets, on which the ink is scarce dry."

Gardiner finds that Cooper's strength lies in "describing action and hitting off the humors of low life"—the highest gifts in "the writer of fiction of a secondary rank." On the other hand, Cooper has little ability to evoke pathos, his descriptions of scenery lack "that deep moral feeling, which weds the soul to beauty wherever it exists," and he occasionally offends a discriminating taste by, for example, personifying a turnpike, "about as violent an appeal to the imagination as can well be made."

> The inventive faculty, that, which if it be not genius is at least its chief characteristic, we cannot but think our author possesses in an eminent degree; and we have rather to complain of that want of good taste, which has crowded so much of violent action into so small a space, than of paucity of incident, or monotony of style.

Finally, Cooper describes people, things, and actions with an "excessive minuteness" that leaves too little to the reader's imagination.[81]

In concluding his essay, Gardiner judges *The Spy* an important if not a great work for "having demonstrated so entirely to our satisfaction" the possibility for an American historical romance. Cooper has "laid the foundations of American romance, and is really the first who has deserved the appellation of a distinguished American novel writer."[82] For all Gardiner's reservations, this is high praise in the pages of a journal that was deigning for the first time to notice an American novel. It is significant not only for what it suggests about the future course of American fiction, but also for what it indicates about the impact of *The Spy*. Whether or not readers were disappointed with Cooper's novel—and Gardiner, for one, had no trouble putting bounds to his enthusiasm— it stirred the imaginations of readers and kindled interest in the territory newly opened to writers. In many instances the authors who inundated publishers with American romances over the next two decades (John Neal, James Hall, Robert Montgomery Bird, John Pendleton Kennedy, William Gilmore Simms, and Nathaniel Hawthorne, to name only the most important) were, properly speaking, not imitators but competitors of Cooper, all certain that they could do a better job of rendering character, dialect, scene, plot. Whatever their relative merits, each of these owes his own excitement and sense of destined glory to *The Spy*.

Less reserved in his expression of enthusiasm was the reviewer for the *Port Folio*. He, too, begins by noting *The Spy* demonstrates "that although we possess no popular traditions to enchain the imagination, yet in the history, the character, and the varied face of our country, there exists an ample fund for interesting narrations." After a summary of the plot, the reviewer raises some objections: the last chapter is "a lame and impotent conclusion," some of the "conversations between inferior characters" retard the flow of the narrative, and Washington should have been kept out of the novel:

He should have worn the disguise of Mr. Harper to the last; for it is offering too great a violence to our veneration for this immortal man to exhibit him, unattended and almost in sight of the enemy, begging for a night's lodging, or skulking in a hut to obtain an interview with a pedlar-spy. . . . *Neo Deus intersit*—is a maxim which must be familiar to our American novelist.[83]

These are minor objections amid general praise. The whole picture the novel presents is "in excellent keeping." Even the death of Isabella Singleton, which had been criticized as a "gratuitous and revolting tragedy," is excused as corresponding to the violence of her falling in love before she was courted. As for the manner of that death, the reviewer cites an actual case of a woman who was killed precisely this way while "she sat in her own parlour, surrounded by her children," and "it is highly probable that the author of 'the Neutral ground,' had this disastrous incident in his eye when he introduced the catastrophe in question." The reviewer praises the portraits of Dunwoodie, Frances, Dr. Sitgreaves, and Caesar, and he approves of the moral tone of the work: "As we wish to bestow on this accomplished writer all the praise that is due to him—both for the credit of our own literature, and in return for the pleasure we have received, we will mention one more very rare quality of his book—we mean its total freedom from indelicacy in word and thought."[84]

These two reviews reveal, the state of American criticism in 1822. The *Port Folio* critic writes from the perspective of Common Sense philosophy and emphasizes the work's freedom from indelicacy, while Gardiner espouses a purer aestheticism and criticizes the personification of a turnpike; Gardiner proposes a historical romance that focuses on the great eras and figures of American history, while the *Port Folio* critic objects to portraying the venerated Washington in a mere novel. These conflicting prescriptions emphasize how remarkable Cooper's achievement was, for he succeeded in winning praise from both critics. He also duly noted their objections; despite his lifelong war with critics, in the 1849 preface he was still answering as best he could their complaints about the feeble last chapter and the representation of historical personages. For all their infuriating rules and jargon, critics, too, were part of the democratic audience.

It is difficult to know whether Cooper benefited from such criticism. In his preface to the first edition of *The Pioneers* he claimed that he could not:

> Just as I have made up my mind to adopt the very sagacious hints of one learned Reviewer, a pamphlet is put into my hands, containing the remarks of another, who condemns all that his rival praises, and

praises all that his rival condemns. There I am, left like an ass between two locks of hay; so that I have determined to relinquish my animate nature, and remain stationary, like a lock of hay between two asses.[85]

Despite this open hostility, Cooper seems to have taken a number of hints from reviews. Certainly he succeeded in investing his landscapes with the deep moral feeling that Gardiner named, and although he never wrote slowly enough to please his critics, he took considerable pains to correct errors in succeeding editions of his works.[86] He seems to have taken Gardiner's hint about the eras of American history that might be fruitfully explored by the novelist, and he continually expanded his gallery of regional characters. Still, when his novels sold well, Cooper felt free to ridicule his critics, and when they sold poorly, he felt compelled by honor to defy them.

The most important benefit, in any case, was the publicity that reviews such as Gardiner's gave to Cooper's work. Brown had not been able to interest reviewers in his works at all, but *The Spy* achieved sufficient notoriety to arouse wide curiosity, and curiosity translated into sales.

Shortly after the American publication of *The Spy* Wiley (again with Cooper's approval) sought an English publisher for the novel. He sent a copy to John Murray, Washington Irving's publisher in London, and a letter to Irving asking him to use his influence with Murray. The plan failed because Irving was ill at the crucial moment. On March 6, 1822, he wrote to Wiley:

I received your letter at a time when I was confined to my room by an indisposition that has afflicted me for many months, and has rendered me incapable of attending to any business. I did not see Mr. Murray until some time afterwards, when he informed me that he had shown the novel to Mr. Gifford, who, however, did not give a sufficiently favorable report to induce him to publish it.[87]

William Gifford, the "acrimonious editor of *The Quarterly Review,* was proverbially harsh on American books and writers" (*L/J,* 1:76), so Irving's unfortunate illness insured that Murray would reject *The Spy.* Irving then offered the book to Henry Colburn: "He told me he had published the previous novel by the same author, and had been promised to have the publication of this one, a copy of which he had been expecting." Unfortunately the delay was fatal to Wiley's project. On February 28, 1822, a pirated edition of *The Spy* was issued by F. and W. B. Whitaker, and Wiley and Cooper lost any possible proceeds from a British edition.

The Spy was reasonably well received in England; it went through two editions in three years and was noticed or reviewed in at least seven different periodicals in 1822. As Cooper had anticipated, it was appreciated chiefly for its portrayal of American scenes and manners. A notice in the London *Monthly Magazine* is representative:

> Amongst the better class of Novels which have lately appeared, may be ranked *The Spy, a Tale of the Neutral Ground,* in three volumes, the scene of which is laid in America during her struggle for independence. This work is, on the whole, cleverly written, and contains some able delineations of American scenery and manners. It displays, perhaps, a little trans-atlantic partiality; but, in the main, it may be considered to present a tolerably fair view of the state of feeling in America at that period.[88]

Although Cooper could not profit directly from the friendly reception accorded *The Spy* in England, he did learn from the episode. In April of 1822 he wrote to Benjamin Coles, a fellow contributor to *The Literary and Scientific Repository,* who was about to go to England. Cooper asked him to visit various London publishers who might be interested in American works, and he urged Coles to investigate British copyright law and find out whether it was possible to obtain both British and American copyrights. By the following June Cooper was ready to seek an English publisher for *The Pioneers,* and he asked Irving to help Coles with the negotiations:

> I was not very sanguine as to the success of the "Spy" in England, nor was I at all surprised when I learnt that the book was referred to Mr. Gifford, that Mr. Murray declined publishing it. If the latter is made sensible of the evil guidance that he has been subjected to, one good purpose, at least, will follow the success which you are so good as to communicate. (*L/J,* 1:75)

Apparently that "one good purpose" did follow, for Murray agreed to publish *The Pioneers*. After *The Spy* Cooper had an English following, and English publication was an important feature of his career.

By mid-1822 *The Spy* was in its third American edition and Cooper's place, as, in Gardiner's words, "the first who has deserved the appellation of a distinguished American novel writer," was assured. Through a careful modification of the generic norms of the novel of purpose, a brilliant Americanization of the setting and characters of *Precaution,* and a profound insight into the social marginality of the essential American hero, he succeeded in capturing an audience for an indigenous American fiction, impressing a broad range of critics, and stimulating a host of imitative and competitive writers. If he had never written again, his accomplishment would still be important, but, as always, he was already at work on a new and innovative novel.

CHAPTER FOUR

Educating the Imagination

As the final crisis of *The Pioneers* approaches, Cooper interpolates a scene in which Richard Jones learns of the panther's attack on Elizabeth and Louisa and of Hiram Doolittle's ill-fated attempted to enter Natty's cabin. First Richard finds Agamemnon sobbing outside the kennel: "Oh! de Lor! Miss 'Lizzy an Miss Grant—walk—mountain—poor Bravy!—kill a lady—painter—oh! Lor, lor!—Natty Bumppo—tare he troat open—come a see, masser Richard—here he be—here he be." Not surprisingly, "all this was perfectly inexplicable to the Sheriff" (*Pioneers*, p. 348), and he turns to Benjamin Pump for an explanation. Richard has instructed Benjamin "to make memoranda, on a slate, of whatever might be thought worth remembering" whenever Richard is absent. Because Benjamin is virtually illiterate, Richard has invented "a kind of hieroglyphical character, which was intended to note all the ordinary occurrences of a day . . . and for the extraordinary, after giving certain elementary lectures on the subject, the Sheriff was obliged to trust to the ingenuity of the Major-domo" (*Pioneers*, p. 349). Accordingly, Richard takes the slate and prepares to transfer its information to his private journal: "Benjamin laid one hand on the back of the Sheriff's chair, in a familiar manner, while he kept the other at liberty, to make use of a fore-finger, that was bent like some of his own characters, as an index to point out his meaning" (*Pioneers*, p. 350).

What follows is a farcical parody of the process by which *reading* yields *meaning*. Signifier and signified, *langue* and *parole* tangle in a linguistic nightmare. Confronted by stick figures representing the panther, Elizabeth, Louisa, and Natty, Richard is at a loss:

> "And what the devil does all this mean?" cried Richard, impatiently.
>
> "Mean!" echoed Benjamin; "it's as true as the Boadishey's log-book"—
>
> He was interrupted by the Sheriff, who put a few direct questions to him, that obtained more intelligible answers, by which means he became possessed of a tolerably correct idea of the truth. (*Pioneers*, p. 353)

For Benjamin, those hieroglyphics *are* the truth, and to question what they mean is to challenge the veracity of their author. For Richard, however, there is no direct connection between hieroglyph and natural fact, the text is susceptible to misreading, and only the physical presence of the author makes it possible for the reader to arrive at a "tolerably correct idea of the truth."

This little parable of the reading process indicates the extent to which Cooper was engaged with the problem of conveying meaning to his readers. The success of *The Spy* had convinced him that he could command a wide audience for his fiction, but he was anxious to develop techniques for instructing that audience in his vision of an American culture. In two reviews from 1822 and in *The Pioneers* itself he experimented with concepts and structures that could support his aims for a democratic fiction.

I

The May 1822 issue of *The Literary and Scientific Repository* printed two new reviews by Cooper. His recent status as a literary figure made him the logical choice for reviewing fiction rather than the nautical and economic books he had treated earlier, and the new reviews assessed two important American publications: Catherine Sedgwick's *A New-England Tale* and Washington Irving's *Bracebridge Hall.* Coinciding with the early stages of the composition of *The Pioneers,* these reviews constitute Cooper's most complete and forceful expression of his belief in a democratic literature. That he preferred Sedgwick's sincere but awkward novel to Irving's smoothly professional sketches is in itself a sufficient indication of the direction of Cooper's imaginative development, but in his discussion of the merits and limitations of the two books he established a theory of the American novel that illuminates his own practice.

Sedgewick's novel bears the subtitle *Sketches of New-England Character and Manners,* and Cooper begins his review by considering the novelist's duty to "illustrate American society and manners."

> Our political institutions, the state of learning among us, and the influence of religion upon the national character, have been often discussed and displayed; but our domestic manners, the social and the moral influences, which operate in retirement, and in common intercourse, and the multitude of local peculiarities, which form our distinctive features upon the many peopled earth, have very seldom been happily exhibited in our literature.

Irving's sketches concern "ludicrous subjects" and limit themselves to one class and community; in fact, the only American examples of the kind of social history Cooper advocates are "a story called Salem Witchcraft, and Mr. Tyler's forgotten, and we fear, lost narrative of the Algerine Captive, both of which relate to times long past."[1] The novelist should be a "true historian" in Fielding's sense of the term:

> We say the historians—we do not mean to rank the writers of these tales, among the recorders of statutes and battles, and party chronicles; but among those true historians which Dr. Moore says, are wanting, to give us just notions of what manner of men the ancient Greeks were, in their domestic affections, and retired deportment; and with whom Fielding classes himself, nearly in these words: "Those dignified authors who produce what are called true histories, are indeed writers of fictions, while I am a true historian, a describer of society as it exists, and of men as they are." (p. 98)

Such a true historian, through "generous sentiments, wide intelligence, and enlightened taste," embodies observations of character and manners in a "new and interesting story" that will "animate our solitude, refresh our weariness, and beguile our cares." But with this amusement comes a more important instruction, and its mode is the central concept in Cooper's theory of the novel:

> [The novelist] carries us out of the world of our self-love, into one resembling, in many particulars, that of our experience, and makes us forget whatever is positively painful in our lot, or wanting to our happiness. This is done by employing the imagination agreeably, by presenting to it such views of the human heart with its affections, and of human life in its appearance, its modes of enjoyment and improvement, of suffering and degeneracy, as interest curiosity, increase our knowledge, correct our false opinions, and, what is more powerful than all, appeal to our sympathies.

The novel is thus a moral fiction that engages the reader's imagination through an essentially realistic portrayal of the details of the fictional world. Reading, like experience, appeals to two innate human capacities: the desire to know; and the need to apprehend imaginatively "that higher truth, the truth of nature and of principles, which is a primitive law of the human mind, and only to be effaced by the most deplorable perversion." Where experience is comprised of contradictory impulses between self-interest and social benefit, so that our sympathies are buried beneath practical and egotistical demands, the novel can simplify, purify, and reinforce our best natures: "A good novel addresses itself very powerfully to our moral nature and conscience, and to those good feelings, and good principles, which Providence has planted within us, constantly to remind us that 'we have, all of us, one human heart'" (pp. 98–99).

The novelist must do more, however, than merely present the higher truths that he or she has perceived in the particularity of the observed world. The art must be attuned to the capacity of the reading audience:

> [The novelist] directs his train of retributions, not only in conformity to the obvious system of Providence, but according to the de-

mand of his readers' probable judgment and moral sense; proving thus his respect for the natural virtue of the common mind, as well as his knowledge of the propriety of the individual characters which he attempts to portray.

The novel, then, is a specifically democratic form whose responsibility is to limit itself to "the nature 'common to man'." High epic, chivalric romance and other forms may represent "the liveliest enjoyments of the fanciful mind," but insofar as they appeal to a more educated and thus a more limited audience, they are less useful as moral instruments.

> Are there not more persons who will be affected, who will remember it for a longer time, and who will experience a more natural pleasure, at the sight of one of Wilkin's simple and expressive pictures, similar to that which describes the oppression of a hard hearted landlord and his suffering tenants, or that of a blind fiddler in a motly family of the common people, producing a coarse but gay delight, than there are who can feel and understand the sublimities of the great masters; and is there not something more sweet and salutary, in the talent which moves and teaches so widely, than in that which enchants and astonishes only a few gifted minds?

Genius inarguably resides with those lofty works that appeal to "a few gifted minds," but genius seems after all to do little good in the world, while the novelist can materially affect the society in which we live: "We love the artist who enters into the concerns and sufferings of the humble, whose genius condescends to men of low estate, and who allies himself to the Father of mercies, when he teaches the callous and the cruel how deep are the wounds they inflict, and how terrible the retribution they may provoke" (p. 100). Thus such writers as Goldsmith, Edgeworth, and Elizabeth Hamilton deserve recognition for serving virtue and increasing human happiness in a manner that "many a venerable folio, and many a splendid epic, adorned by great names, and honoured by great critics, can never effect."

The theory that Cooper here espouses is a powerful inversion of the terms of the American debate over a republican art. Form is not to be appropriated from classical literature and imposed on native materials; rather it develops naturally out of the novelist's observation. More importantly, a firm foundation of moral utility supports the structure; Cooper argues that the very qualities of popular appeal and cheap reproduction that were the despair of conservative critics serve the fundamental needs of a democratic society and are therefore superior to the elitism of traditional art. He shares Brown's hope that the novel would appeal to the common reader as well as those who study and reflect, but unlike Brown, Cooper has a clear notion of the artist's need to "enter into the concerns and sufferings of the humble" and to observe "the demands of his reader's probable judgment and moral sense." Firmly oriented to the requirements of an actual audience, Cooper subscribes to a practical theory of a democratic fiction.

In discussing *A New-England Tale* Cooper focuses on those elements of the novel that illustrate Sedgwick's perception of the common life of New England. Foremost among these is her portrayal of "Crazy Bet," the only character whom Sedgwick attempted to sketch from life. Crazy Bet is a "natural," a madwoman whose hypersensitive mind annihilates the conventions that buffer the ordinary ideas of God, nature, and society. Cooper is especially interested in Crazy Bet's language, which is filled with "expressions the most original and affecting," and he emphasizes Sedgwick's success in recording it:

> The style of the maniac's broken discourse displays a fine power of imagination, and an equal command of expression in the recorder of the character, if the language imputed to her be not taken from the original; and, in relation to the poor creature, it reminds us of those flowers which are said to spring up from the soil recently deluged by the fiery showers of a volcano, that derive their glowing colors and their sweet odours from the elements which have changed beauty to ashes and joy to mourning. (p. 108)

Another character whom Cooper finds worthy of "particular notice" is Mary Hull, a servant. Like Caesar in *The Spy*, Mary Hull exemplifies those servants who comprehend their own best interests in the interests of those they serve. America has grown away from its original simplicity, and as masters have arisen for the first time from the servant class, a certain amount of insubordination and jealousy has resulted. Still, the American servant enjoys unusual advantages, and "the best of this class are the most cultivated and intelligent." Cooper's point is that servants should not be kept ignorant; the nature of a democratic society demands that servants be educated in the same way as their masters:

> If the elevation of character by means of enlarged knowledge is a certain and universal effect; if moral excellence is the supreme good, and if this is required of all God's people of every rank; surely all men are entitled, by some provision of their country, by common consent, and by the active cooperation of all persons of any influence in society, to such a share of literary and moral instruction, as shall define their duties, create for them some literary enjoyment, and improve their understanding: so that even the humblest individual may feel himself exalted by the intellectual pleasures, and by his share of rational and worthy influence improve the succeeding generation. (p. 129)

Other elements which Cooper finds interesting include the pretentious obscurity of New England names ("Hortensia, Olympia and Philologus"), a visit to a mountaineer's cabin, and a midnight sojourn to the grave of a suicide—an episode that Cooper compares to "the peril and forelorness of some of C. B. Brown's heroes in their lonely and hazardous wanderings." Although he dutifully summarizes the plot of *A New-England Tale*, what attracts Cooper's attention are fringe elements, the observation of remarkable characters and scenes, action of unusual intensity, and episodes that affirm his interest in democratic fiction. He concludes his review by quoting Crazy Bet's deathbed scene, "both on account of the interest she inspires, and on that of the pathos with which the close of her life is described, and the book is terminated."

If Cooper made *A New-England Tale* the occasion for expressing his belief in the power of democratic literature, he used *Bracebridge Hall* as an opportunity to voice his reservations about the course Irving had chosen to pursue. "We commenced the perusal of this work with no ordinary anticipations," he begins; national and regional pride predispose him to view Irving's work favorably, the *Sketch Book* has found favor with English literati, and "the appearance of the volumes . . . and the price the author is said to have received for the manuscript, (to say nothing of the price of the volumes themselves), had no little agency in exciting our imagination as to the merits of the work."[2] But he finds that his expectations have been disappointed and that, though *Bracebridge Hall* will probably prove popular, its success will be based more on fashion than on intrinsic merit (p. 133).

 Cooper castigates *Bracebridge Hall* on every point, from its title to its overall conception. It was a mistake, he argues, to give the work a new title when it is but a continuation of the *Sketch Book,* and no author can afford merely to repeat himself:

> It seems to be a conceded point, that the reputation of a living author cannot be stationary. He must advance in merit, or he will be supposed to decline. In other words, he cannot sustain his reputation, by barely equaling, in the same line of composition, that which he has already produced. He must either cultivate a new field, or produce a richer harvest from the old.

Irving's topics are "trite and commonplace" and result in "elaborate trifling" and "important nothingness." As an example, Cooper quotes Irving's description of his feelings on first approaching London, the semimythical city of his childhood reading. Those feelings center on Newberry's bookshop because Newberry had been the publisher of "all the picture books of the day, Tom Thumb's Folio, Giles Gingerbread, and Jack the Giant Killer; and out of his abundant love for children, he demanded nothing for the paper and print, and only a penny half-penny for the binding!" Of this alleged generosity, Cooper dryly comments, "How it escaped D'Israeli, in his Curiosities of Literature, we know not, nor have we now time to enquire" (p. 134).

 The weakness of individual detail is compounded by the weakness of the work's design:

> It is a sort of series, or rather a given number, of sketches and descriptions of squires and maids and matrons and bachelors and lovesick girls and school masters and priests and apothecaries and doctors and dogs; intermingled with stories, both long and short, having no other connection than that of continuity, and no other order than that of succession. (p. 135)

Many of the portraits and tales are witty and just, but Cooper complains of "a few instances" when Irving has "overstept the modesty of nature, and passed from the ludicrous to the absurd." "The fair Julia," the heroine of the hall, Cooper finds "rather an insipid article": "Indeed, all the love scenes of our author, are puerile and mawkish; characterized by a morbid sensibility, and by a fastidious and artificial arrangement of common-place details, language, and scenery." In addition, Irving has occasionally indulged a certain streak of indelicacy which is likely to offend his potential audience—an audience that Cooper still envisions as primarily female. Cooper cites the story of "The Stout Gentleman," a tale about a man who placates his angry landlady by taking her to bed:

> It has, however, another fault, which, considering the class of readers to whom our author must mainly look, as well for the profit, as the fame of his production, (we mean the fair and the fashionable), is still more objectionable. There is a half-hidden looseness, an indelicacy of allusion in the story, which should have found no place in a book destined, if not designed, as an ornament to the sopha, and as a modest companion at the parlour window. (pp. 136–39)

Finally, Cooper praises the "prudence and delicacy" with which Irving writes of English politics, classes, and landscape, though the praise strikes an ironic note when Cooper cites Irving's professed attachment to republican principles: "He eulogizes the aristocracy of Great Britain; descants upon the dignity of descent, and the generous pride of illustrious ancestry!" With a cautionary fable, Cooper warns Irving that relying on an English audience can be disastrous to his political principles:

> The English, though a proud, are a refined people, and generous minds are neither insensible to praise, nor of the obligation it confers. Even Mr. Walsh was once a favourite; his unbounded admiration of England and indiscriminate abuse of France, softened the hearts of the most implacable reviewers; and while they acknowledged the justness of his observations and the purity of his style, they candidly confessed, that he had said more for them, than they could say for themselves.[3] But Mr. Walsh subsequently corrected

his opinions, and so did the reviewers. He lost his admiration of the
English, and with it he lost his information, his talents, and purity
of style. (pp. 140–43)

No American author can afford to stake his livelihood on a British
audience unless he is prepared to flatter its prejudices and to
suppress his observation.

Taken together, these two reviews provide a reasonably
complete picture of the ideas that occupied Cooper while he
worked on *The Pioneers*. He could not merely repeat the formulas
he had developed for *The Spy;* in any event, the novel had already
inspired a host of imitations, and Cooper could hardly imitate the
imitators.[4] Nor, despite the pleas of Wiley, could he surrender
himself to the writing of mere tales and sketches after the manner
of either Opie or Irving; his ambition demanded an extended work
of sufficient complexity to provide richness. He still conceived of
the audience for fiction as female and genteel, and he retained the
sense that moral purity was necessary to his work, but political
responsibility and the concept of a democratic fiction had begun to
assume a more important place in the hierarchy of his values. *The
Pioneers,* like some of *Bracebridge Hall,* relies on childhood memories, and, to judge by his remarks on the "common-place" and
"infantile" quality of Irving's recollections, Cooper determined to
make his own as fresh and "manly" as he could. The strictures
against Irving's caricatures, too, must have served as a reminder
that in portraying regional and ethnic characters Cooper did not
want to be carried beyond the "modesty of nature." Clearly, he
wanted to provide his tale with a vigorous, attractive heroine and
with love scenes that avoided the "puerile and mawkish."

These were not the only goals Cooper set himself in
writing *The Pioneers*. He also intended to enlarge the literary
independence of his American audience by encouraging what he
understood as a healthy lack of reliance on the strictures and
judgments of professional critics. In preparing for the English
publication of his new novel, Cooper offered to write a new preface
for it: "I have an object in my present preface that is altogether
confined to this Country."[5] Common people might respond spontaneously to the simple, natural pictures of Wilkins, but they could

be bullied by self-proclaimed experts into deprecating their own responses and denying the democratic artist his proper audience. Throughout his career Cooper was alert to this danger, and he took every opportunity to enjoin his countrymen to use their own responses as the measure of value, not to surrender to the opinions of reviewers and editors. In *Notions of the Americans* he could (rather idealistically) claim that "So far, then, from the journals succeeding in leading the public opinion astray, they are invariably obliged to submit to it. . . . [Their] principles must be in accordance with the private opinions of men, or most of their labour is lost."[6] By the time he wrote *The American Democrat,* however, the battle for intellectual independence seemed lost, and Cooper could only inveigh against the ascendency of demagogues.[7] In the early stages of his career Cooper was optimistic about the possibility of nurturing the independent spirit in America.

The preface to the first edition of *The Pioneers* is a letter (dated January 1, 1823) to "Mr. Charles Wiley, *Bookseller,*" and it reflects Cooper's pleasure both with the remarkable success of *The Spy* and with the book he has just completed. The tone is jaunty and self-confident, and much of Cooper's anxiety about his audience has been replaced by a more focused anxiety about the niggling objections and critical pretensions of reviewers.

Cooper's mood is suggested by a brief résumé of his career in letters:

> The first book was written, because I was told that I could not write a grave tale; so, to prove that the world did not know me, I wrote one that was so grave nobody would read it; wherein I think that I had the best of the argument. The second was written to see if I could not overcome this neglect of the reading world. How far I have succeeded, Mr. Charles Wiley, must ever remain a secret between ourselves. The third has been written, exclusively, to please myself; so it would be no wonder if it displeased every body else; for what two ever thought alike, on a subject of the imagination! (*Pioneers,* p. 3)

From this beginning Cooper develops his argument that reviewers display a lamentable "discrepancy of taste" that justifies an author's ignoring them completely. But Cooper does not ignore them; he accuses reviewers of clothing the tritest ideas "in a language so obscure and metaphysical, that the reader is not about to comprehend their pages without some labour." This obscurity is the source of a general contagion in the reading public, for common readers often take their opinions from reviews, although they may not be sure what precisely those opinions are: "It is delightful, to see the literati of a circulating library get hold of one of these difficult periods! Their praise of the performance is exactly commensurate with its obscurity." A case in point is the term "keeping," which is common "in the mouths of all Reviewers, readers of magazines, and young ladies, when speaking of novels."[8] Whatever a reviewer wishes to rebuke is "out of keeping," and the word loses all meaning. For Cooper, however, "keeping" has a very specific meaning:

> the writer of a tale, who takes the earth for the scene of his story, is in some degree bound to respect human nature. Therefore, I would advise any one, who make take up this book, with the expectation of meeting gods and goddesses, spooks or witches, or of feeling that strong excitement that is produced by battles and murders, to throw it aside at once, for no such interest will be found in any of its pages. (*Pioneers*, p. 4)

Having warned against lurid expectations, Cooper does little to suggest what the reader *could* anticipate, aside from the hint that "it was mine own humour that suggested this tale; but it is a humour that is deeply connected with feeling." The purpose of the preface, clearly, is to induce readers to ignore reviewers (just as the author does) and to approach the new novel in an open, conscientious spirit. For his true reviews, Cooper will look to his profits:

> The "Pioneers" is now before the world, Mr. Wiley, and I shall look to you for the only true account of its reception. The critics may write as obscurely as they please, and look much wiser than they are; the papers may puff or abuse, as their changeful humours dictate; but if you meet me with a smiling face, I shall at once know that all is essentially well. (*Pioneers*, pp. 4–5)

This mercantile policy may seem rather crass, but it expresses Cooper's understanding of the operations of the capitalist market in a democratic society. Behind it is his faith in a democratic art, the faith he expressed more loftily in his review of Sedgwick. That art which has the broadest appeal, brings the most natural pleasure, and serves to alter human society will also be the most profitable for the artist as long as wealth and critical opinion are relatively evenly distributed in a democracy. Whenever either wealth or opinion is accumulated by a few individuals, whether they be Wall Street brokers or newspaper editors or magazine critics, the livelihood of a democratic artist is threatened. The 1823 preface marks the opening of Cooper's lifelong war against reviewers, and it displays the extent to which that war was motivated by Cooper's commitment to the concept of democratic art. If the nation's wealth were to be commanded by a few aristocratic individuals, the artist would be forced to cater to them in a return to the old patronage system; if the reception of art were to be determined by a few critics and reviewers, the artist would be forced to cater to *them* in a new but no less pernicious patronage system. When Cooper prematurely bade farewell to his reading public in 1834, he believed that the latter condition had come about, that he had been effectively cut off from his true audience and was therefore forced to cease writing:

> So far as I stand opposed to that class among you which forms the public of a writer, on points that, however much in error, I honestly believe to be of vital importance to the well being and dignity of the human race, I can only lament that we are separated by so wide a barrier as to render any further communion, under our old relations, mutually unsatisfactory.[9]

Publicly, then, Cooper expressed every confidence in his ability to touch, with simple and expressive pictures, his common reader. Privately, however, he expressed some doubts. On November 29, 1822, he wrote to John Murray, who had agreed to publish *The Pioneers* in London:

> I had announced the work as a "descriptive tale" but perhaps have confined myself too much to describing the scenes of my own

youth—I know that the present taste is for action and strong excitement, and in this respect am compelled to acknowledge that the
two first volumes are deficient, I however am not without hopes
that the third will be thought to make some amends—[10]

The danger of writing a book exclusively to please oneself is that
no reader will ever find its scenes and actions interesting, that the
author's personal involvement will render his work merely personal and garrulous at the expense of the reader's excitement. The
danger seemed worth risking, however, because of the opportunity
to act as Fielding's true historian, and Cooper's developing sense of
his own powers gave him reasonable assurance that *The Pioneers*
would succeed in the marketplace: "If there be any value in truth,
the pictures are very faithful, and I can safely challenge a scrutiny
in th[is] particular—But the world must be left to decide for itself,
and I believe it is very seldom that it decides wrong—" (*L/J,* 1:85).

II

Cooper called his new novel "A Descriptive Tale," and it
is this descriptive quality that D. H. Lawrence praised in a famous
passage:

Perhaps my taste is childish, but these scenes in
Pioneers seem to me marvelously beautiful. The raw village street,
with woodfires blinking through the unglazed window-chinks, on a
winter's night. The inn, with the rough woodsman and the drunken
Indian John; the church, with the snowy congregation crowding to
the fire. Then the lavish abundance of Christmas cheer, and turkey-
shooting in the snow. Spring coming, forests all green, maple-
sugar taken from the trees; and clouds of pigeons flying from the
south, myriads of pigeons, shot in heaps; and night-fishing on the
teeming, virgin lake; and deer-hunting.
Pictures! Some of the loveliest, most glamorous pictures in all literature.[11]

Although *The Spy* had contained a few rudimentary descriptions of
nature, that novel never approached the panoramic vistas and pal-

pable sense of nature for which Cooper was to become famous. What were the sources of his new impulse to write a descriptive tale?

In an important article, Thomas Philbrick noted three direct influences on the structure of *The Pioneers*. The first was James Kirke Paulding's *The Backwoodsman,* where Cooper found the lines for his title-page motto, although "the poem was notorious in this country for its ineptitude." More important, Philbrick argues, were Irving's *Bracebridge Hall* and Thomson's *The Seasons. Bracebridge Hall* presents the story of the Gypsy chieftain Starlit Tom, who is arrested for stealing sheep, tried before Squire Bracebridge, and treated with "great mildness and indulgence" by the kindly Squire. The Bracebridge episodes in Irving's *Sketch Book* concern the celebration of Christmas: "the reunion of the family, the feasting, and the church service."[12] Some of Cooper's secondary characters, especially Elnathan Todd and Richard Jones, may be derived from Irving's sketches of British characters. In these adaptations Cooper was attempting to correct the discontinuity for which he had criticized Irving:

> the pages of *The Sketch Book* and *Bracebridge Hall* bring into haphazard juxtaposition a substantial portion of the diverse materials from which *The Pioneers* was to be constructed: romantic outcasts, voracious Yankees, paternalistic proprietors and bustling bachelors, manor-house manners and tavern politics, village games and county churches. [Cooper's] task was to assemble those materials into a coherent and meaningful structure, to impose upon them systems of relationship and patterns of development that Irving's casual sketching did not permit.[13]

The principle of organization Cooper chose, according to Philbrick, was Thomson's *The Seasons*. Like Thomson's poem, Cooper's novel moves through the cycle of the year: "the time scheme of the novel is carefully designed to achieve Thomson's major effect, a sense of the incessant flux in nature and human activity and of the sharp contrasts in the scenes that the seasonal cycle brings successively into view."[14] Thus Cooper merged the resources of the novel with those of eighteenth-century descriptive poetry.

James Franklin Beard, citing Cooper's boyhood acquaintance with Virgil's *Ecloques,* argues that the pastoral tradition also contributed importantly to *The Pioneers:*

> Virgil transformed the pastoral from a mode for gratifying the
> human longing for a simplified, Arcadian existence to a medium
> for exploring the inconsistencies and dissatisfactions implicit in
> that longing, a stage for dramatizing the most complex states of
> mind and the most baffling contradictions. Employing such devices
> as multiple plots, ironic juxtapositions, symbolic elaboration of
> character, contests, and complicated forms of wordplay, Virgil and
> his successors evolved conventions adaptable to any genre and sus-
> ceptible of exquisitely refined statement.[15]

The pastoral tradition combines with a broad spectrum of
other concerns to produce the hybrid form Northrop Frye calls
"romance-anatomy," and the results is that *The Pioneers* is "our
closest early approach to prose epic."[16]

Cooper himself defined "descriptive tale" in other
terms. Writing a rebuttal to critics who had accused him of portraying himself as an American aristocrat in *Home As Found,*
Cooper drew attention to the original purpose of *The Pioneers:*
"*The Pioneers* is announced, in its title page, as a 'Descriptive
Tale'; descriptive, not in Mr. Jordan's sense of a literal account of
persons and things; but descriptive as regards general characteristics, usages, and the state of a new country" (*L/J,* 4:253). If we take
seriously the motive imputed in 1842 for a novel written twenty
years earlier, we must look to the extraordinary profusion of travelers' accounts and explorers' journals published in the Federal
period. The most famous of these were Crèvecœur's *Letters from
an American Farmer* (1782), William Bartram's *Travels through
North and South Carolina, Georgia, East and West Florida* (1792),
and the journals of the Lewis and Clark expedition, but there were
many others. The London publisher Richard Phillips specialized in
travel accounts from all parts of the world and printed a number of
American journals: F. A. Michaux's *Travels to the Westward of the
Allegany Mountains* (1805), Perrin du Lac's *Travels through the
Two Louisianas and Among the Savage Nations of the Missouri*
(1807), *Travels in the Interior Parts of America . . . by Captains*

Lewis and Clark, Doctor Sibley, and Mr. Dunbar (1807), and
Thomas Ashe's Travels in America (1809).[17] More meaningful for
Cooper were those accounts of travels in upstate New York. Foremost among these, for obvious reasons, was his father's *A Guide in
the Wilderness* (1810), a handbook for founding viable pioneer
communities and a preface to the history of Cooperstown. De Witt
Clinton's *Private Canal Journal* (1810) was the result of the survey
preparatory to building the Erie Canal. Mrs. Grant's *Memoirs of an
American Lady* (1808) concerned life in Albany. Cooper definitely
used Mrs. Grant's book as a source for *Satanstoe*,[18] but he may also
have used her discussions of the history and culture of the Mohawk
Indians and of the "gentle treatment of slaves among the Alba-
nians" in *The Pioneers*,[19] and Mrs. Grant tells the tale of a "Settler
who resided some Time among" the Indians and became a kind of
moral standard for the community.[20]

    The pioneering spirit represented by these accounts
was immeasurably enhanced in the early nineteenth century by
the territorial acquisitions and expeditions that gave rise and expression to the American doctrine of manifest destiny. The Cumberland Road, begun in 1811, and the Erie Canal, begun in 1817,
had opened the American interior to settlers, and in 1824 an obser-
vor emphasized the "ease and comfort" with which the westward
migration was conducted, comparing the Cumberland Road to "a
street through some populous city—travelers on foot, on horse-
back, and in carriages are seen mingling on its paved surface."[21] In
1803 the Louisiana Purchase more than doubled the size of American territory, and the Lewis and Clark expedition set out with the
dual purpose of collecting scientific information and opening the
Missouri River country to American fur traders. In 1811 John Jacob
Astor sent the *Tonquin* around Cape Horn to establish a trading
post at the mouth of the Columbia River. The early 1820s saw the
opening of the Santa Fe Trail, the founding of the Rocky Mountain
Fur Company, and the military expedition of the Missouri Legion,
designed to intimidate the Arikaras and other Indians into allowing fur traders access to the Missouri River. In 1821 Stephen Austin
planted the first Anglo-American settlement in what was to become the Texas Republic. The first decades of the nineteenth cen-

tury mark the birth of that extraordinary fermentation of expansionist energies that would not flag until the close of the frontier.

Expansionism was not without its critics. The Whig Party advocated a policy of cultivating the existing territories rather than adding to them. When Joel Barlow, that advocate of the French Revolution, wrote an enthusiastic poem "On the Discoveries of Captain Lewis," it was quickly parodied in Boston's *Monthly Anthology* by no less a personage than John Quincy Adams. The parody assails the expedition on a number of points. Of its heroic daring, Adams wrote:

> Heroic, sure, the toil must be
>   To travel through the woods, sir;
> And never meet a foe, yet save
>   His person and his goods, sir!

Adams treated the expedition's scientific mission as a personal aberration of Thomas Jefferson:

> He never with a Mammoth met,
>   However you may wonder;
> Nor even with a Mamoth's bone,
>   Above the ground or under—
>
> . . . .
> And from the day his course began,
>   Till even it was ended,
> He never found the Indian tribe
>   From Welchmen straight descended. . . .

Adams' main target was the impulse to aggrandize explorers at the expense of those who work to improve the quality of human life. In a note he claimed that "our intention is not to depreciate the merits of Captian Lewis's publick services," but it is clear that he regarded those services as relatively insignificant, and he objected strenuously to Barlow's recommendation that the name of the Columbia River be changed to "Lewis"; Lewis had merely looked at, not improved, the Oregon Territory:

And must we then resign the hope
　　These Elements of changing?
And must we still, alas! be told
　　That after all his ranging,
The Captain could discover nought
　　But Water in the Fountains?
Must Forests still be form'd of Trees?
　　Of Rugged Rocks the Mountains?

We never will be so fubb'd off,
　　As sure as I'm a sinner!
Come—let us all subscribe, and ask
　　The HERO to a dinner—
And Barlow stanzas shall indite—
　　A bard, the tide who tames, sir—
And if we cannot alter *things*
　　By G—, we'll change their names, sir!

In his concluding stanza Adams links the French Revolution,
Thomas Jefferson, Joel Barlow, and the Lewis and Clark expedition
as representatives of the muddle-headed populism against which
he struggled all his public life:

True—Tom and Jöel now, no more
　　Can overturn a nation;
And work, by butchery and blood,
　　A great regeneration;—
Yet, still we can turn inside out
　　Old Nature's Constitution,
And bring a Babel back of *names*—
　　Huzza! for REVOLUTION![22]

　　　When Cooper sat down "to amuse myself" with a tale of
pioneer life, then, he was simultaneously exploiting the popularity
of those travelers' accounts and explorers' journals that described
the frontier and entering into the debate over the advisability of
expansionist policies. Out of these two concerns arose the theme
of the novel. John McWilliams has argued that *The Pioneers* is
about "the nature of political justice and the necessity of law on

the American frontier,"[23] but that facet of the book depends on a more fundamental question: who owns America? The question is pursued through the conflict between Judge Temple and Natty Bumppo, but it can only be resolved in the marriage of Oliver Edward Effingham and Elizabeth Temple. Before the resolution is achieved, Cooper analyzes the apparently irreconcilable differences between America's past and its future, and the landscape of violence is once again the scene for dramatizing those differences.

III

The opening of the novel establishes a panoramic view for the reader. It is a geographical and historical perspective that gradually narrows until it is focused on a sleigh traveling to Templeton on Christmas Eve, 1793. The first paragraph surveys mountains and rivers, agriculture, education, religion, and government in New York State; the sense of historical perspective emerges from the narrator's insistence on the time in which he writes (1821–22) and on the clearly definable *beginning* of history in the region: "Only forty years have passed since this territory was a wilderness" (*Pioneers,* p. 16).[24] After the episode of the deer hunt and a chapter detailing Judge Temple's personal history, Elizabeth Temple (with the reader) surveys the valley from the mountaintop; the perspective gradually contracts to Templeton and finally to "the castle, as Judge Temple's dwelling was termed in common parlance" (*Pioneers,* p. 43).

The aerial perspective contracting to a near view of the castle accomplishes a number of things, all of them important to the reader's understanding of the conflict over the ownership of the American landscape. First, it establishes the castle as the visual and moral center of that landscape. We are told that the castle "came to be the model, in some one or other of its numerous excellencies, for every aspiring edifice within twenty miles of it" (*Pioneers,* p. 43), and if the lawyers, shopkeepers, and doctor are Templeton's nobles, Judge Temple is "its king" (*Pioneers,* p. 42). All that matters in the valley emanates from and returns to this castle.

Second, the contracting perspective gathers to the castle the visual features of the valley—the beautiful, tree-covered mountains, the snowy plains, the fruit trees planted by the vanished Indians, and the tawdry industry suggested by the more or less ugly houses of the village. Cooper adopts this effect from Book 1, Chapter 4, of Fielding's *Tom Jones,* where the grandeur and beauty of Squire Allworthy's estate flows centripetally into the man himself, "a human being replete with benevolence, meditating in what manner he might render himself most acceptable to his Creator, by doing most good to his creatures."[25] The emphasis that Cooper places on the incongruity of Templeton and the castle leavens Fielding's effect with irony, however, and presages an incongruity in Judge Temple's character.

Third, the reader's role is allied with that of Elizabeth as she surveys a scene dimly remembered but dramatically altered by the growth of the village. In the unfolding of the plot Elizabeth and the reader are to share a critical judgment tempered by sympathy for both disputing parties. Rather than condemning Judge Temple's duplicity or Oliver Edwards' romantic excesses from an objective perspective, the reader is to share a daughter's forgiveness of her father's pride, a woman's forgiveness of her lover's precipitancy.

Fourth, the movement from aerial view to mountaintop to Templeton is experienced as a literal and figurative *descent.* We move from the beauty of nature to the incongruous architecture of the "composite order," from the moral expansiveness of sky and forest to the claustrophobic and overheated confines of the castle. This sense of contraction and confinement powerfully prepares the reader for the conflict between Judge Temple's vision of a tamed agrarian landscape and Natty Bumppo's vision of a life coherent with nature.[26]

With these effects established, Cooper focuses at length on the castle itself. Because walls are solid stone, Richard Jones, Judge Temple's cousin and architect, can only exercise his genius on the porch and roof. Jones' ineptitude gives a comic surface to what is essentially a solid and comfortable structure. "A roof, Richard contended, was a part of the edifice that the ancients always endeavoured to conceal, it being an excrescence in architecture that was only to be tolerated on account of its usefulness" (*Pioneers,* pp. 43–44). Accordingly, Richard plans a flat roof until Temple points out that it could not support the weight of a winter's snows. The peaked roof eventually erected proves to be "the most conspicuous part of the whole edifice," and Richard tries to mend the error by painting the roof—first sky-blue, then "a cloud-color," then "invisible green." Finally Richard abandons his attempt to conceal the roof and paints it "sunshine," the platform is decorated with "gaudily painted railings," urns and moldings, and the four chimneys become "four exceedingly conspicuous objects." Richard modifies his architectural theory to embrace the accomplished fact:

> as his eye became gradually accustomed to the object, he grew better satisfied with his labours, and instead of apologizing for the defects, he commenced praising the beauties of the mansion house. He soon found hearers; and as wealth and comfort are at all times attractive, it was, as has been said, made a model for imitation on a small scale. . . . Thus it is ever with fashion, which even renders the faults of the great, subjects of admiration. (*Pioneers,* p. 45)

The porch is equally successful; its stone platform has sunk into the ground, and the pillars, instead of supporting the roof, dangle from it. In addition the house is surrounded by "stubbs," the charred skeletons of trees killed by the slash-and-burn technique used to clear the area for building. Elizabeth is forcefully impressed with what a descent she has experienced:

> when the horses of her father turned, with a rapid whirl, into the open gate of the mansion-house, and nothing stood before her but the cold, dreary stone-walls of the building, as she approached them through an avenue of young and leafless poplars, Elizabeth felt as if all the loveliness of the mountain-view had vanished like the fancies of a dream. (*Pioneers,* p. 59)

The interior of the castle, too, is an incongruous mélange. Everything the house contains suggests superfluity, excess, redundancy. The hall is dominated by "an enormous stove, the sides of which appeared to be quivering with heat"; the sideboard is "groaning under the piles of silver plate"; the tables are "prodigious" and the sofa is "enormous"; Benjamin Pump consults the barometer "with prodigious exactitude" (*Pioneers*, p. 63). The side doors are crowned with pediments and pedestals, each bearing a small bust in blackened plaster of Paris: a Homer, a Shakespeare, an urn "holding the ashes of Dido," a Franklin, a Washington, and either Julius Caesar or Dr. Faustus ("there were good reasons for believing either"). These busts are at once the tutelary idols of the Temple household and an ironic comment on Temple's role as a pioneer. On the one hand they illustrate the ambition to create a retrospective golden age in the American wilderness; the founding fathers take their places adjacent to representatives of those values worth preserving from the past. At the same time the "ashes of Dido" and the ambiguous Caesar/Faustus figure evoke memories of the dangers of pioneering. We recall the misery Aeneas left in his wake, the tragic hubris of Caesar and Faustus.

The walls are covered with a "dark, lead-coloured English paper, that represented Britannia weeping over the tomb of Wolfe," but the hanging was done by Richard, and so of course it is not properly aligned:

> Each width contained the figure, with the slight exception of one arm of the General, which ran over on to the next piece, so that when Richard essayed, with his own hands, to put together this delicate outline, some difficulties occurred, that prevented a nice conjunction, and Britannia had reason to lament, in addition to the loss of her favourite's life, numberless cruel amputations of his right arm. (*Pioneers*, p. 64)

This image of impotence compounds the sense of Pyrrhic victory commemorated in the wallpaper.

The castle's interior reflects an undirected, superabundant energy wasting its powers in a futile attempt to rebuild Europe on the frontier, and its exterior is an affront to nature, as the epigraph to chapter 3 (in which the house is first described) indicates: the epigraph praises "nature's handy work" but concludes, "Yet man can mar such works with his rude taste, / Like some sad spoiler of a virgin's fame." Judge Temple's enterprise, which includes burning down native trees and replacing them with imported poplars, is specifically a "rape of the land."[27]

The incongruities of the house mirror the incongruities of Judge Temple's character. He is a conservationist and a despoiler, possessor and dispossessor of the valley, the illegitimate source of the law. Several details of his life link him with an ironic version of the Mosaic myth of the journey to the Promised Land. His first view of the valley echoes Moses' view of Palestine:

> I left my party, the morning of my arrival, near the farms of the Cherry Valley, and, following a deer-path, rode to the summit of the mountain, that I have since called Mount Vision; for the sight that there met my eyes seemed to me as the deceptions of a dream. The fire had run over the pinnacle, and, in a great measure, laid open the view. The leaves were fallen, and I mounted a tree, and sat for an hour looking on the silent wilderness. (*Pioneers*, p. 235)

When his band of pioneers suffers near starvation, Temple (with the help of the Lord) feeds them:

> It was not a moment for inaction. I purchased cargoes of wheat from the granaries of Pennsylvania; they were landed at Albany, and brought up the Mohawk in boats; from thence it was transported on pack-horses into the wilderness, and distributed amongst my people. Seines were made, and the lakes and rivers were dragged for fish. Something like a miracle was wrought in our favour, for enormous shoals of herrings were discovered to have wandered five hundred miles, through the windings of the impetuous Susquehanna, and the lake was alive with their numbers. These were at length caught, and dealt out to the people, with proper portions of salt; and from that moment, we began to prosper. (*Pioneers*, pp. 234–35)

Of course, Judge Temple is also the bringer of the law, and, like Moses, he cannot truly possess the Promised Land, for his ownership is based on an equivocal claim from the Revolution, a claim that can only be legitimized by the merging of his line with the Effinghams.

These details of the Mosaic myth are by no means Cooper's invention; they are taken from the experience of his father, William Cooper. The arrival at Lake Otsego and the miracle of the wheat (supplied by the New York legislature, not by Judge Cooper) and herrings are from William Cooper's *A Guide in the Wilderness*.[28] Lest the reader find these events too mythologized for easy credence, Cooper added a footnote to the 1832 edition of the novel: "All this was literally true" (*Pioneers*, p. 235n). Moreover, Judge Cooper's patent to the Cooperstown land, purchased at a mortgage sale, had been "complicated by the Tory interests of Governor William Franklin and the claims of heirs of George Crogan, the original patentee."[29] The parallels between Judge Temple and Moses were not created by art but by the mythology of the American frontier as the Promised Land, a mythology that extended from William Bradford's *Of Plymouth Plantation* to Joel Barlow's *Vision of Columbus*.[30] In 1785 Timothy Dwight, who was to become president of Yale College in 1795, published *The Conquest of Canaan,* a biblical-epical allegory of the American Revolution. In the early nineteenth century the rhetoric of the Puritan errand into the wilderness was adapted to a new purpose, and a new series of visionaries tried again to prove that the Indians were the ten lost tribes of Israel; the attempt gave rise to such works as Elias Boudinot's *Star in the West* (1816), Ethan Smith's *View of the Hebrews* (1823), and Joseph Smith's *Book of Mormon* (1830).[31] Virtually every successful American settlement could point to its local Moses, Aaron, and Joshua.

Cooper's contribution was the transforming of the myth into comic legend. Judge Temple's vision is not of a land of milk and honey but of an industrial Europe: "To his eye, where others saw nothing but a wilderness, towns, manufactories, bridges, canals, mines, and all the other resources of an old country, were constantly presenting themselves" (*Pioneers*, p. 321). The realization of his vision is entrusted to and subverted by Richard Jones. Jones is clearly a projection of one aspect of Judge Temple; for all his conservationist rhetoric, the Judge continually yields to "the excitement of the moment" (*Pioneers*, p. 259) and reveals himself as another waster and spender at the pigeon shoot, the fishing scene, and elsewhere. After these orgies of exploitation he may, as Elizabeth notes with surprise, suffer remorse, "as if he actually thought that a day of retribution was to follow this hour of abundance and prodigality" (*Pioneers,* p. 262), but the hour has been his own work. Judge Temple's social projects become Richard's architectural monstrosities (mansion house, church, and jail), and Richard even manages to subvert the miracle of the wheat and herrings; he recalls,

> I was the man who served out the fish and the salt. When the poor devils came to receive their rations, Benjamin, who was my deputy, was obliged to keep them off by stretching ropes around me, for they smelt so of garlic, from eating nothing but the wild onion, that the fumes put me out, often, in my measurements. (*Pioneers,* p. 235)

A further incongruity in Judge Temple's character derives from another source. Because of the obvious example of William Cooper, critics have seen Temple as a portrait of Cooper's father and have analyzed it as an instance of filial revenge. As Henry Nash Smith remarks in a frequently cited sentence, "When an author introduces a central character resembling his father, one does not have to be very much of a Freudian to conclude that the imagination is working on a deeper level than usual."[32] This ready identification would have been less obvious to Cooper's reader in 1823 than another, more prominent model for Judge Temple: De Witt Clinton, an unsuccessful presidential candidate in 1812, mayor of New York City from 1803 to 1815, and governor of New York for most of the period between 1817 and 1828. Cooper had actively campaigned for Clinton in the 1820 election,[33] and he must have been thoroughly familiar with the two marks Clinton left on American cultural life: the Erie Canal and the spoils system of political appointment. Clinton's *Private Canal Journal* (1810), in language much like that of William Cooper's *Guide in the Wilderness,* records his journey through New York's western counties in quest of a route for the Erie Canal, and from 1810 to 1817 Clinton served on the Canal Commission. When the Canal opened in 1825 it initiated a land boom that fueled the American economy for twelve feverish years, until the Panic of 1837.[34] Judge Temple's vision of "towns, manufactories, bridges, canals [and] mines" is more akin to Clinton's than to that of William Cooper, whose hand-book for pioneers focuses much more practically on problems of survival. Clinton's other innovation, the spoils system, became a permanent fixture of American political life when Andrew Jackson brought it to the White House in 1829. The first budding of this system can be seen in the sheriff's position that Judge Temple obtains as a Christmas present for Richard Jones.

Judge Temple, then, adumbrates the political and cultural trend of New York at the end of the eighteenth century. As he is the center of the opening landscape, so is he the center of the political, social, and spiritual life of his community. His name puns on "Templar" (*Pioneers*, p. 37) and "temple" (both these words have double meanings, too), and the law and the religion of Templeton ramify from his opinions. Yet in treating Judge Temple's accomplishments ironically, Cooper prepares the reader for an alternative to his vision.

Natty Bumppo and his companions represent that alternative. If the language of *The Pioneers* forces the reader to perceive Temple and his castle as the nadir of an artificially structured space, it represents Natty as curiously diffuse, ubiquitous, centrifugal rather than centripetal. His first appearance in the novel is by one of those miraculous transformations that Elizabeth marvels at. After her father has missed the deer in the opening scene, two more shots ring out: "A loud shout was given by the unseen marksman, and a couple of men instantly appeared from behind the trunks of two of the pines, where they had evidently placed themselves in expectation of the passage of the deer" (*Pioneers*, p. 21). Natty always appears from and returns to the forest which surrounds Templeton; he is a socially marginal character in a literal as well as a moral sense.[35]

Thus Natty's cabin is the antithesis of the densely centering force of Temple's castle. The cabin is located across the lake from Templeton; unlike the castle, it is never really described except as a mysterious "forbidden ground" which is as silent "as if the foot of man had never trod the wilderness" (*Pioneers*, p. 288). The cabin is so perfectly blended with its surroundings that it is virtually invisible. Judge Temple's original view of the valley from

Mount Vision gives no hint that anyone lives near the lake. After gazing down "with a mingled feeling of pleasure and desolation" for an hour, Temple descends into the valley, and only then does he see smoke curling up from the eastern shore.

> "It was the only indication of the vicinity of man that I had then seen. After much toil, I made my way to the spot, and found a rough cabin of logs, built against the foot of a rock, and bearing the marks of a tenant, though I found no one within it.—"
>
> "It was the hut of Leather-stocking," said Edwards quickly.
>
> "It was; though I, at first, supposed it to be a habitation of the Indians." (*Pioneers,* p. 236)

The castle embodies a botched version of European history, but Natty's cabin is an integral part of the wilderness and its natural inhabitants, the Indians.

In *The Spy* Cooper reinforced Harvey Birch's social marginality with references to European myth and legend. In *The Pioneers* Natty Bumppo's marginality is manifested in his combination of white and Indian characteristics. Like the Judge, he wears a fox-skin cap, though Natty's is "much inferior in finish and ormaments." His shirt is "of the country check," but over it he wears a deerskin jacket:

> On his feet were deer-skin moccasins, ornamented with porcupine's quills, after the manner of the Indians, and his limbs were guarded with long leggings of the same material as the moccasins, which, gartering over the knees of his tarnished buck-skin breeches, had obtained for him, among the settlers, the nick name of Leatherstocking. (*Pioneers,* p. 23)

Natty's first action in the novel is his idiosyncratic "inward chuckle" or "inward laugh," and he confronts the Judge like a crudely contained natural force: "As the speaker concluded he drew his bare hand across the bottom of his nose, and again opened his enormous mouth with a kind of inward laugh" (*Pioneers,* p. 21).

Natty's idiom, too, is a blend of white and Indian speech. That idiom has suffered a wealth of unfriendly criticism.

Richard Poirier cites it as an example of "Cooper's laziness, his apathetic mingling, in his hero's dialogue, of a semi-literate vernacular, of which the author is needlessly proud, with a pretentiously literary phraseology about which he ought to be embarrassed."[36] But Natty's idiom is not at all the result of laziness. Cooper wanted to combine a popular tradition of the eloquence of Indian oratory with the garrulity of a frontier character. The most famous example of Indian oratory, in Cooper's time as in ours, was Logan's speech delivered to Lord Dunmore in 1774. Throughout much of the nineteenth century it was a standard item in school texts, and students were forced to commit it to memory.[37] Logan's speech and its background were first presented by Thomas Jefferson, who wanted to defend the American Indian against the common European view that they were a degenerate race:

> The principles of their society forbidding all compulsion, they are led to duty and to enterprize by personal influence and persuasion. Hence eloquence in council, bravery and address in war, become the foundations of all consequence with them. . . . I may challenge the whole orations of Demosthenes and Cicero, and of any more eminent orator, if Europe has furnished more eminent, to produce a single passage, superior to the speech of Logan, a Mingo Chief, to Lord Dunmore, when governor of this state.[38]

De Witt Clinton, in an address to the New York Historical Society (December 6, 1811), similarly emphasized that Indian eloquence was a consequence of their political liberty. "Popular, or free governments have, in all ages, been the congenial soil of oratory." Moreover, Indian eloquence was not the result of artificial rules or rhetoric; it was indigenous, natural, vibrant—the full expression of their culture:

> Their models of eloquence were to be found, not in books, but in the living orators of their local and national assemblies; their children, at an early period of life, attended their councils [sic] fires, in order to observe the passing scenes, and to receive the lessons of wisdom. Their rich and vivid imagery was drawn from the sublime scenery of nature, and their ideas were derived from the laborious operations of their own minds, and from the experience and wisdom of their ancient sages.[39]

For such nationalists as Jefferson and Clinton, Indian oratory represented not only a rhetorical tradition firmly fixed in the American landscape, but also a political tradition of democracy, especially as it was practiced by the Five Nations of the Iroquois Confederation. Cooper invokes this background in Natty's very first speech in *The Pioneers:*

> No—no—Judge, . . . you burnt your powder, only to warm your nose this cold evening. Did ye think to stop a full grown buck, with Hector and the slut open upon him, within sound, with that pop-gun in your hand? There's plenty of pheasants amongst the swamps; and the snow birds are flying round your own door, where you may feed them with crumbs, and shoot them at pleasure, any day; but if you're for a buck, or a little bear's meat, Judge, you'll have to take the long rifle, with a greased wadding, or you'll waste more power than you'll fill stomachs, I'm thinking. (*Pioneers,* p. 21)

Occasionally Natty's pungent language echoes directly the stoic resignation of Logan's speech, as when he tells the Reverend Grant, "I never know'd preaching come into a settlement, but it made the game scarce, and raised the price of gun-powder; and that's a thing that's not as easily made as a ramrod, or an Indian flint" (*Pioneers,* pp. 135–36).

In addition to metaphorical language, Cooper also draws some details of personality from Logan in portraying Natty. We recall that Logan's speech begins by invoking his reputation for hospitality: "I appeal to any white man to say, if ever he entered Logan's cabin hungry, and he gave him not meat; if ever he came cold and naked, and he clothed him not."[40] When Judge Temple tells of his first trip to his valley, Edwards asks with particular emphasis how he was received by Natty:

> "And how did the Leather-stocking discharge the duties of a host, sir?"
> "Why, simply and kindly, until late in the evening, when he discovered my name and object, and the cordiality of his manner very sensibly diminished, or, I might better say, disappeared. . . . Natty treated me hospitably, but coldly, I thought, after he learnt the nature of my journey. I slept on his own bear-skin, however, and in the morning joined my surveyors again." (*Pioneers,* pp. 236–37)

Natty's personality and language tap the popular tradition of Indian eloquence and natural democracy represented most notably in Jefferson's book, but also in Clinton's address and (as has often been noted) in John Heckewelder's *Account of the History, Manners, and Customs, of the Indian Natives who once inhabited Pennsylvania and the Neighboring States* (1819).[41] Thus Natty is portrayed as the antithesis of the European and feudel Judge Temple. Natty, too, claims ownership of the valley, though on far different terms than the Judge. Temple's vision of manufactories and canals is countered and outweighed by "all creation" in the Catskills. There, with "mountains bigger than the 'Vision,' seeming to be haystacks of green grass," Natty finds "the best piece of work that I've met with in the woods; and none know how often the hand of God is seen in the wilderness, but them that rove it for a man's life." In describing the scene, Natty attains his greatest eloquence in *The Pioneers:*

> It is a spot to make a man solemnize. You can see right down into the valley that lies to the east of the High-Peak, where, in the fall of the year, thousands of acres of woods are afore your eyes, in the deep hollow, and along the side of the mountain painted like ten thousand rainbows, by no hand of man, though not without the ordering of God's providence. (*Pioneers*, p. 294)

Here the concept of a possessionless ownership of the land through a natural relation to its beauty contrasts vividly with the squalid incongruities of Templeton.

By associating Natty Bumppo with ascent, circumference, nature, and Indian eloquence, Cooper has granted him moral as well as physical ascendancy over Judge Temple and his town. Yet it is an ascendancy with severe limitations of its own. Beyond all its attractions, Natty's aesthetic relation to nature is essentially sterile for precisely the same reason that it is attractive: its social marginality. The centrifugal character has no children. Here again Cooper draws on the popular image of Logan, whose speech concludes by recalling the murders of his "women and children": "Who is there to mourn for Logan?—Not one."[42] This *ubi sunt?* formula is present in *The Pioneers* largely through the presentation of Natty's other self, Chingachgook. As Terence Martin has argued, "Cooper has doubled Natty's consciousness to include that of the savage Chingachgook."[43] In *The Pioneers* the relationship between Natty and Chingachgook is the remnant of an unrecorded history which will be detailed in future Leatherstocking novels, but their twinned nature is unmistakable as it is defined in contrast to the social world of Templeton. Not only in the hunting scenes but also at the Christmas Eve services and at the Bold Dragon, Chingachgook and Natty stand apart.

Chingachgook has a double nature, represented by his two names, also. "Old John and Chingachgook were very different men to look on," Natty observes. The difference between the two is the difference imposed by the renaming impulse that John Quincy Adams found so ridiculous. However ridiculous, the Christian name attaches to a real effect, which is not merely the ruin of Chingachgook but the violation of the wilderness as well:

> "Oh! he was Christianized by the Moravians, who was always over intimate with the Delawares," said Leather-stocking. "It's my opinion, that had they been left to themselves, there would be no such doings now, about the head-waters of the two rivers, and that these hills mought have been kept as good hunting-ground, by their right owner, who is not too old to carry a rifle, and whose sight is as true as a fish-hawk, hovering—"

But the renaming of Chingachgook, like all Christian naming, neither recognizes nor changes the essence of nature. While Chingachgook is dying, the Reverend Grant tries to see him in Christian terms: "The offspring of a race of heathens, he has in truth been 'as a brand plucked from the burning.'" Natty corrects Grant's perception and returns Chingachgook to the Logan tradition: "it's no burning that ails him. . . . Flesh isn't iron, that a man can live for ever, and see his kith and kin driven to a far country, and be left to mourn, with none to keep him company" (*Pioneers*, p. 419).

Chingachgook's role as the last of the Mohicans is powerfully symbolized in his death scene. Elizabeth ascends Mount Vision with the keg of powder she has bought for Natty. There she finds Chingachgook, dressed and painted as a warrior and waiting to die. When she shows him the powder, Chingachgook looks "earnestly at the gift":

> This is the great enemy of my nation. Without this, when could the white men drive the Delawares! Daughter, the Great Spirit gave your fathers to know how to make guns and powder, that they might sweep the Indians from the land. There will soon be no redskin in the country. When John has gone, the last will leave these hills, and his family will be dead. (*Pioneers,* p. 403)

Almost immediately they are enveloped by the smoke and heat of the forest fire. The fire itself is a manifestation of the feverish passions of the citizens of Templeton as well as an element that consumes and transforms the world of *The Pioneers.*[44] It is also the agent of Chingachgook's death, for as he sits with the powder between his thighs, the fire causes it to explode in a literalization of Chingachgook's accusation: the white man's powder has stripped him of his paternity and left him to die alone and sterile.

In Chingachgook's fate Natty sees the image of his own, for the hunter's life is as sterile as the Indian's. Natty's meditation on Chingachgook's death is a kind of yearning after death, a recognition that there is nothing for him to nourish and cultivate in the new world of Templeton except the dying Major Effingham and that there remains no joy except escape:

> Red skin, or white, it's all over now! He's to be judged by a righteous Judge, and by no laws that's made to suit times, and new days. Well, there's only one more death, and the world be left to me and the hounds. Ahs! me! a man must wait the time of God's pleasure, but I begin to weary of life. There is scurcely a tree standing that I know, and it's hard to find a face that I was acquainted with in my younger days. (*Pioneers,* p. 423)

As in *The Spy,* however, the socially marginal hero, though sterile himself, acts as a midwife to the future of America. The fire on Mount Vision precipitates the mutual recognition of Elizabeth and Oliver Edwards, and in that recognition lies the only hope for the marriage and fertility of the irreconcilable conflicts represented by the castle and the cabin. But first they must be delivered from the fire, and here Natty enacts his symbolic function. As Edwin Fussel notes, "During the forest fire, Natty Bumppo wraps [Elizabeth] in buckskin, an explicit symbol of transcendence through emblematic investure in the garb of reality."[45] Elizabeth is reborn at Natty's cave in the healing rain that extinguishes the forest fire, and Edwards becomes Oliver Edward Effingham:

> The moment of concealment is over, Miss Temple. By this time tomorrow, I shall remove a veil that perhaps it has been weakness to keep around me and my affairs so long. But I have had romantic and foolish wishes and weaknesses; and who has not, that is young and torn by conflicting passions! (*Pioneers*, p. 424)

The fulfillment of Natty's role, then, is a new perception of reality that permits Elizabeth and Edwards to see each other and themselves without veils or foolish wishes. In order to understand fully the preparations for their rebirth, we shall have to examine a corollary to Cooper's treatment of his theme, a corollary that involves the education not only of Elizabeth and Edwards, but of the reader of *The Pioneers*.

IV

The minor plot of *The Pioneers* concerns the resolution of the apparently irreconcilable conflicts projected by the theme. Central to the minor plot is the love story of Elizabeth Temple and Oliver Edwards, a story that begins in the quickened interest of their first meeting, founders on a series of psychological and circumstantial factors, climaxes in the face of death on Mount Vision, and (at least formally) reaffirms the social harmony of Templeton in marriage. While the bare outlines of the minor plot are perfectly conventional, Cooper's treatment of it reveals the same anxieties about the function of democratic literature and the role of criticism that we saw in his reviews of Sedgwick and Irving and in his preface; the great issue of the minor plot is interpretive activity in all its forms—reading and misreading. How are people, circumstances, or documents "read," and how does reading lead to truth?

We can better understand how thoroughly Cooper explores the problem of misreading if we adopt for a moment Roland Barthes' conception of the five codes under which all the signifiers of a "readable" text group themselves—in other words, the set of norms, rules, and constraints according to which a narrative is understandable, readable.[46]

1. Hermeneutic code: "the various (formal) terms by which an enigma can be distinguished, suggested, formulated, held in suspense, and finally disclosed."

2. Signifier code: semes (units of semantic significance) which combine with other semes to create characters, ambiences, shapes, and symbols. Essentially the signifier code consists of a sufficient knowledge of the language in which the text is written so that the reader recognizes connotative elements such as femininity, wealth, and so on.

3. Symbolic code: elements which provide entry into the "symbolic field"; "this is the place for multivalence and for reversibility."[47] These elements allow the reader to perceive that they are part of a pattern of meaning that is more abstract or greater or more fundamental than that of the signifier code.

4. Proairetic code: the code of actions and behavior as determined by the discourse rather than by the characters. It is by this code that we can summarize the plot of a story.

5. Cultural codes or reference codes: references to a body of knowledge or science. In one culture, "He shook his head," means he disagreed; in another it means the opposite.[48]

Since Barthes deduces his five codes from his reading of a classic text by Balzac, it is not surprising to find that Cooper is quite aware of their function in the interpretive process. In fact, in *The Pioneers* Cooper attempts to heighten the reader's awareness of and structure his response to the functions subsumed by the five codes by providing a negative reader analogue, a kind of ideal misreader, in the figure of that general factotum of authority, Richard Jones. When Monsieur Le Quoi bitterly claims that the present French government gives liberty to no one "except to de ladi," Richard says, "Yes, yes, to the women, I know, . . . that is your Sallick law. I read, sir, all kinds of books; of France, as well as

England; of Greece, as well as Rome" (*Pioneers,* p. 93). In fact Salic law prevented women from succeeding to the throne, and Richard is not likely to have read of it in some book of France (the law existed in the Teutonic code) but in Shakespeare's *Henry V,* where the "Law Salique" has been deliberately misread by French factions who want to deny Henry's claim to the French throne (thus Richard's association of the law and France). Asking for an interpretation of the law, Henry provides an exquisitely ironic comment on Richard's reading:

> And God forbid, my dear and faithful lord,
> That you should fashion, wrest, or bow your reading,
> Or nicely charge your understanding soul
> With opening titles miscreate, whose right
> Suits not in native colors with the truth.
> (*Henry V,* 1.2.13–17)

Richard has misread both the cultural code of *Henry V* and Le Quoi's *bon mot* (signifier).

Similarly, Richard misreads the other codes. When the Reverend Grant declines the Judge's invitation to spend the night at the castle because "a clergyman must not awaken envy or distrust, by dwelling under so splendid a roof as that of Judge Temple," Richard is delighted: "You like the roof, then, Mr. Grant, ... I am glad to find one man of taste at last" (*Pioneers,* p. 132); here Richard misreads the signifier "roof." He misreads the hermeneutic code in his certainty that Edwards is a half-breed (Elizabeth shows better understanding by refusing to judge prematurely); the proairetic code in his interpretation of the incident on the mountainside, when Edwards saves the sleigh by jerking the horses back into the road; the symbolic code in his attempt to imitate a spire of the London Cathedral in the steeple of the village church: "after much difficulty, Mr. Jones had the satisfaction of seeing an object reared, that bore, in its outlines, a striking resemblance to a vinegar-cruet" (*Pioneers,* p. 118).

The important thing about all of these readings is that they are motivated by self-interest, pretentiousness and ignorance. Richard is not a complete fool, after all; he is capable of real insights when he is not blinded by self-importance. As Judge Temple puzzles over Edwards' hostility, he remarks,

> "I know not what there is in my dwelling, to frighten a lad of his years, unless it may be thy presence and visage, Bess."
> "No, no," said Richard, with great simplicity; "it is not cousin Bess." (*Pioneers*, p. 204)

By emphasizing the "simplicity" of Richard's observation, Cooper offers a clue to the appropriate method of arriving at truth. If we set aside selfish motives, pretentious theories, and our fear of being ignorant, it we patiently approach a text on its own terms, if we become those naive readers who prefer homely, moral art to the rarified effusions of genius, then we will discover the truth of the text. So long as we insist on reading as critics, imposing on the text our critical vocabularies and pretentious theoretical concepts, we will be building a vinegar cruet for our church steeple. *The Pioneers* animates the frustration with criticism that Cooper expressed in his preface.

Just as Richard represents an exemplary misreader, Elizabeth is an exemplary reader analogue. We have already seen how Elizabeth's perspective governs the reader's experience of the opening events of the novel. She has been away from Templeton and her father long enough for them to impress her as freshly as they do us, but in perceiving them from her perspective we also absorb her essential sympathies. More importantly, the reader shares Elizabeth's interest in the enigmas surrounding her father and Oliver Edwards, and we adopt our attitude toward those enigmas from Elizabeth. Richard is certain that Edwards is a halfbreed, but Elizabeth is skeptical, and so we are skeptical, too. In order for the plot of hidden identities and secret documents to work, we must feel an ever-increasing curiosity about the solutions, but we must withhold any premature judgments, and this is precisely what Elizabeth does. Her behavior guides the reader.

Another aspect of the special relation between Elizabeth and the reader is suggested by Leland Person's argument that one of Natty Bumppo's functions in *The Pioneers* is "to inculcate a conservative vision of the future in those who will assume responsibility for the land." Natty heaps scorn on the citizens at the pigeon shoot, downs a bird with a single shot and withdraws; at the fishing expedition he takes Edwards and Elizabeth into an alternative expedition of "symbolic importance as a religious ceremony or initiation," "a night-sea journey into the underworld and the ideal realm of myth"; he saves Elizabeth from both the wilderness savagery of the panther and the Templetonian savagery of the fire. In Person's reading both Elizabeth and Edwards are "soundly instructed in the wisdom of the forest, until they can emerge at the end of the novel as the agents of a reconciling vision of the American future and the progenitors of a race and a culture."[49]

But the reader has been instructed, too. The marriage of Elizabeth and Edwards is only a fiction, after all. Cooper's real purpose in *The Pioneers* is to make his *readers* the agents of a reconciling vision of the American future, to educate our imaginations—in the words of his review of *A New-England Tale*, to "increase our knowledge, correct our false opinions, and, what is more powerful than all, appeal to our sympathies." It is for this reason that the danger of misreading figures so largely in *The Pioneers*. A Richard Jones can defeat the designs of the most moral author by imposing his preconceptions onto the narrative, and too many readers of *The Spy* did just that.

The enigma of Judge Temple is created by the reader's sympathy with Natty and his companions. It is soon clear that the Judge's wounding of Edwards is not an adequate motive for the depth of the youth's resentment, that the wound is merely a metonymy for some more grievous injury. The nature of that injury is indicated through a number of scenes in which something important obviously transpires, though its meaning eludes the Judge. Chingachgook, summoned to treat Edwards' wound, confronts the Judge: "The children of Miquon [William Penn] do not love the sight of blood; and yet, the Young Eagle has been struck, by the hand that should do no evil!" When the Judge protests his innocence, Chingachgook makes this oracular comment:

> "The evil spirit sometimes lives in the best heart," returned John, "but my brother speaks the truth; his hand has never taken life,

when awake; no! not even when the children of the English Father, were making the waters red with the blood of his people." (*Pioneers*, p. 87)

"When awake" is the key phrase, for it suggests that the Judge is guilty of some murder committed unconsciously. In fact, the reader has already been supplied with a basis for comprehending Chingachgook's words. We know that Temple served the American cause during the Revolution "in various civil capacities" although he "never seemed to lose sight of his own interests," and after the war he was able to purchase confiscated Tory lands "at, comparatively, low prices" (*Pioneers*, p. 36). We also know that the Indians have been dispossessed of their lands by peaceful as well as forceful means: "The wars of a portion of the latter [Europeans], are celebrated among us, as the wars of King Philip; but the peaceful policy of William Penn, or Miquon, as he was termed by the natives, effected its object, with less difficulty, though not with less certainty" (*Pioneers*, p. 84). In equating King Philip's War with the peaceful policies of the Quakers, the narrative prepares us to believe that Judge Temple is perfectly capable of an unconscious or indirect violence, if it serves his interests. His religious scruples prevent his owning slaves, so Agamemnon, his sleigh-driver, belongs to Richard. These equivocations suggest that Temple is equally equivocal in his business transactions.

The possibility that Temple has injured Edwards gathers important political and social dimensions during the scene at the Bold Dragon. Temple reports on the progress of the French Revolution and the activities of the New York State legislature in a peculiar juxtaposition, as if they were somehow related. And so they are: the Jacobins, "as blood-thirsty as bull-dogs," have beheaded their king and are "rushing from one act of licentiousness to another," executing the queen and despoiling the province of La Vendee; the legislature has passed game laws protecting fish and deer, laws that the Judge approves as "loudly called for, by judicious men." All men are blood-thirsty and must be restrained by the rule of the law. When Natty scoffs at the new laws, the Judge rebukes him:

"Armed with the dignity of the law, Mr. Bumppo," returned the Judge, gravely, "a vigilant magistrate can prevent much of the evil that has hitherto prevailed, and which is already rendering the game scarce. I hope to live to see the day, when a man's rights in his game shall be as much respected as his title to his farm." (*Pioneers*, p. 160)

But if the Judge's property rights are based on the American Revolution, the law that respects them is only another form of Jacobin licentiousness, the rule of the strong. It is the farmers, not the hunters, who have made game scarce, Natty claims, and Major Hartmann replies, "ter lant is not mate, as for ter teer to live on, put for Christians" (*Pioneers*, p. 161).

Hartmann's assumption is the fundamental justification for Judge Temple's enterprise—to bring European culture to the American landscape. This assumption is quickly brought into question by a transformation that the people of Templeton utterly misread: Indian John, who has quietly been drinking cider laced with whiskey, becomes Chingachgook, the Great Serpent of the Delawares. Where Richard hears only the "damned dull music" of an Indian song, there is the pride and hatred of a Logan confronting his enemy. Natty asks him, "And why have you slain the Mingo warriors? was it not to keep these hunting-grounds and lake to your father's children? . . . and does not the blood of a warrior run in the veins of a young chief, who should speak aloud, where his voice is now too low to be heard?" Chingachgook's answer to these rhetorical questions is to reach for his tomahawk, and Natty must stop him from killing the Judge immediately. At this climax, Richard's comment reflects ironically on Chingachgook's dispossession as well as the whites' inability to understand any culture but their own: "Well, old John is soon sowed up. Give him a berth, Captain, in the barn, and I will pay for it" (*Pioneers*, p. 166). The bloodthirsty forces of revolution and the vigilant magistrate confront each other in a mutual ignorance that is nearly absolute.

Every turn of the plot serves to intensify the growing animosity between the antagonists, and each degree of increasing tension is marked by a failure of the interpretive faculties. The Judge receives a letter announcing the death of Edward Effingham, but Cooper conceals its contents from us by the simple expedient of having Richard interpret it:

> "'Since the receipt of the last, I'"—Here a long passage was rendered indistinct, by a kind of humming noise, made by the Sheriff. "'I grieve to say, that'—hum, hum, bad enough, to be sure—'but trust that a merciful Providence has seen fit'—hum, hum, hum; seems to be a good, pious sort of man, 'duke; belongs to the established church, I dare say; hum, hum—'vessel sailed from Falmouth on or about the 1st of September of last year, and'—hum, hum, hum. 'If any thing should transpire, on this afflicting subject, shall not fail'—hum, hum; really a goodhearted man, for a lawyer—'but can communicate nothing further at present.'—Hum, hum'. 'The national convention'—hum, hum—'unfortunate Louis'—hum, hum—'example of your Washington'—a very sensible man, I declare, and none of your crazy democrats." (*Pioneers*, p. 276)

Little content escapes from Richard's critical reading, which converts the letter into a comment on the personality, religion, and politics of its writer. We are left to assume, with Edwards, that the news is of some business venture and that the Judge's exclusion of his secretary from the affair is highly suspicious. When Edwards tries to probe Mr. Van der School, the Judge's lawyer, for information, he meets with interpretive language at its most obfuscatory—the language of law:

> I shall be always glad to see you, sir, at my office, (as in duty bound, (not that it is obligatory to receive any man within your dwelling, (unless so inclined,) which is a castle,) according to the forms of politeness,) or at any other place; but the papers are most strictly confidential, (and, as such, cannot be read by any one, (unless so directed,) by Judge Temple's solemn injunctions,) and are invisible to all eyes; excepting those whose duties (I mean assumed duties) require it of them. (*Pioneers*, p. 282)

These papers (the Judge's will) thus become a secret document whose import is withheld until the climax of the novel. In the meantime Edwards can only intrepret the withholding as a sign that the Judge does not trust him.

Misinterpretation also renders Natty's cabin a fortress. Richard and his unsavory assistants interpret the signs of digging

around the cave on Mount Vision as evidence that Natty has discovered silver and is hoarding it in his cabin. Again the language of
the law serves to obscure rather than to clarify motives and purposes. Richard and Hiram Doolittle obtain a search warrent osten-
sibly to investigate Natty's poaching, but the true purpose is to
penetrate at last into the "forbidden ground," as Natty recognizes
at once:

> "Did Marmaduke Temple put his name to that bit of paper!" said
> Natty, shaking his head;—"well, well, that man loves the new ways,
> and his betterments, and his lands, afore his own flesh and blood.
> But I won't mistrust the gall: she has an eye like a full-grown
> buck! poor thing, she didn't choose her father, and can't help it."
> (*Pioneers*, p. 336)

The intensifying pressure of the citizen's greed gradually forces the circumferential diffusion of Natty's life into a point,
a locus of secret meaning. Thus the opposition between Temple
and Natty, originally signaled through contrasting spatial associations, becomes at last a matter of the secret meaning which each
harbors from all others. Natty's secret is Major Effingham, in
whose person resides the remnants of two defeated forces in American history: the Indians and the Tories. Effingham is not only a
retired major of the British army, but he is also the adopted son of
Chingachgook, and the Indians have granted ownership of the
valley to the man they call Fire-eater. Natty's secret, then is the
secret of those dispossessed and forgotten contributors to the
present America. Judge Temple's secret is the guilty knowledge of
those contributors, a supposed awareness that his present wealth
and power derive from the same bloodthirsty activity that he pi-
ously condemns in the Jacobins. As long as the antagonists protect
their respective secrets, no reconciliation between them is possible. For the citizens of Templeton, "value" means simply "money";
what Natty defends so vigorously can only be silver, and his secret
is subjected to a series of constricting circles. The Sheriff and his
posse encircle the cabin to arrest Natty, but it has already burned
in the first manifestation of the fire that represents their feverish
greed; they encircle Natty to conduct him to jail; the forest fire

encircles the cave to which Natty and his secret have retreated, and after the fire is quenched the village militia takes its place. The constriction of the landscape which opened *The Pioneers* here reaches its greatest concentration.

The militia's assault takes a strangely semantic turn. Billy Kirby, good-natured as ever, negotiates a truce, but Richard, "burning with a desire to examine the hidden mysteries of the cave" (*Pioneers*, p. 430), demands immediate surrender and produces a warrent for the arrest of Benjamin. For the first time, Benjamin reveals his true name:

> "Look, you, Master, or Captain, thoff I questions if ye know the name of a rope, except the one that's to hang ye, there's no need of singing out, as if ye was hailing a deaf man on a topgallant-yard. Mayhap you think you've got my name in your sheepskin; but what British sailor finds it worth while to sail in these seas, without a sham on his stern, in case of need, d'ye-see. If you call me Penguillan, you calls me by the name of the man on whose land, d'ye-see, I hove into daylight; and he was a gentleman; and that's more than my worst enimy will say of any of the family of Benjamin Stubbs."
>
> "Send the warrent round to me, and I'll put in an alias," cried Hiram, from behind his cover.
>
> "Put in a jackass, and you'll put in yourself, Mister Doobut-little," shouted Benjamin. . . . (*Pioneers*, p. 431)

The skirmish begins as a war of words, appropriately enough. Nor is it mere name-calling, for the issues of names and aliases, names and realities, language and law lie at the heart of the conflict that this skirmish mirrors. In the comic action that follows, the warriors live out parodies of their conceptions of war: Benjamin fires a swivel from a shipdeck, Captain Hollister leads a cavalry charge, and Hiram Doolittle exposes his rear to the attacks of the enemy. Yet it is Judge Temple who puts the skirmish into perspective: "Silence and peace! why do I see murder and bloodshed attempted! is not the law sufficient to protect itself, that armed bands must be gathered, as in rebellion and war, to see justice performed!" Richard explains that he has collected a "posse comitatus," but the Judge corrects him: "Say rather a posse of demons" (*Pioneers*, p.

435). All veils are dropped at the cave: the vigilantes, not their victims, are the Jacobins of Templeton.

The enlightenment that ensues is conveyed in the reading of Temple's secret document, his will. Cooper stresses the clarity of Temple's account; after an introduction in "the usual forms, spun out by the ingenuity of Mr. Van der School . . . the pen of Marmaduke became plainly visible." It is an exemplary readable text: "In clear, distinct, manly, and even eloquent language, he recounted his obligations to Colonel Effingham. . . . recounting in a clear narrative, the events which our readers must now be able to connect" (*Pioneers,* pp. 442–43). In short, the Judge's will is an epitome of *The Pioneers,* and its reading effects the emotional climaxes and the rites of reconciliation toward which the entire narrative has been moving. The revelation of the secret document removes the stain of guilt tarnishing the American present and ensures that the dispossessed Indian and Tory traditions will be assimilated to the American future.

A final scene recapitulates the lesson of proper reading. Elizabeth and Edwards find their tutor, Natty Bumppo, at the graves of Effingham and Chingachgook. Natty asks them to read the epitaphs: "I should like to know what 'tis you tell these people, that be flocking into the country like pigeons in the spring, of the old Delaware, and of the bravest white man that ever trod the hills" (*Pioneers,* p. 451). He asks Edwards to show him his own name on Effingham's stone and traces the engraved letters "with deep interest." But when Edwards reads Chingachgook's stone, all Natty's deference vanishes, and he corrects Edwards' pronunciation of "Mohican" and "Chingachgook": "'Gach, boy; 'gach-gook; Chingachgook; which, interpreted, means Big-sarpent. The name should be set down right, for an Indian's name has always some meaning in it" (*Pioneers,* p. 452). The last instructions that the illiterate woodsman gives to his cultured pupils are in reading.

Elizabeth and Edwards, properly inculcated in interpretive methodology, are the inheritors of the contested American landscape, and their marriage signals a new sense of national identity that integrates the disparate traditions of patriots, Tories, and Indians in a new relation to the land and the law. Yet the real future of America lies not with fictional characters and symbolic reconciliations but with the readers of *The Pioneers,* the men and women who will live that future. In his review of *A New-England Tale* Cooper described a good novel as that which "addresses itself very powerfully to our moral nature and conscience . . . constantly to remind us that 'we have, all of us, one human heart.'" That is the goal of *The Pioneers.* By merging the resources of the explorer's journal with those of the American novel he had invented in *The Spy,* Cooper advanced his claim to be Fielding's true historian, "a describer of society as it exists and men as they are," and by teaching us to read *The Pioneers,* he sought to teach us to be Americans.

V

Two innovations in Cooper's publishing practices preceded the appearance of *The Pioneers.* The first of these was the securing of British copyright. Cooper had been too slow in investigating British copyright law for *The Spy,* and he was determined not to repeat the error. He entrusted negotiations to Benjamin Coles, who wrote to Henry D. Sedgwick (Catherine Sedgwick's brother) on June 26, 1822: "The booksellers are anxious to obtain his next work the Pioneers and publish it dividing the profits with him—Murray proposed this to Irving who spoke with him at my suggestion and I am to call & see Murray with Irving when he comes to town which will be in a day or two."[50] The popularity of *Precaution* and *The Spy* superseded Murray's reliance on Mr. Gifford's critical opinions. At issue was the means of obtaining British copyright; English law was hazy about the protection of works by aliens, but the common practice gave copyright to any work that was published first in England. Thus Murray wrote Coles on July 10 that "Mr. Cooper should take care that it is first published here."[51] Coles misunderstood the American copyright law, which protected the works of American citizens regardless of priority of publication, and feared that Murray's method might endanger Cooper's copyright in America. He proposed that *The Pioneers* be put on sale in America one or two days before in England, and Murray agreed. The specific terms of the contract provided that Murray should publish *The Pioneers* at his own expense and divide the profits equally with Cooper.[52]

The second innovation was not Cooper's idea. William Leet Stone, who had served his apprenticeship in Cooperstown, was by 1822 one of the publishers of the New York *Commercial Advertiser*. He printed two prepublication excerpts from the novel: the Christmas turkey shoot, on January 18, 1823; and Natty's killing of the deer on the lake, on January 25. When these printings were criticized as puffs, Stone tried to exonerate Cooper of any complicity: "not a single remark of our's has been made with his previous knowledge; and it was not until after repeated solicitation, that we obtained the extracts given before the work was published."[53] While Cooper may not have been guilty of puffing his work, Stone clearly implies that Cooper cooperated by supplying extracts, and a comparison of the texts demonstrates that the author supplied corrections in the printer's copy, "perhaps intending to polish those parts of the novel the public would see first."[54] The obvious intention was to stimulate reader interest, a plan that must have resulted in part from the fact that the first notices of impending publication had appeared in the summer of 1822 before an outbreak of yellow fever, that old enemy of commercial life, forced a six-month delay.

Despite the fact that he was no longer a tyro in the publishing business, Cooper encountered numerous difficulties with *The Pioneers*. For one thing, his nonliterary affairs continued to distract his energies. On June 22, 1822, his whaling ship returned with a cargo of 16,532 gallons of oil, and Cooper had to dispose of both cargo and ship. Meanwhile, the United States Attorney's office had decided that Cooper owed the U.S. Navy $190 and demanded payment; Cooper, in typical fashion, decided that the Navy owed *him* back pay, and over a three-year period he argued his case vigorously in a series of letters to Secretaries of the Navy. There were further complications to Cooper's uncertain financial condition, complications that Beard summarizes as "a series of family crises and an endless maze of debts, suits, decrees, and foreclosures."[55] The Angevine farm where Cooper and his family had been living was under the trusteeship of Cooper's brothers-in-law, apparently to prevent it ever being attached for Cooper's debts. When one trustee died and he quarreled with the other, Cooper demanded that a new trustee be appointed, in accordance with a provision of the deed. The surviving brother-in-law, with the concurrence of his father, refused, and as soon as the fever epidemic had subsided Cooper moved his family to New York City and broke off all relations with the De Lancey family (*L/J,* 1:87n1).

Amid all this, Cooper read proof, finding a discouraging number of errors. He and Wiley decided that the first printing was too small to satisfy demand, and a second was made before publication. Although no definite figures exist, the combined printings seem to have been in excess of 5,000 copies. Corrected sheets for about two-thirds of the novel were sent to Murray on November 29, 1822, and a complete set of corrected sheets followed on January 15, 1823 (*L/J,* 1:85–86, 91–92). The American edition finally appeared on February 1, 1823; the British, on February 26.

Publication of *The Pioneers* was a major cultural event in the United States. By noon on February 1, 3,500 copies had been distributed, and newspapers reported the arrival of the novels at major ports:

> Booksellers quoted the early sales figure to stimulate further sales; and newspaper notices of the arrival of shipments—Philadelphia on February third, Baltimore on the fifth, Washington on the seventh—testified to a lively interest and a demand at times outrunning supply. Copies were "hourly expected" in Boston on February seventh, and a new shipment replenished the short supply on the seventeenth.[56]

The excitement was so widespread that even Ralph Waldo Emerson, whose general attitude toward novels was a studied indifference, expressed his interest in a letter to John Boynton Hill:

> Since Scott has failed to equal himself in his two last works our young novelist has grown the greater; I suppose you know that the

Spy, translated into French, is popular at Paris; but of the "Sources of the Susquehannah," his second birth, I have heard nothing. What is the reason? Have you never yet sanctioned it with a 'bon!'[57]

American reviewers were almost unanimous in their enthusiasm for the new novel. *Niles' Weekly Register* printed a short notice rather than a long review because "the book will be read, whether the receivers like it or not." This notice considered *The Pioneers* to be an emphatic refutation of Sydney Smith's slur: "'Who reads an American book?' was the late modest and liberal demand of the editors of the *Edinburgh Review*. The 'Pioneers,' we venture to say, will be read by tens of thousands even in Great Britain." The chief virtues of the novel were its immediacy and its realism.

> The character and grouping is excellent, and will furnish many delightful scenes for the painter; and the great merit is, that there is *probability* in the highest wrought parts of the book—the chief things, indeed, seem as if familiar to us, and we have only to admire the satisfactory manner in which they are presented.[58]

Reviewers frequently isolated these qualities for praise, and many notices began with a résumé of frontier experience: "To understand and relish the beauties of the Pioneers, it is necessary to take into view the habits and manners of early settlers."[59]

The most thoughtful of the early reviews appeared in the *Port Folio*. The anonymous reviewer begins by trying to establish the generic norms of the novel. Echoing Cooper's preface, he warns that the reader "must not expect to be astonished by a succession of prodigious adventures, or perplexing incidents and harassing entanglements. His feelings will not be excited by any romantic trials of friendship or love." Rather, the novel must be judged by its own generic designation, "a descriptive tale"; "It might, indeed, be called historical; for the historian can scarcely find a more just and vivid delineation of the first settlements of our wilderness." We know that new settlements spring up like mushrooms on the frontier, but we do not know how:

> The Pioneers affords us much of this information, imparted with a fidelity and vividness that carry the reader into the midst of the

scenes, and make him acquainted with every individual who is introduced. These individuals will all be found in good keeping; not deformed by caricature nor frittered away by extravagance. Each one speaks and acts with perfect fitness and congruity, and they are, as we can testify from personal observation, the very kind of persons who may be expected to be found in such situations.[60]

With these criteria the reviewer focuses on characters and scenery. Oliver Edwards is the only implausible figure in the book: "though he seems to be treated as a person of some consequence by his own friends, [he] does not strike us as entitled to much commendation." Such regional characters as Richard Jones, Remarkable Pettibone, and Elnathan Todd are accurately represented, but the reviewer reserves his highest praise for Natty Bumppo, Ben Pump, Chingachgook, and Elizabeth. Natty is "modeled from the effigies of old Daniel Boone" and is certainly a hero "if courage, fidelity, and a spirit of independence, unbroken by a life of suffering, can make him so":

> This demi-savage is constantly seen in bold relief, separated from all the others by the singularity of his opinions, the inflexibility with which he maintains them, and a manliness of spirit and wild virtue, that command respect even in a being so rude and so humble, so ignorant and unpolished. (*Port Folio*, pp. 232–33)

Ben Pump is praised for his generous heart: "His voluntarily going into the stocks to keep Leather-stockings in countenance and break the weight of his disgrace, is an admirable thought and quite sailor-like." Chingachgook forms "a fine and striking portrait":

> He represents, with barbarous dignity, in his seventieth year, the last remnant of a powerful race, over whom his ancestors bore sway. The stubborn, but fallen power and pride;—the lofty sentiments of personal dignity;—the enduring, uncomplaining patience of ruin and despair;—the feverish and convulsive recurrence to his former state;—the deep sense of his wrongs, all softened, though not subdued by his conversion to Christianity, are depicted with a strong and accurate pencil. (*Port Folio*, pp. 233–34)

The reviewer finds Elizabeth a "fine spirited girl" who combines delicacy and propriety with great decision and firmness;

she "belongs, upon the whole, to a high order of heroines." However, it is in connection with Elizabeth that the reviewer levels his only negative criticism of *The Pioneers*. Her "painful struggles" between loyalty to her father and love for Edwards "might have been described with much effect," but they are not, and in this omission Cooper has lost the opportunity to captivate the "wondering females" in his audience:

> Never, Mr. Cooper, never while you live, if you wish to sleep in a whole skin, throw aside such incalculable treasures. For want of a few pages of this description, which we all know you could have thrown off with as much ease as a fine woman scatters civil speeches among a crowd of admirers, you have inflicted a task upon the patience of many of your fair readers, who dare not remain in ignorance of "the new American novel;" certain prodigiously wise critics have pronounced you dull, and the learned fraternity of dandies, have voted you incontinently *a sad bore!* (*Port Folio,* pp. 235–36)

The remainder of the review consists of extracts illustrating the spirit of pioneer life, as indeed did most reviews: the turkey shoot, the fishing expedition, the killing of the deer in the lake, Natty's view of all creation, the panther's attack, and the fire on Mount Vision were reprinted with regularity. In the *Port Folio* and in other reviews Cooper could see the reaction to the goals he had set for himself in writing *The Pioneers*: he was accepted as a true historian of American society, he had created a heroine who was vibrant and spirited, and even his omission of tender romance accorded with his desire to avoid what he saw as puerile and mawkish love scenes.

But despite its overwhelmingly positive critical reception, Cooper was disappointed by the sales of *The Pioneers*. His 1843 letter to Griswold called *The Pioneers* "only moderately successful; its present popularity being in a great degree factitious. It never has been a work of *loyal* success, though criticism has rather favoured it. At first, it was thought a failure" (*L/J,* 4:342). Cooper's comment is rather surprising, given the fanfare that greeted publication. The early excitement seems to have created expectations that succeeding months failed to fulfill. While 3,500 copies were distributed by noon on the first day of publication, the original two printings of 5,000 copies sufficed for two years. The third edition appeared in 1825 and the fourth was issued by Carey, Lea and Carey in 1827 after Cooper had sold them the copyright. After that it was reprinted thirteen times during Cooper's life; it was only slightly less popular than *The Last of the Mohicans.* If the early sales were less than the clamor had led him to expect, the blame lay largely with Cooper's refusal to negotiate a larger discount rate for his distributors. In 1823 Carey & Lea had a virtual monopoly on the booktrade to the interior and the South, and Henry Carey's decision not to handle *The Pioneers* had a decisive effect (see chapter 3 above). The English reception of *The Pioneers* was even more disappointing. Murray printed an edition of 1,000, but by September of 1823 only 800 had been sold, and as late as July of 1826, when Cooper visited London, there were still six unsold copies remaining. Murray told a friend of Cooper that British readers had little interest in the descriptions of local scenery and that many believed the games and customs represented in the novel had been lifted from Scott: "he said there was no one here, who possessed the requisite knowledge of the scenery &c therein described, to review the work, as it should be done."[61] Cooper's share of the profits amounted to only 134 pounds.[62] Thus the sales figures for *The Pioneers,* amazing though they were by the standards of just two years before, could not satisfy Cooper's growing ambition to become the universal novelist of democratic society.

Still, the novel had a profound impact on American cultural life. Robert Lemelin, for example, sees Cooper's novel as central to a nascent tradition of apprehending the American self in the American landscape. Of Natty's prospect view of creation he writes,

> There is no personification or pathetic fallacy actually, but the description has a sacramental character. Antebellum Americans were led to believe that they should find their points of observation and from seeing nature learn something about their inner selves. Nature was the medium through which the national character was to be filtered and defined. Cooper's description is representative of the passages travel and descriptive books chose to illustrate the

American genius for description, but beyond their praising nature description the writers unconsciously were codifying a pathway to the national identity.[63]

As *Niles' Weekly Register* had predicted, the book "excited a sensation among the artists, altogether unprecedented in the history of our domestic literature."[64] Thomas Doughty, William Dunlap, Thomas Cole, Henry Inman, and Gideon Fairman are only the most famous of the painters and engravers who undertook to illustrate scenes from the novel. Cole's *A View of the Two Lakes and Mountain House, Catskill Mountains, Morning* (1844) represented the creation over which Natty had waxed eloquent; by the time Cole painted it, the site (Pine Orchard near the town of Catskill) had become a tourist Mecca, at least in part owing to the fame of Cooper's description. James Franklin Beard has argued that *The Pioneers* was a precipitating factor in the birth of the Hudson River Valley School of painting.[65]

Above all, however, the creation of Natty Bumppo was seen as Cooper's great contribution to world literature. Richard Henry Dana wrote Cooper on April 2, 1823, that Natty creates

a grateful and very peculiar emotion made up of admiration and pity and concern. So highly is his character wrought that I was fearful lest he would not hold out to the end. But he *does* grow upon us to the very close of the last scene, which is, perhaps, the finest, certainly the most touching in the book. A friend of mine said at Natty's departure, "I longed to go with him."[66]

And Honoré de Balzac, reviewing *The Pathfinder* in 1840, called Leatherstocking a "grand original conception":

Leatherstocking is a statue, a magnificent moral hermaphrodite, born between the savage and the civilized states of man, who will live as long as literature endures. I question whether the extraordinary works of Sir Walter Scott furnish a creation so grandiose as that of the hero of the Savannahs and the forests of America.[67]

The Pioneers represented a major victory in Cooper's campaign to create an audience for American fiction. His reviews of Sedgwick and Irving had given him the opportunity to explain to both himself and his readers the social utility of the novel he envisioned, and in the preface to *The Pioneers* he irrevocably aligned himself with common readers against the prescriptive jargon of the critics. In the novel itself he courted a whole new class of readers by assimilating the substance of pioneer and travel narratives; he structured the novel in such a way that it taught his audience how to read an American novel and warned them against the danger of misreading; finally, the theme of *The Pioneers* instructed his readers in what it meant to inhabit the American landscape, to inherit American history—to be an American. As a result, *The Pioneers* has a richness, complexity, and scope that Cooper himself rarely equalled, and that was unsurpassed in American fiction before the great novels of Hawthorne and Melville.

CHAPTER FIVE

Cooper's Audience

Cooper died just as he was achieving permanent recognition. His death was marked by memorial addresses and letters from Daniel Webster, William Cullen Bryant, Herman Melville, and others, and in fewer than ten years Stringer and Townsend began to publish their great edition of Cooper's collected novels with illustrations by America's foremost graphic artist, F. O. C. Darley. The dedication of that edition, printed at the beginning of *The Pioneers,* is eloquent testimony to the fact that Cooper had become something of a national treasure:

> To the American People, this illustrated edition of the works of the first American novelist is respectfully dedicated by the publishers.

The importance of Cooper's protracted grappling with the problem of audience cannot be overestimated. Quite simply, Cooper created the community of readers whose taste would dominate the market for fiction in America (and for American fiction abroad) throughout the nineteenth century. Most of the fiction we recognize as most characteristic and valuable in the period was designed for Cooper's audience and is unthinkable outside the horizon of expectations Cooper had established. When we encounter the generic conventions of romance in the works of Hawthorne, Melville, Lippard, Stowe, Warner, James, Howells, Twain, Norris, and Crane—and whether these writers thought of themselves as realists or romantics, all used at least some of those conventions—we are seeing the effect of Cooper's audience on the American artist.

By 1823 the patterns of Cooper's creative activity were firmly established. His exploration of the cultural life of his nation, his adaptation of popular subliterary forms to the purposes of his novels, his presentation of a socially marginal hero as the essential American, his involvement with the details of publication, his manipulation of the newspapers for publicity, and his preference for the reactions of common readers (as expressed in sales figures) to those of critics in reviews are permanent features of Cooper's career. In *The Pilot* (1824) he took what he found valuable in Scott's *The Pirate,* corrected what displeased him, merged it with the Byronic hero, American history, and his own experience, and invented the sea novel, a form he later perfected in *The Red Rover* (1827) and *The Water-Witch* (1830). After *The Narrative of the Life of Mary Jemison* joined a long tradition of captivity narratives as a bestseller in 1824, Cooper adapted the flight-and-pursuit plot and the cultural-conflict theme of captivity narrative to his frontier novels: *The Last of the Mohicans* (1826), *The Prairie* (1827), *The Wept of Wish-ton-Wish* (1829), *The Pathfinder* (1840), and *The Deerslayer* (1841). Natty Bumppo always held the place of honor in his gallery of marginal heroes, but there were many others: John Paul Jones; Lionel Lincoln; Submission, the regicide; Jacopo, the Bravo. Cooper's relations with his various publishers were marked by unusual loyalty on both sides. He remained with Charles Wiley while Wiley's firm teetered on the brink of bankruptcy, and he held a number of unpaid notes at the time of Wiley's death in 1826. Cooper then signed an agreement with Carey and Lea of Philadelphia and remained with them for seventeen years. Carey often felt that Cooper was wasting his talent on absurd political or personal propaganda and tried to persuade him to return to the more popular and profitable mode of his earlier novels, but Carey's firm continued to publish his books at a loss for much of that seventeen years. But Cooper never surrendered his own involvement in the details of publication. During his years in Europe (1827–33) he arranged for English publication and authorized translations of his works in Germany, France, and Italy. When readers ignored his doctrinal and travel narratives of the thirties, he reverted to his most popular character and themes in *The Pathfinder* and *The Deerslayer*. When the depression of 1837 devastated the book market to the point that Cooper's income from each book was cut in half, he wrote twice as fast and published two novels a year throughout the forties. When national literary magazines arose to fill the vacancy created by the slow circulation of bound books, Cooper serialized his fiction. Through all these adjustments, Cooper remained true to his original principle of literary success: if his publisher greeted him with a smiling face, all was well; as the smiles became rarer and turned to thoughtful frowns, Cooper strove to adapt his work to the new conditions—to reengage, re-educate, and reestablish his audience.

The exact nature of Cooper's audience is elusive. We know what Bryant and Melville, Balzac and Belinsky had to say about his works.[1] We can cull reviews from contemporary journals and newspapers and try to establish a specific intellectual milieu for the reception of his novels. But the Melvilles and Belinskys constitute a tiny and often arbitrary minority, and reviewers are often little more than a claque whose actual judgments, positive or negative, have little influence on the circulation of a book. "Publishers have always recognized the unreliability of critical opinion as a trade index. They do not care what a critic says as long as he says it."[2] Reception studies that focus on contemporary reviews have only limited value for determining an author's standing with his audience. Yet mass audiences leave few records of their enjoyment of or distaste for particular books; where they exist, publishers' cost books and the records of circulating libraries may offer the only reliable guidance. Thus something of Cooper's audience may be adduced from the fact that Carey and Lea "had developed the Southern Atlantic, Pennsylvania, and Ohio Valley market so extensively by the time of Cooper's arrival in 1826 that in terms of geographical coverage its distributive facilities were unmatched."[3] Much of Cooper's audience resided in those regions distant from the Eastern seaboard, so that when Henry Carey refused to handle *The Pioneers* or when *The Bravo* was published after the winter freeze had halted canal and river traffic, sales were seriously affected. We might assume, then, that Cooper's audience was largely rural, parochial, populist, Jacksonian.

Another body of evidence, however, suggests that Cooper's audience was in fact much larger and less parochial. Unfriendly reviewers fought a rearguard action against the advancing mass of Cooper enthusiasts; readers displayed an early and continuing interest in the "real-life" prototypes of Cooper's fictional heroes; painters tried to ride Cooper's coattails into the public eye; and dramatizations of Cooper's novels held the stage throughout the nineteenth century. Each of these contributes to our understanding of Cooper's readers.

The early and persistent enthusiasm for *The Spy* and the consequent excitement that greeted announcements of *The Pioneers* could not fail to alert the American contingent of those "Scotch Reviewers" who had irritated Byron. Cooper's popularity alone was grounds for suspicion; the publicity accorded each new edition of *The Spy* and the approaching appearance of *The Pioneers* was so great that literary columns adopted a kind of shorthand in reporting it: " 'The Pioneers' of the Susquehannah, a new novel by the author of 'The Spy,' is just about to be published at New York. 'The Spy' has passed through its third edition. 'Who reads an American book?' "[4] Such popularity was bound to arouse those critics who regarded themselves as watchdogs whose role was to improve the public taste and literary performance.

Moreover, *The Pioneers* challenged the critics directly twice over. First, in his preface Cooper had chosen to make popularity his measure of literary success and to ignore the arbiters of public taste; he had dared to call them asses and to doubt the objective principles upon which criticism was founded. Second, the prepublication printing of extracts from the novel in the *New York Commercial Advertiser* (and the reprinting of those extracts by other newspapers) seemed very much like an attempt to bypass altogether the judgment of reviewers by appealing directly to the reading public.

Both measures provoked righteous ire. James Gates Percival, whose name became synonymous with "failed poet" and whom Van Wyck Brooks has called a "walking suicide,"[5] equating Cooper's popular success with his own failure, denounced the pre-publication excerpts and their wide following in a bitter renunciation: "I ask nothing of a people who will lavish their patronage on such a vulgar book as the Pioneers. They and I are well quit. They neglect me, and I despise them."[6] More temperate, though no less alarmed, was the reviewer of *The Pioneers* in *The Minerva,* a New York magazine. Insisting on his intention to give a work "a fair and impartial review," he began by objecting to "the manner in which this book has been brought before the public attention":

> For some months before the appearance of the PIONEERS, we have had our curiosity kept alive, and our anticipations strongly excited, by the *puffs,* which have, from time to time, appeared in one of our daily papers. Praise has been dealt out most liberally on the book long before we had an opportunity of judging whether there were or were not a just foundation for that praise.

Allowing a book to gather common praise amounted to a usurpation of the proper role of critics: "The only *proper* means for an author to claim the public approval, is to rely on the merits of his work, and to offer his pages as a criterion by which he is to stand or fall in the estimation of the reading world." It is clear that by "the reading world" the reviewer meant first of all professional critics and their readers; otherwise, it would be absurd to object to the printing of excerpts and announcements in newspapers, a practice that can only succeed if readers find their appetites whetted by the isolated episodes they encounter.

The *Minerva* reviewer also objected to Cooper's preface. He found the claim that Cooper had written exclusively to please himself "a contemptible affectation" and Cooper's complaints about the incomprehensibility of reviewers' jargon inexcusable: "Because his own mental powers are not sufficiently great to comprehend the meaning of their language, must he anathematize the skills of all others?" But the reviewer reserved the bulk of his scorn for Cooper's determination to take the measure of his success by the profits he earned rather than by the reviews:

> We are well aware that the mass of authors generally "Rack their brains for *lucre,* not for fame;" but this is the first time we have known any of them, even from Walter Scott down to the smallest scribbler in Grubb-street, so candid as to acknowledge the motives which induced them to write. We had, all along, stupidly enough, imagined, that an author of talents looked for the *honours* of success; that he was actuated more by the noble thirst for fame and reputation, than by the love of dollars and cents, until Mr. Cooper kindly assured us to the contrary in his *peroratio.*[7]

Again, by "fame and reputation" the reviewer clearly meant reputation in a reading community consisting of professional critics and their audience, a community whose taste had been fashioned and refined by the moral, social, and critical preoccupations of Common Sense philosophy. Behind his attack on Cooper lay his anxiety about the new reading community—rural, Western and Southern, democratic and populist in political and cultural matters—that Cooper was rapidly developing. If authors succeeded in making a direct, unmediated connection with their audience, the critic's watchdog role would cease to function.

Such rearguard actions, fought in the interest of a preindustrial, aristocratic concept of the artist, confirm Cooper's success in establishing an entirely new relation to his audience. That he was the first (and before 1850 the only) American writer to earn a living exclusively from his writing is directly attributable to his appeal to the provincial, untrained audience that professional critics feared.

That audience, uninhibited by any coherent theory of mimesis, showed an intense, naive curiosity about the American "reality" that lay behind Cooper's fictions. Kennedy Williams has pointed out that the period of Cooper's career saw the first flowering of a broad-based interest in American and local history. In 1800 the nine-year-old Massachusetts Historical Society was the oldest of only five such societies in the nation; by 1860 there were one hundred eleven, and at least ninety of these published their pro-

ceedings.[8] Over the same period George Bancroft and Francis Parkman brought epic scope and romantic historiography to their
studies of American history, and, as David Levin has shown, both
the scope and the method owed a great deal to the historical
romances of Cooper and Scott.[9] History and historical fiction both
bred and gratified a national antiquarian appetite for "wiping the
dust from the urns of our fathers—gathering up whatever of illustrious achievement, of heroic suffering, or unwavering faith,
their history commemorates, and weaving it all into an immortal
and noble national literature," as Rufus Choate remarked in
1833.[10] Beginning with the veritable legend of the patriotic spy,
Cooper's fictions attached themselves to this appetite. Reviewers
regularly vouched for the veracity of events from the novels; as we
have seen, W. H. Gardiner praised Cooper's use of ethnic characters
and American landscapes, and the *Port Folio* review of *The Spy*
cited an actual case of a woman killed in her parlor by a stray
bullet, a possible model for the death of Isabella Singleton. The
Port Folio reviewer of *The Pioneers* (surely the same critic) praised
the novel for its "exact knowledge" of life in a frontier town and
related in a footnote an adventure of his own which paralleled
Natty's killing of the deer on the lake: "we have . . . contended
successfully on the lake with the pride of the forest":

> the party consisted of three. . . . When the deer dashed into the
> lake, the poet in a wrapt phrenzy, seized the helm of the batteau,
> the Editor took the prow, and the traveller plied the oars. After an
> animated chace of some minutes, the animal was overtaken, and as
> we had no fire-arms or grappling irons, we caught him by the horns
> and pressed him under the water, while our contributors manfully
> seconded us by urging the bark on his back. Situated as we were,
> but one person could struggle with our prey, and he would have
> escaped, had not the traveller, who is *a bit of a bleeder,* contrived to
> introduce the point of a penknife into his jugular vein.[11]

Cooper's socially marginal characters also seemed to
reveal something essentially American to his American readers;
Harvey Birch and Natty Bumppo took on an independent life in the
mythos of American culture, the first through a series of specula-
tions about the prototype for Cooper's spy and the last through the

inevitable connection to Daniel Boone. As early as February 1823 *Nile's Weekly Register* printed an account of a petition to the Massachusetts legislature by one David Gray for compensation for "extraordinary services" in the Revolution: "The Boston Centinel says—'It appears from evidence produced by the petitioner, that he was employed during the revolutionary war to act as a spy, and is the identical personage so celebrated in the popular novel of "The Spy" under the name of Harvey Birch.'"[12] The *Port Folio* review of *The Pioneers* remarked that Natty "has been modelled from the effigies of old Daniel Boone,"[13] and in 1825 *Nile's Weekly Register* printed a letter about a frontiersman named Augustine Friend who was "popularly known in the western country as having once been the companion of the celebrated Daniel Boone":

> There is something very remarkable in the appearance, the character and habits, of this old hunter, but, as you have no doubt read the Pioneers, and are, consequently, already intimately acquainted with the "Leather Stocking," I shall not trouble you with more description. I may be mistaken, but it seems to me that this old man of the hills, with his fondness for his dogs, his rifle, and the mountain wilds, and his indifference to society, with his antipathies to "clearings," must, without doubt, have set to the author of the Pioneers when drawing his admirable character of Natty Bumppo.[14]

The patriotic spy and the philosophical frontiersman participated in the emergence of a national "type," a process Richard Slotkin has labeled "The Evolution of a National Hero."[15] The interplay between Cooper's characters and their real-life prototypes and parallels resulted from the need of his audience to make fiction serve life, their need to locate themselves in the portrait of the essential American character that Cooper progressively drew. The frontier had receded across the Mississippi, but readers could discover a regional history, just as Cooper had, in the adventures of his heroes, and an important part of that discovery was the affirmation of Cooper's fictions in real spies and hunters.

While the literary periodicals carried on their various campaigns for and against Cooper's novels, a generalized effect spread from them through literary and subliterary circles. The most convincing indicator of Cooper's success was that he created the audience which bought, read, debated, and remembered American fiction throughout the nineteenth century. The many collected editions of Cooper's novels represent their status as living classics, but their numerous progeny in painting and drama are equally important measures of their widespread cultural influence.

The Pioneers, with its new approach to the representation of the American landscape, had an immediate impact on American art, as painters and engravers sought to capitalize on the novel's popularity by associating themselves with its scenes. The Port Folio reported on the remarkable number of artists who began illustrating The Pioneers as soon as it was published:

> The Pioneers.—The new novel, entitled The Pioneers, seems to have excited a sensation among the artists, altogether unprecedented in the history of our domestic literature. We learn from New York that Mr. Dunlap has on his easel a painting from the work, in oil five or six feet square; and there is another, of similar size, by a competitor, whose name has not been mentioned to us. In Philadelphia, Mr. Fairman and Mr. Childs, have several designs in hand, which are intended for the embellishment of The Port Folio. We have seen at the Athenaeum in this city, an illustration of the Panther scene, which had been particularly selected for the attention of artists by the writer of a review of The Pioneers in a late number of the Port Folio. It is a painting in water colours by Mr. Thompson, of Susquehanna County. . . . In short, poetry and painting seem to have combined with criticism, in rewarding our author for the engaging manner in which he has depicted our own fire-sides. In assigning to Mr. Cooper a high station among the novelists of the present day readers and critics cheerfully concur; and no discordant notes are heard but from prejudice or malignity.[16]

Through 1823 and 1824 the Port Folio published a series of vignettes from The Spy and The Pioneers; drawings were by Henry Inman as well as Fairman and Childs.[17] Famous scenes from The Pioneers provided inspiration for oil paintings by Thomas Doughty, William W. Walcutt, Tompkins H. Matteson, John Quidor, George Loring Brown, and Thomas Cole.[18] If few of these artists ever achieved permanent status, it is nevertheless true that they owed much of their contemporary fame as well as their niches in history to their association with Cooper's name.

A similar popularity was enjoyed by the dramatists and actors who adapted Cooper's novels to the theater. *The Spy* was produced at The Broadway Circus in New York on September 9, 1822, but audience enthusiasm was greatest for adaptations of Cooper's sea tales. *The Pilot; or, a Storm at Sea,* a "nautical burletta" by Edward Ball, was produced at the Adelphi Theatre in London on October 21, 1826, and at the Chatham Theatre in New York on March 21, 1828;[19] the English actor T. P. Cooke, famous for his nautical roles, played in *The Pilot* 562 times during his career.[20] *The Red Rover* was dramatized in four separate versions between 1828 and 1831, the first only forty-four days after the appearance of the novel. A fifth version, *An Entirely New and Original Burlesque, Being the Very Latest Edition of a Nautical Tradition Told by one of the Floating Population to the Marines Who Entitled it* THE RED ROVER; *Or, I Believe You, My Bouy!* by Francis Cowley Burnand, the editor of *Punch,* was performed in London as late as December 26, 1877. As John D. Gordan has noted, "That *The Red Rover* could inspire a successful travesty half a century after the novel first appeared and over a quarter of a century after Cooper's death indicates a more enduring popularity than has hitherto been suspected."[21] The popularity of the novels inspired dramatizations, all of which depended to some degree on a knowledge of the novels for a coherence the scripts lacked, and the popularity of the plays reinforced the popularity of the novels among a largely nonreading public, a fact that accounts in part for the continuing growth of Cooper's audience throughout the nineteenth century.

While negative reviews and items of literary gossip suggest that Cooper's readers were provincial and populist, the popularity of illustrations and dramas based on his novels indicate a more sophisticated urban audience. Paintings were executed and shown in New York, Philadelphia, and Baltimore, not in Pittsburgh or Cincinnati. Acting companies went on the road, of course, but adaptations of *The Spy, The Pilot,* and *The Red Rover* always played in New York first. Cooper's appeal, then, was not limited to any one type of reader or region of the country, and the population of the Eastern seaboard was as important to his success as markets in the interior.

The enduring effect of Cooper's popularity was the permanent change it wrought in the taste of the novel-reading audience in America. Modern critics have (sometimes begrudgingly) granted Cooper a place at the source of the American novel, but they have generally done so by emphasizing the "mythic" qualities of his work—its generic affinity with romance, its frontier mythos, its American Adam, its democratic humanism, its portrayal of a special intimacy between a white hero and his dark double.[22] Such readings attempt to locate Cooper's importance somewhere behind or beyond his texts, which are commonly regarded as embarrassingly flawed by their sentimental love plots, their eighteenth-century prolixity, their fastidious attention to distinctions of class and manners. Thus both Richard Chase and R. W. B. Lewis define their studies as explorations of a native American mythology, and Richard Slotkin prefaces his fine investigation of violence in American culture with a Jungian explication of the mythology of the hunt, as if the popularity of Natty Bumppo could be explained by reference to a Collective Unconscious rather than to the historical and literary antecedents that Slotkin so skillfully traces in the rest of his book. Behind every such attempt to explain Cooper's value looms the daunting figure of Mark Twain, who taught us once and for all just how ridiculous the surface of Cooper's fiction can be.

Attempts to circumvent Twain miss the point of "Fenimore Cooper's Literary Offenses." The object of Twain's attack is not Cooper, after all, nor his work; both were safely past amending. Rather, Twain was attacking the audience that Cooper had created and that inexplicably continued to prefer the novels of Cooper and his literary heirs to those of the realists, who were attempting to create an audience of their own. Twain's essay is a pedagogical tract designed to show us how to read, a manifesto in the form of an attack on an established figure, no different in spirit than T. S. Eliot's famous assault on Milton. Its greatest value lies in its identification of the conventional features of Cooper's fiction, the features that define the horizon of expectations for Cooper's readers: the inflated diction, the arcane Indian lore, the improbable feats of tracking and marksmanship, the painstakingly contrived episodes of danger, the melodramatic behavior of its heroes and heroines. That Twain felt it necessary to castigate these excesses over fifty years after the appearance of *The Deerslayer* is still another indication of the persistence of the audience Cooper created.

In Cooper's own day, other novelists were not slow to comprehend the opportunity that Cooper's success represented. In May 1823 *Niles' Weekly Register* announced a work "of the same kind" as *The Spy* and *The Pioneers:* "'The Wilderness' lately appeared in New York, and the whole edition was disposed of in four weeks." The first issue of *The New-York Mirror* not only reviewed *The Wilderness* (which it found distinctly inferior to *The Pioneers*) but also initiated a serial novel entitled *Whigs and Tories: A Moral Tale,* which drew its plot of love, politics, and rebellion and its moral intent from *The Spy.*[23] The electrifying effect of Cooper's first novels can be seen in the reaction recorded by the irascible John Neal. Neal had already composed a quantity of Byronic poetry and an autobiographical novel and had ghost-written most of Paul Allen's *History of the American Revolution* when he came across *The Spy:* "I had got charged to the muzzle with the doings of our Revolutionary fathers," wrote Neal, "while writing my portion of 'Allen's History,' and wanted only the hint, or touch, that Cooper gave in passing, to go off like a Leyden jar, and empty myself at once of all the hoarded enthusiasm I had been bottling up, for three or four years." The explosion produced *Seventy-Six,* a novel combining realistic battle scenes with three conventional love stories, an abortive seduction, and a duel. Though Neal is now nearly forgotten, Benjamin Lease notes that during the 1820s he was successful enough to be regarded as Cooper's chief American rival. Indeed, one lady reader became "so infatuated with Neal's pungent style that she lost her taste for all other books and died with a copy of *Seventy-Six* in her hand."[24]

Cooper's influence endured for several decades, and most aspiring American novelists assumed that they were writing for Cooper's audience. Nathaniel Hawthorne may seem to have little in common with Cooper, yet his first novel, *Fanshawe* (1828), owes its descriptions of nature, its flight-and-pursuit plot, and the alienation of its eponymous hero to Cooper's example. Indeed, the socially marginal artist-heroes of Hawthorne's fiction—Dimmesdale, Holgrave, Coverdale, Kenyon—represent an alternative version of Harvey Birch and Natty Bumppo: the essential American as student, poet, sculptor. Other versions of the uncouth woodsman as hero also appeared: Supple Jack Bannister in William Gilmore Simms' *The Kinsman* (1841) and Nick in Robert M. Bird's *Nick of the Woods* (1837). When Herman Melville dropped the writing of autobiographical narratives and essayed a philosophical allegory, *Mardi* (1849), he projected a marginal American hero (Taji), a contrasting dark-fair pair of women (Hautia and Yillah), and a flight-and-pursuit plot, all tailored for the readers who had welcomed *The Last of the Mohicans* and *The Red Rover.* Even *Uncle Tom's Cabin* (serialized 1851–52), which is commonly considered outside the male-dominated tradition of the American novel,[25] employs the bifurcated fair-dark heroines (Eva and Topsy), socially marginal heroes (notably George Harris), and the horror of the hunted human in ways quite familiar to Cooper's readers.

The point of these comparisons is not that Cooper "influenced" Hawthorne, Melville, and Stowe, but that each of these later writers was quite aware of what the reading public expected to find in a new novel, and each strove according to his or her own temperament to satisfy the prevailing taste. For these and a host of lesser figures throughout the nineteenth century, that meant a taste formed by Cooper's novels.

Early in the twentieth century, as notions of the autonomous artist who wrote for a select few began to dominate literary thought, W. C. Brownell observed that recent critics had erred in applying realist or symbolist standards to Cooper's fiction:

Cooper wrote as well as, and builded better than, any one required of him—and though genius, *ex hypothesi,* escapes the operation of evolutionary law, literary or any other artistic expression is almost as much a matter of supply and demand as railroads or any other means of communication; the demand, that is, produces, controls, and gives its character to the supply. The theory that art is due to artists leaves the origin of artists unexplained.[26]

Early in his career Cooper had decided that Adam Smith's prediction had been correct: that in the post-industrial era the production of art was as subject to the effects of economic law as was the production of pins. In the new world and under the new dispensation, an artist's success depended on his or her ability to fulfill existing demand and to create new demand for the new product. Beginning with an audience that he knew well, the gentleman farmer James Cooper produced an imitation English novel that won the respect of readers. Within three years, with two more novels, he transformed both himself and his readers: he became America's national author, the only American who could support himself by his writing, the American whose works could be found "in Constantinople, in Egypt, at Jerusalem, at Ispahan";[27] and his readers demanded a new kind of fiction suited to the continent. He adapted his literary structures from models he knew to be popular—novels by Opie, Austen, Scott—but he drew his substance from subliterary narratives, legends, traditions, the gossip of the nation. From these disparate materials he forged the American novel and taught his audience to read it.

APPENDIX

The 1801 Review of *Wieland*

The first issue of *The American Review, and Literary Journal* (1801) contains the beginning of an extensive review of Charles Brockden Brown's *Wieland*. Although this review has occasionally been cited by Brown's critics, it has not stirred much interest save for its identification of the historical source for Wieland's religious delusion. The anonymous reviewer is generally assumed to have been a friend or associate of Brown.[1]

In the second chapter of this book, I have assumed that the reviewer was Brown himself. The first time I read the review, I was convinced that its style, theoretical concerns, and privileged information all were Brown's, and subsequent readings have only strengthened my conviction. Convincing other readers that I am right, however, has been more difficult than I at first imagined. In the last analysis, it may not matter whether Brown is the actual author; an associate writing under his influence or direction would have had access to the source material the review reprints, could have been tutored in Brown's theory of fiction, and might have been inspired to imitate Brown's style; the applicability of the final result to our reading of *Wieland* would be the same. Nevertheless, I remain sure that Brown is the author, and my purpose here is to present the evidence as forcefully as possible. The 1801 review is reprinted so that the reader of this study may judge as well.

I

The American Review succeeded the Monthly Magazine and American Review (1798–1800). While Brown was the editor of the earlier journal (it was founded by his friends in an attempt to help Brown earn a living as a man of letters), his role in The American Review has never been clearly established. William Dunlap's biography, the basic source for all information about Brown's life, simply skips over those months following the last issue of the Monthly Magazine.[2] David Lee Clark notes that "Brown returned to New York by the middle of September [1800] and remained there until he had edited the last issue of the Monthly Magazine (December 1800). What he did with himself during the next six months has not been determined."[3]

We can be certain, however, that Brown wrote for The American Review and that, whoever was acting as editor, Brown was considered a specialist on literary matters for the journal. In a letter dated July 8, 1802, Brown complains about the work expected of him:

> The review is exceedingly behind hand, & my friends have imposed on me the task of reading & reviewing half a dozen books, which, without their injunctions, I should never have looked into. This had been an irksome undertaking, & which nothing but a kind of necessity could reconcile me to. To criticize without reading would be absurd, & to read not for instruction or amusement, would be galley slavery. The next number is very long in making its appearance, & I suppose will scarcely issue from the press in less than a fortnight.[4]

Self-promotion through anonymous reviews was not an uncommon practice at the turn of the nineteenth century. In 1816 Sir Walter Scott reviewed *Tales of My Landlord* in the *Quarterly Review,* which he had helped to found, and John Neal wrote *two* anonymous reviews of his *Rachel Dyer* for the same number of *The Yankee,* of which he was the founder and editor.[5] Brown, previous to 1801, had gone to unusual lengths to promote *Wieland.* On December 15, 1798, just two months after the publication of the novel, he had sent a presentation copy to Thomas Jefferson, then Vice President and the foremost man of letters in the country, together with a letter asking for a puff. Jefferson's reply was over a year in coming and included the admission that he had not yet had time to read *Wieland.*[6] Shortly after this disappointment, Brown's publisher took copies of *Wieland, Ormond,* and *Arthur Mervyn* to the Minerva Press in England in the hope that English publication and a few favorable English reviews would stimulate domestic curiosity about Brown's work. Unfortunately, the Minerva Press had a reputation for printing trash, and the only review that English publication generated (*The Anti-Jacobin Review,* August 1800) treated Brown with contempt.[7] Nonetheless, these efforts indicate that Brown was well acquainted with the need to whet the public appetite for a new novel, and given the opportunity afforded by his less direct involvement with *The American Review,* he was free to make another (and final) attempt to promote *Wieland.*

Finally, it should be noted that two years had passed between the publication of *Wieland* and the appearance of the 1801 review. In that time Brown's five other published novels had failed; his career as a writer of fiction, already severely modified by his decision to limit himself to the domestic novel in *Jane Talbot* and *Clara Howard,* had ended; his *Monthly Magazine* had folded from lack of financial support; the enormous excitement and lofty ambition that had brought him to New York in 1798 had led to obscurity and failure. In these circumstances a reassessment of the moral and artistic resources of the novel would be natural for Brown, and the review of *Wieland* undertakes such a reassessment.

II

The 1801 review consists of an introduction that sketches a theory of fiction, a body that summarizes and quotes extensively from *Wieland,* and a conclusion that assesses the novel's strengths and weaknesses. The theory of fiction is consistent with that expressed in Brown's prefaces and other theoretical writing, and the plot summary displays a privileged knowledge of the sources Brown used in writing *Wieland*. Throughout the review, the style is Brown's; occasionally there are verbal echoes of Brown's prefaces.

Theory of Fiction

The introductory portion of the review argues six main points for a theory of fiction. These points are summarized below and juxtaposed with corresponding points from Brown's other writing.

1. Ancient romances were very popular but were "pernicious to morals and taste," and these were the ancestors of the modern novel (*1801*, 1:333).

In a brief note entitled "Novels" (*The Literary Magazine*, 1805) Brown compares the novel and poetry as imaginative forms: "The modern novel well executed, possessing the essential characters of poetry, perhaps even more perfectly than the ancient romance, certainly deserves a place among the works of genius." The novel is a species of poetry in the sense that "fancy collects, judgment combines, and taste expresses in suitable language, images furnished by Nature."[8] Similarly, the 1801 review argues that novelists and romancers have the same liberty as poets in affecting the imaginations of readers: "Fiction and fancy belong equally to both, and while the laws of nature are not violated, or the bounds of probability exceeded, both equally deserve to escape censure" (*1801*, 2:34).

2. Novels excite "curiosity and sympathy" and offer an unparalleled opportunity to illustrate truths "by examples which come home to the apprehension and feelings of every class of men, and in which every reader, in some degree, finds the sentiments of his own heart and the incidents of his own life, reflected before him" (*1801*, 1:333).

Brown's advertisement for the unpublished *Sky Walk* (1798) shows a similar interest in appealing to "every class of men." There Brown argues that the American novelist must treat "our ecclesiastical and political system, our domestic and social maxims" in order to "lay some claim to the patronage of his countrymen"; he must write not merely to amuse "the idle and thoughtless" but also "the man of soaring passions and intellectual energy."[9] "A Student's Diary . . . Number V: Novel-Reading" (1804) presents a dialogue between the student and a woman who advocates novel-reading. She maintains that the enlightened mind "loves to contemplate human life in the mirror which genius holds up to it" and that the "brightest" property of human nature "is to be influenced more by example than by precept."[10]

3. An innate love of novelty and a need for relief from "the tedious uniformity of life" motivate people to read and enjoy "works of imagination," and while "amusement only is sought in opening a volume, effects the most serious and durable may be produced on the imagination and heart of the reader" (*1801,* 2:334).

The novel-reading advocate of "A Student's Diary" implies this same motivation for opening a novel: "Boys and girls, and men and woman [*sic*] whose judgments are no better than those of boys and girls, read and relish them. The food is suited to the palate, and they derive a pleasure from it which at least is innocent." The Student, less assured of the innocence of *all* novels, is willing to grant that "the merit of a score of these is . . . so great, that they are the first and principal objects to which I would direct the curiosity of a child or pupil of mine" ("Diary," p. 405). The "Advertisement" to *Wieland* tells the reader that this is an epistolary novel addressed to a "small number of friends, whose curiosity, with regard to it, had been greatly awakened,"[11] and in the prefatory letter "To I. E. Rosenberg" in *Ormond* the writer admits, "I am well acquainted with your motives, and allow that they justify your curiosity" (*Ormond,* p. 3).

4. While most novelists write from "desire of gain, or the hope of some portion of literary fame," the fact remains that the novel is an "obvious and popular means of inculcating and enforcing the principles of morality" (*1801,* 1:334).

The "Advertisement" to *Wieland* notes that the author's purpose "is neither selfish nor temporary, but aims at the illustration of some important branches of the moral constitution of man" (*Wieland*, p. 3). The novel-reading woman of "A Student's Diary" allows that "Novelists, in general, write for the sake of a subsistence. . . . The herd of romance-writers, are, for the most part, goaded by necessity into authorship." Still, the Student concludes, "I cannot but say, however, that my fancy has received more delight, my heart more humanity, and my understanding more instruction from a few novels I could name, than from any other works" ("Diary," pp. 404–5). In the "Preface" to *Arthur Mervyn* Brown contends, "It is every one's duty to profit by all opportunities of inculcating on mankind the lessons of justice and humanity." He goes on to analyze how didacticism works:

> Men only require to be made acquainted with distress for their compassion and their charity to be awakened. He that depicts, in lively colours, the evils of disease and poverty, performs an eminent service to the sufferers, by calling forth benevolence in those who are able to afford relief, and he who pourtrays examples of disinterestedness and intrepidity, confers on virtue the notoriety and homage that are due to it, and rouses in the spectators, the spirit of salutary emulation.[12]

5. Observing the popularity of Gothic novels, the author of *Wieland* ("almost the first American" novelist) has "sought to profit by this love of the marvelous, to display and illustrate some remarkable properties in the physical and moral constitution of man." He has chosen a "real but extraordinary faculty [ventriloquism]" to "constitute a machinery . . . more dignified and instructive than ruined castles, imaginary spectres, and the monkish fictions of modern romance" (*1801*, 1:334).

The "Advertisement" to *Wieland* attempts to stimulate the reader's interest in the marvels the novel portrays: "The incidents related are extraordinary and rare. Some of them, perhaps, approach as nearly to the nature of miracles as can be done by that which is not truly miraculous" (*Wieland*, p. 3). The substitution of striking fact for the "wonder-working powers of gothic machinery" is extolled in the well-known preface to *Edgar Huntly:*

One merit the writer may at least claim: that of calling forth the passions and engaging the sympathy of the reader by means hitherto unemployed by preceding authors. Puerile superstition and exploded manners, Gothic castles and chimeras, are the materials usually employed for this end. The incidents of Indian hostility and the perils of the Western wilderness are far more suitable; and for a native of America to overlook these would admit of no apology.[13]

6. "Whatever may be thought of the practical utility of this species of narrative, the praise of a vigorous and creative fancy, and of strong talents for moral description, cannot be denied to our author" (*1801,* 1:334).

This emphasis on a "vigorous and creative fancy" is frequently found in Brown's theoretical writing. The advertisement for *Sky Walk* promised "lofty eloquence," "the exhibition of powerful motives, and a sort of audaciousness of character" that would "enchain the attention and ravish the souls of those who study and reflect" (*Rhapsodist,* p. 136). Elsewhere he asserts that "it is the business of moral painters to exhibit their subject in its most instructive and memorable forms" (*Wieland,* p. 3) and stresses that he is "ambitious of depicting in vivid and faithful colors" the perils of the Western wilderness (*Edgar Huntly,* p. 29). "The Student's Diary" maintains that the purest gratification of taste is to "view human characters and events, depicted by a vigorous and enlightened fancy" ("Diary," p. 404).

Some of these points, of course, are critical commonplaces of late eighteenth-century thought. Two of them, however, are peculiarly Brown's: the interest in replacing Gothic machinery with natural marvels, and the high value placed on the creative imagination beyond any "practical utility" a novel may have.

Summary of *Wieland*

The summary of *Wieland* in the 1801 review is notable for its identification of the sources for the "extraordinary and rare" incidents in the plot: the elder Wieland's spontaneous combustion, the younger Wieland's religious delusion, and Carwin's ventriloquism. A footnote in chapter 2 of *Wieland* refers the reader to "one of the Journals of Florence" and to the "Journal de Medecine" for cases of spontaneous combustion. The "Advertisement" suggests that though Theodore Wieland's delusion is a rare case, it is nonetheless based on fact: "If history furnishes one parallel fact, it is a sufficient vindication of the Writer; but most readers will probably recollect an authentic case, remarkably similar to that of Wieland" (*Wieland*, p. 3). A lengthy footnote also attests to the authenticity of ventriloquism, with references to the Abbé de la Chappelle and to Dr. Burney (*Wieland*, p. 198n). Brown considered the factual basis of his marvels important enough to interrupt the flow of his narrative with outside authorities. They provide the basis for his transformation of Gothic machinery into something dignified and instructive.

The 1801 review is even more anxious to persuade the reader of this factual basis. Instead of a reference to Italian and French journals (which must seem fantastic to most American readers in any case), we have a translated account of spontaneous combustion from "the fourth volume of the *Literary Magazine*"— an account which takes up three pages of the review (*1801*, 1:337–39). The "authentic case" of religious delusion is cited from the *New-York Weekly Magazine* (*1801*, 1:336). Carwin's ventriloquism is discussed extensively as well; the review calls it an "extraordinary faculty . . . the reality of which cannot be denied, but whose effects are not generally known, nor easily to be explained" (*1801*, 2:31–32).

While we might attribute the precise identification of *Wieland*'s sources to one of Brown's friends, the space given to those sources and the insistent tone in which they are offered as a validation of the machinery of the novel betray more anxiety to persuade than we would expect, even from a friend. The whole subject is central to Brown's career as a novelist.

Style

Virtually every critic who has written on Brown has complained about his style. Ernest Marchand has summarized its distinctive features:

When Brown can think of a mouth-filling Latin derivative, he prefers it to a more common word. . . . He is clear enough, but often redundant. He makes a sparing use of initial periodicity, balance, and antithesis; and since his sentences are, in the main, of moderate length (even, for pages at a time, markedly short), they lack the heavy rolling groundswell of the Johnsonian period. A peculiarity is his excessive use of the passive voice, which soon forces itself on the attention of the reader.[14]

To be sure, Brown had more than one style and tried to make style conform to the subject he was treating.[15] The voice of his prefaces and journal writing is far less bizarre than that of Arthur Mervyn. Yet the peculiarities of vocabulary, syntax, and rhetoric remain.

The first paragraph of the 1801 review betrays many of those peculiarities. Some of Brown's favorite latinisms are here: "pertinacious," "incorrigible," "pernicious," "inundation." The two-part parallel structures characteristic of Brown's style abound: "resign or suppress"; "of licentiousness in the prelate, or of unreasonable prejudice in the brethren"; "pertinacious and incorrigible"; "the censures of the pious and the frowns of the moralist"; "religion and morals"; "contempt and neglect"; "morals and taste"; all these contribute to the sense of redundancy that Marchand notes. The first two sentences employ the passive voice, and the most common verb is some form of "to be." Initial periodicity, balance, and antithesis all make appearances but, as Marchand remarks, to little effect. The style here and throughout the review is Brown's.

There are also a number of instances where the 1801 review echoes not only the preface to *Wieland* (as we might expect from an unusually sympathetic critic) but Brown's other theoretical writings as well:

"inculcating and enforcing the principles of morality" (*1801,* 1:334);

"inculcating on mankind the lessons of justice and humanity" (*Mervyn,* p. 3);

"to display and illustrate some remarkable properties in the physical and moral constitution of man" (*1801,* 1:334);

"aims at illustration of some important branches of the moral constitution of man" (*Wieland,* p. 3);

"He has availed himself of a real but extraordinary faculty, heretofore unnoticed by the novelist" (*1801*, 1:334);

"One merit the writer may at least claim: that of calling forth the passions and engaging the sympathy of the reader by means hitherto unemployed by preceding authors" (*Huntly*, p. 29);

"a vigorous and creative fancy" (*1801*, 1:334);

"a vigorous and enlightened fancy" ("Diary," p. 404);

"The principal incidents, however incredible and shocking, are founded on well authenticated facts, and are sublime and tragical in the highest degree" (*1801*, 1:335);

"An event so extraordinary and deplorable" (*1801*, 1:339);

"The extraordinary and shocking death of the father" (*1801*, 2:28);

"The incidents related are extraordinary and rare" (*Wieland*, p. 3);

"Possessed of the extraordinary faculty of *ventriloquism,* the reality of which cannot be denied, but whose effects are not generally known, nor easily to be explained" (*1801*, 2:30–31);

"The power which the principal person is said to possess can scarcely be denied to be real. It must be acknowledged to be extremely rare; but no fact, equally uncommon, is supported by the same strength of historical evidence." (*Wieland*, p. 3);

"Carwin is an extraordinary being, and in some degree, incomprehensible" (*1801*, 2:37);

"Ormond will, perhaps, appear to you a contradictory or unintelligible being" (*Ormond*, p. 3).

In every point of thought and style, the 1801 review reveals Brown's hand. Even if the review is actually by one of Brown's friends, its form and substance suggest that Brown supervised its composition so closely that the difference is negligible. I would therefore maintain that we must accept it as Brown's last attempt to promote *Wieland.*

The 1801 Review

The text of the 1801 review follows. It is reprinted in its entirety, except for long extracts from *Wieland;* I have indicated those omissions in brackets. Original page numbers are also indicated, by volume and page number, in brackets within the text.

ARTICLE X.

Wieland, or the Transformation. An American Tale. 12 mo.
pp. 298. T. & J. Swords. 1798.

A Greek Bishop is said to have been the first *romance* writer. His work was condemned by an ecclesiastical synod, as dangerous to the morals of youth; and the author, rather than resign or suppress his book, relinquished his bishoprick. This was a proof either of licentiousness in the prelate, or of unreasonable prejudice in his brethren. The readers of romances have been no less pertinacious and incorrigible in their attachment to this species of writing than this dignified instructor of mankind; for, in spite of the censures of the pious and the frowns of the moralist, it continued, for many ages, to be popular in Europe until the spread of purer religion and morals, and the general cultivation of classical literature, brought them into contempt and neglect. The ancient romances were certainly pernicious to morals and taste; and every sober man who has any regard for either must rejoice that they have been exploded; though he may yet find some cause for censure in that form of fictitious history which has succeeded, and may deplore the ravages made by the inundation of modern novels.

It is a circumstance of considerable weight in favour of novels, that men of undoubted piety and benevolence have been writers as well as readers of them. No species of composition is more universally read, since none so powerfully excites curiosity and sympathy, the active principles of every human being. Truths inculcated in the more solemn forms of instruction make slighter impressions, and have less influence on the great mass of mankind, than when practically illustrated by examples which come home to the apprehension and feelings of every class of men, and in which every reader, in some degree, finds the sentiments of his own heart and the incidents of his own life, reflected before him. It is not surprising, therefore, that men of deep insight into the springs of human action, as well as rigid moralists, have approved and practised this mode of teaching virtue. Like every other power over the imaginations and conduct of men, when exercised by the ingenious and benevolent, it is conducive to the noblest purposes, but, in the hands of the licentious and immoral, it is liable to be abused and perverted. [1:333]

The love of *novelty* is universal and inextinguishable, and it is in works of imagination that it finds its most ample gratification. To this passion, so deeply rooted in human nature, is every species of composition, narrative or dramatic, real or fictitious, principally indebted for its interest and success. The bulk of mankind, restless and impatient, seek, in the variety and change of real or imaginary objects, relief from the tedious uniformity of common life. While amusement only is sought in opening a volume, effects the most serious and durable may be produced on the imagination and heart of the reader. It is only to be desired that these effects should be always favourable to the cause of virtue.

To condemn wholly this mode of writing, and to proscribe novels from the world, would evince more zeal than justice or good sense. It cannot be denied that the greater number of novel writers appear to have had no better motives than the desire of gain, or the hope of some portion of literary fame, and have paid little attention to the moral effects of their productions. Yet why should the benefactors of the human race, those who seek to inform, instruct and direct the conduct of men, regard this class of writers with unmingled contempt, and wholly neglect so obvious and popular means of inculcating and enforcing the principles of morality?

The author of Wieland is almost the first American who has adventured in this path of literature, and this production is the first of the kind which has attracted much public attention. Observing the great avidity with which some popular British novels are read, and which are indebted for much of the interest they excite to the wonder-working powers of gothic machinery, he has sought to profit by this love of the marvellous, to display and illustrate some remarkable properties in the physical and moral constitution of man.

He has availed himself of a real but extraordinary faculty, heretofore unnoticed by the novelist, and imperfectly known to the natural philosopher. The effects produced by such a power are sufficiently mysterious and wonderful to keep curiosity active, and to constitute a machinery, if such it may be called, more dignified and instructive than ruined castles, imaginary spectres, and the monkish fictions of modern romance.

Whatever may be thought of the practical utility of this species of narrative, the praise of a vigorous and creative fancy, and of strong talents for moral description, cannot be denied to our author. [1:334]

The principal incidents, however incredible and shocking, are founded on well authenticated facts,* and are sublime and tragical in the highest degree.

The first and second chapters are occupied in relating some incidents in the life of the *elder* Wieland, and his extraordinary death. This part of the narrative is lucid and impressive; and though not immediately connected with the principal story, yet the strong effect of these events on the mind of the younger Wieland, is conducive to the part which he acts in the dreadful scenes that follow.

The elder Wieland is represented as a gloomy and visionary enthusiast, who retires to a solitary edifice to perform his accustomed midnight devotions, and there receives the stroke of death, under circumstances so mysterious as to be thought miraculous by his children— This event is thus described:

[Extract from *Wieland,* pp. 16–18; this extract occupies the rest of 1:335, all of 1:336, and half of 1:337.]

Reference is made, in a note, to two cases similar to the one here related, reported in a Journal of Florence, and in the "Journal de Medecine," by Messrs. Merille and Muraire. We find these cases mentioned in the fourth volume of the *Literary Magazine* (p. 336), part of which we shall extract for the satisfaction of the curious and philosophical reader.

"Don G. Maria Bertholi, a priest, residing at Mount Valere, in the district of Livizzano, went to the fair of Filetto, on account of some

*See *New-York Weekly Magazine,* vol. ii, pp. 20–28.

business which he had to transact, and after spending the whole day in going about through the neighbouring country, in order to execute commissions, in the evening he walked towards Fenille, and stopped at the house of one of his brothers-in-law, who resided there. No sooner had he arrived than he desired to be conducted to his apartment, where he put a handkerchief between his shoulders and his shirt, and when every body retired, he began to repeat his breviary. A few minutes after a loud noise was heard in Mr. Bertholi's chamber, and his cries having alarmed the family, they hastened to the spot, where they found him extended on the floor, and surrounded by a faint flame, which retired to a greater distance in proportion as it was approached, and at length disappeared entirely. Having conveyed him to bed, such assistance as seemed necessary was given him. Next morning I was called, and after examining the patient carefully, I found that the teguments of the right arm were almost entirely detached from the flesh, and hanging loose, as well as the skin of the lower part of it. In the space contained between the shoulders [1:337] and the thigh, the teguments were as much injured as those of the right arm. The first thing, therefore, to be done, was to take away those pieces of skin, and perceiving that a mortification was begun in that part of the right hand which had received the greatest hurt, I scarified it without loss of time; but notwithstanding this precaution, I found it next day, as I had suspected the preceding evening, entirely sphacelous. On my third visit, all the other wounded parts appeared to be in the same condition. The patient complained of an ardent thirst, and was agitated with dreadful convulsions. He voided by stool bilious putrid matter, and was distressed by a continual vomiting, accompained [sic] with a violent fever and delirium. At length, the fourth day, after a comatose sleep of two hours, he expired. During my last visit, whilst he was sunk in the lethargic sleep of which I have spoken, I observed, with astonishment, that putrefaction had already made so great progress, that his body exhaled an insupportable smell. I saw the worms which issued from it crawling on the bed, and the nails of his fingers drop of themselves; so that I thought it needless to attempt anything farther, whilst he was in this deplorable condition.

"Having taken care to get every possible information from the patient himself respecting what had happened to him, he told me that he had felt a stroke, as if somebody had given him a blow over the right arm with a large club, and that, at the same time, he had seen a spark of fire attach itself to his shirt, which, in a moment, was reduced to ashes, though the fire did not in the least injure the wristbands. The handkerchief which he had placed upon his shoulders, between his shirt and the skin, was perfectly entire, without the least appearance of burning; his drawers were untouched, but his night-cap was destroyed, though a single hair of his head was not hurt.

"That this flame, under the form of elementary fire, burnt the skin, reduced the shirt to ashes, and entirely consumed the night-cap, without in the least touching the hair, is a fact which I affirm to be true; besides, every symptom that appeared on the body of the deceased announced severe burning. The night was calm, and the circumambient air very pure; no bitumenous smell could be perceived in the chamber, nor was there the least trace of fire or of smoke. A lamp, however, which had been full of oil was found dry, and the wick almost in ashes. We cannot reasonably suppose this fatal accident to have been occasioned by any external cause, and I have no doubt, that if Maffei were still alive he would take advantage [1:338] of it to support an opinion which he entertained, that lightning is sometimes kindled within the human body, and destroys it.

"The above observations respecting Mr. Bertholi, naturally bring to our remembrance the fate of the unfortunate Countess Cornelia Bandi, of Verona, concerning whom the Canon Bianchini has published the details collected by Dr. Cromwell Mortimer, Fellow of the Royal Society of London, with some similar facts, to which we may add others more recent, such as the observations which Mr. Merille and Mr. Muraire inserted in the *Journal de Medecine,* for the months of February and May, 1783.

"The authors of these different observations, almost of the same nature, remark, that those subjected to such accidents were, for the most part, advanced in years, remarkably fat, and had been much addicted to the use of spirituous liquors, either in their drink, or applied in frictions to the body; whence they have concluded, that these people had perished by their whole substance spontaneously taking fire, the principal seat of which had been the entrails or the epigastric viscera, and that the exciting cause was naturally found in the phlogiston of the animal humours, called forth by that of the spirituous liquors combined with the latter."

It will be perceived that the incidents related of Wieland are the same which accompanied the death of the unfortunate Bertholi.

An event so extraordinary and deplorable, it may well be supposed, produced the most deep and awful impressions on the family of Wieland.

Young Wieland regarded the death of his father as the effect of supernatural agency, and, possessing an ardent imagination, it assumed a predominant influence over his future character, and fashioned his mind to melancholy and superstition.

Such a cast of mind, and such incidents as are here introduced, serve to render more probable the subsequent events of this affecting story.

Having said so much on the introductory chapters, we must be excused for deferring our account of the remainder of this volume to our next number; when we shall more particularly examine its merits as a literary production, and the claims of its author as a writer and moralist.

The rarity of this species of writing among us, as well as the nature and character of the performance, will, we trust, be a sufficient apology for the length to which this review may be extended. [1:339]

ART. VI. *Wieland, or the Transformation.*
Continued from vol. i. p. 339, and concluded.

The extraordinary and shocking death of the father of young Wieland was shortly followed by the death of his mother. Left with his sister, the supposed narrator of the tale, to the care of a maiden aunt, he passed his youthful days in the acquisition of knowledge, and in the society of his sister, and her intimate friend and companion, *Catharine Pleyel.* On arriving at full age he married Miss Pleyel, and having chosen agriculture as his occupation, he took possession of the farm and mansion of his father. Six years of uninterrupted happiness passed in retirement; during which time he was blessed with four [2:28] lovely children. His social circle was further enlarged by the presence of Henry Pleyel, his wife's brother, and Miss CONWAY, a young lady whom misfortune had placed under the care of the aunt.

One evening, while his family and friends were assembled together, Wieland having occasion to visit the building which had been the scene of his father's death, is stopped on his approach, by the voice of his wife issuing from the building before him, warning him not to come thither, "for danger is in the path." The astonished husband returns to his house, where he finds his wife seated as he had left her, and surrounded with friends, who were witnesses that she had not moved from her chair. This incident is viewed in various lights by the friends of

Wieland. The reality of the voice, however, is soon put beyond dispute, when Wieland and Pleyel are jointly addressed in a manner still more mysterious and impressive; and the latter is assured of the death of a lady at Leipsic, by whom he was beloved, and to whom he was preparing to return: he delays his departure a few weeks, when he received undoubted intelligence, in the ordinary way, of her death.

"These incidents, for a time, occupied all our thoughts. In me they produced a sentiment not unallied to pleasure, and more speedily than in the case of my friends were intermixed with other topics. My brother was particularly affected by them. It was easy to perceive that most of the meditations were tinctured from this source. To this was to be ascribed a design in which his pen was, at this period, engaged, of collecting and investigating the facts which relate to that mysterious personage, the Daemon of Socrates."

A personage is now introduced, who is the mysterious and secret mover of the scenes which follow. His first appearance and person are thus described:

[The rest of 2:29 through 2:33 prints extracts from *Wieland,* pp. 50–51, 53, and 84–86, describing Carwin and the incident in which Clara discovers Carwin in her closet.]

Invited to a midnight interview by the author of her perplexity and distress, urged by an irresistible desire to discover the source of the mysterious circumstances which surround and overwhelm her, she determines to meet *Carwin* at her own house, which she had recently left for the purpose of residing with her brother. After visiting the habitation of her brother, and finding it deserted, she repairs to her own dwelling, where, instead of *Carwin,* the first object which strikes her astonished sight is the lifeless corpse of the beloved wife of her brother extended on her own bed. While she is pouring forth her grief at this spectacle, Wieland enters the apartment, and by his looks discovers that some dreadful madness had seized his brain. Before he has time to add another victim to his frenzy, he is alarmed by the footsteps of friends and neighbours, and flies before his astonished sister could comprehend the meaning of the scene, or the purpose of his visit. After a most painful suspense, she learns that all the children of her brother had fallen by the same ha[n]d which had slain their mother. Her senses forsook her, and it was not until a long time, when her reason was restored, and her tranquillity in some degree regained, that she was informed of the real assassin of her brother's family. She had supposed Carwin to be the author of the ruin, until her uncle, one day, put into her hands a paper which contained a record of the speech delivered by Wieland at his trial, in which he avows the object of his infatuated zeal, and details, in terms the most affecting, the unnatural and inhuman acts he was prompted under the influence of a deluded imagination, to perpetrate.

The perusal of this paper gave such a shock to the feelings of Miss Wieland, that she was with difficulty rescued from the grave. Time, however, and the assiduous attentions of her uncle, got the better of her malady; and by his advice, she prepared to visit Europe for the recovery of her health. Previous to her departure she resolved to behold once more her long deserted mansion.

Here, to her utter astonishment, *Carwin* reappears. His presence deprives her, for some time, of sense and motion; on recovering her recollection, she, at length, yields to his intreaties to be heard in his defence, and listens to an explanation of [2:33] the mysterious sounds which had assailed her ears, and of the motives which impelled him to produce them.

This developement is not perfectly satisfactory. The motives assigned for the conduct of Carwin appear to us insufficient, nor are the effects described explained by adequate causes. This defect may be ascribed to an imperfect knowledge of the nature and operation of that power which the author has chosen for raising the wonder, and exciting the curiosity of his readers. We are inclined to believe that no possible exertion of the faculty given to Carwin, nor any application of the human organs, could ever produce the effects here supposed.

Many intelligent persons absolutely deny the existence of any peculiar or distinct faculty of this kind, but regard the instances of ventriloquism which have appeared, as nothing more than an improved power of imitation, or an artful suppression and modification of the common voice, aided by the ordinary laws of sound. The strong assertions on both sides leave the matter in doubt, though, relying on the authority of reputable witnesses, we have been disposed to admit its reality to a certain extent.

But the writers of novels and romances may be fairly indulged in the same liberty in use of the means of affecting the imagination of their readers, which poets have uniformly claimed and exercised. Fiction and fancy belong equally to both, and while the laws of nature are not violated, or the bounds of probability exceeded, both equally deserve to escape censure.

During the conversation with *Carwin, Wieland,* who had been confined as a *maniac,* having found means to elude the vigilance of his keepers, enters the apartment. His appearance is described; and the dialogue between him and Carwin, in which the latter declares himself to be the author of those mysterious sounds, those solemn warnings, which the gloomy imagination of Wieland had mistaken for supernatural agency, is interesting and impressive. His rage subsides into gentleness; his belief is for a moment shaken; and a faint glimmering light of truth seems breaking on his benighted intellect. At his command Carwin retires. Left with his sister, Wieland resumes the purpose of completing the work of death, by her destruction. A scene painfully affecting ensues. Carwin suddenly returns, and is called on by the sister to exert his fatal power to avert the impending blow.

[2:34 through 2:36 contain an extract of the scene in which Carwin stops Wieland from harming Clara and Wieland commits suicide, *Wieland,* pp. 229–232.]

Such are the leading incidents in the story of Wieland. The episode of Miss *Conway,* and the attachment between *Pleyel* and Miss *Weiland* [*sic*], which serve to diversify the scenes, and relieve the mind from the horror and distress of the general tale, are passed over in the rapid sketch we have given.

It will imply some commendation of the author's powers of narration, when we say, that having begun the perusal of this volume, we were irresistibly led on to the conclusion of the tale. The style is clear, forcible and correct. Passages of great elegance might be selected, and others which breathe a strain of lively and impassioned eloquence.

It is impossible not to sympathise in the terror and distress of the sister of Wieland. Persons of lively sensibility and active imaginations may, probably, think that some of the scenes are too shocking and painful to be endured even in fiction.

The soliloquies of some of the characters are unreasonably [2:36] long, and the attention is wearied in listening to the conjectures, the reasonings, the hopes and fears which are successively formed and rejected, at a moment when expectation is already strained to its highest pitch. These intellectual conflicts and processes of the imagination show fertility of conception, and the art of the narrator; but this act is too often exercised in suspending the course of action so as to render the reader restless and impatient. The generality of readers love rather to be borne along by a rapid narrative, and to be roused to attention by the quick succession of new and unexpected incidents.

The characters which are introduced are not numerous; nor are they such as may be easily found in the walks of common life. Carwin is an extraordinary being, and, in some degree, incomprehensible. If his prototype is not in nature, he must be acknowledged the creature of a vigorous fancy, fitted to excite curiosity and expectation. The author seems to have intended to exhibit him more fully to view; but not having finished the portrait, or doubtful of the effect of the exhibition, has reserved him for some future occasion, when he may be made the hero of his own story. The consequences produced by the exercise of the powers imputed to him were not foreseen, and were beyond the reach of his controul [*sic*]. Their exertion was from the impulse of caprice, or for a momentary self-gratification. He is the author of the most dreadful calamities, without any malicious or evil intention.—The reader sees the misery and ruin of an amiable family, by ignorant and deluded beings, undeserving the severity of punishment.—The endowments of such a being as Carwin, if they can possibly exist to the extent here imagined, are without advantage to the possessor, and can be of no benefit to mankind. This seems to be the principal lesson taught by the delineation of such a character.

Wieland and his family, in retirement, devoted to contemplation and study, and mixing little in the varied scenes of enlarged society, furnish few of those instructive facts and situations which may be supposed to occur in the usual progress of life. The even tenor of their existence is not broken by the stronger impulses of social feeling, or agitated by the conflict of violent passions. Their repose is disturbed, and their imaginations excited, by unknown and invisible agents. Comparisons, therefore, with the actual or probable situation of the reader, are not often suggested, nor are many precepts of instruction to be derived from examples too rare for general application. Against the [2:37] freaks of a *ventriloquist,* or the illusions of a madman, no rules can be prescribed for our protection. No prudence or foresight can guard us against evils which are to flow from such causes. The example of Wieland may teach us, indeed, the necessity of placing due restraints on the imagination; the folly of that presumptuous desire which seeks for gratifications inconsistent with the laws of existence and the ordinary course of nature; and to be content with the light which is set before us in the path of our moral and religious duties, without seeking for new illuminations. From the exhibition, however, of an infatuated being, deluded by the suggestions of a disturbed intellect, into the commission of acts the most unnatural and horrid, it is doubtful whether any real good is to be derived. But whether benefit or harm, or how much of either is to be received from tales of this kind, we are not prepared to decide, and they are questions not easily solved. The good or ill effect of a book, in most cases, depends on the previous disposition and character of the reader.

The author has certainly contrived a narration deeply interesting; and whatever may be its faults, and some we have ventured to remark, *Wieland*, as a work of imagination, may be ranked high among the productions of the age. [2:38]

NOTES

Preface

1. Quoted in René Wellek, "The Fall of Literary History," in Richard E. Amacher and Victor Lange, eds., *New Perspectives in German Literary Criticism: A Collection of Essays* (Princeton: Princeton University Press, 1979), p. 419.

2. For a convenient survey of reader-response criticism, see two collections, both of which contain extensive and excellent bibliographies: Susan R. Suleiman and Inge Crosman, eds., *The Reader in the Text: Essays on Audience and Interpretation* (Princeton: Princeton University Press, 1980), and Jane P. Tompkins, ed., *Reader-Response Criticism: From Formalism to Post-Structuralism* (Baltimore: Johns Hopkins University Press, 1980).

3. Jauss' literary history is expounded in a series of works; see his *Literaturgeschichte als Provokation* (Frankfurt am Main: Suhrkamp, 1970); "Literary History as a Challenge to Literary Theory," Elizabeth Benzinger, tr., in *New Literary History* (1970), 2:7–37; "Racines und Goethes Iphigenie. Mit einem Nachwort über die Partialität der rezeptionsästhetischen Methode," in Rüdiger Bubner et al., eds., *Theorie literarischer Texte* (Göttingen: Vandenhoeck & Ruprecht, 1973), pp. 1–46; *Ästhetische Erfahrung und literarische Hermeneutik I: Verusche im Feld der ästhetischen Erfahrung* (Munich: Fink, 1977).

4. René Wellek, for one, finds Jauss' literary history subject to the same objections as more traditional methods: "The new literary history promises only a return to the old one: the history of tradition, genres, reputations, etc., less atomistically conceived as [sic] in older times, with greater awareness of the difficulties of such concepts as influence and periods but still the same old one." "The Fall of Literary History," pp. 430–31.

5. Charvat's lecture, "Literary Economics and Literary History," was first delivered to the English Institute in 1949 and is reprinted in Matthew J. Bruccoli, ed., *The Profession of Authorship in America, 1800–1870: The Papers of William Charvat* (Columbus: Ohio State University Press, 1968).

6. For a more recent argument in favor of using the contractual conception of reader-text relations as a pragmatic solution to methodological problems, see Ross Chambers, *Story and Situation: Narrative Seduction and the Power of Fiction* (Minneapolis: University of Minnesota Press, 1984), pp. 1–49.

1. Toward a Democratic Fiction

1. Susan Fenimore Cooper, *Pages and Pictures from the Writings of James Fenimore Cooper* (New York: W. A. Townsend, 1861), p. 15.

2. *Pages and Pictures,* p. 17.

3. See James D. Hart, *The Popular Book: A History of America's Literary Taste* (Berkeley: University of California Press, 1950), pp. 73–78; Frank Luther Mott, *Golden Multitudes: The Story of Best Sellers in the United States* (New York: Macmillan, 1947), pp. 64–70. In 1826 Carey & Lea printed 9,000 copies of *Woodstock* and sold 8,000 on the day of publication; see David Kaser, *The Cost Book of Carey & Lea, 1825–1838* (Philadelphia: University of Pennsylvania Press, 1963), p. 30.

4. Margaret Fuller, "American Literature. Its Position in the Present Time, and Prospects for the Future," in Perry Miller, ed., *Margaret Fuller: American Romantic. A Selection from Her Writings and Correspondence* (Ithaca, N.Y.: Cornell University Press, 1963), pp. 231, 234.

5. Howard Mumford Jones, *The Theory of American Literature,* revised ed. (Ithaca, N.Y.: Cornell University Press, 1965), pp. 79–80.

6. Raymond Williams, *Culture and Society, 1780–1950* (1958; rpt. New York: Harper Torchbooks, 1966), p. 32.

7. Quoted in Williams, p. 34.

8. Thomas Carlyle, *Sartor Resartus: The Life and Opinions of Herr Teufelsdröckh* (Indianapolis: Odyssey Press, 1937), pp. 40–41.

9. *On Heroes, Hero-Worship, and the Heroic in History,* bound with Ralph Waldo Emerson, *Representative Men* (Garden City, N.Y.: Doubleday-Dolphin, n.d.), p. 151.

10. Jean-Jacques Rousseau, *Emile,* in *Œuvres complètes* (Paris: Gallimard-Pléiade, 1969), 4:454–55. For an interesting discussion of the doctrine of *Emile* see Allan Bloom, "The Education of Democratic Man: Emile," *Daedalus* (1978), 107:135–53. For the cultural significance of *Robinson Crusoe* see Ian Watt, *The Rise of the Novel: Studies in Defoe, Richardson and Fielding* (Berkeley: University of California Press, 1957), pp. 60–92.

11. Richard Slotkin, *Regeneration Through Violence: The Mythology of the American Frontier, 1600–1860* (Middletown, Conn.: Wesleyan University Press, 1973), pp. 316–19. See also Oliver F. Emerson, "Notes on Gilbert Imlay, Early American Writer," *PMLA* (1924), 39:406–39.

12. Quoted in Slotkin, p. 317.

13. *The Poetry and Prose of William Blake,* David V. Erdman, ed. (New York: Anchor-Doubleday, 1965), p. 52. On Blake's political allegory in *America* see Erdman, *Blake: Prophet Against Empire* (Princeton: Princeton University Press, 1954), pp. 53–60 and 234–41.

14. Karlheinz Rossbacher, *Lederstrumpf in Deutschland: Zur Rezeption James Fenimore Coopers beim Leser der Restaurationzeit* (Munich: Wilhelm Fink, 1972), pp. 13–18.

15. Rossbacher, p. 14; translation is mine.

16. Antoine-Nicolas de Condorcet, *Sketch for a Historical Picture of the Progress of the Human Mind,* June Barraclough, tr. (London: Weidenfeld and Nicolson, 1955), pp. 197–98.

17. *The Influence of Literature upon Society Translated from the French of Madame de Staël-Holstein to which is Prefixed a Memoir of the Life and Writings of the Author* (New York: William Pearson, 1835), p. 12. The translator's introduction is signed,

"D. Boileau, Brompton Road, Nov. 1st, 1811." The text is a translation of *De la littérature considérée dans ses rapports avec les institutions sociales* (Paris: Crapelet, 1800).

18. *The Influence of Literature upon Society,* pp. 80–85.

19. *The Influence of Literature upon Society,* p. 68. For a review of Staël's influence in American, see Jones, *Theory of American Literature,* pp. 64–68.

20. For an analysis of the anxieties of this period, the "Didactic Enlightenment," see Daniel F. May, *The Enlightenment in America* (New York: Oxford University Press, 1976), pp. 307–62.

21. Robert E. Spiller, "The Verdict of Sydney Smith," *American Literature* (1929), 1:3.

22. *The Edinburgh Review* (1820), 33: 79–80.

23. *The Edinburgh Review,* p. 80.

24. Quoted in Marius Bewley, *The Eccentric Design: Form in the Classic American Novel* (New York: Columbia University Press, 1963), p. 32.

25. *Letters of Shahcoolen* (1802; rpt. Gainesville, Fla.: Scholar's Facsimiles & Reprints, 1962), pp. 81–83.

26. Reprinted in *The American Literary Revolution 1783–1837,* Robert E. Spiller, ed. (New York: New York University Press, 1967), p. 87.

27. Alexis de Tocqueville, *Democracy in America,* Henry Reeve, tr., revised by Frances Bowen and Phillip Bradley, 2 vols. (New York: Knopf, 1963), 2:52.

28. Merrill D. Peterson, *The Jefferson Image in the American Mind* (New York: Oxford University Press, 1960), p. 394.

29. Peterson, p. 394.

30. Peterson, pp. 415 and 416.

31. See Benjamin T. Spencer, *The Quest for Nationality: An American Literary Campaign* (Syracuse, N.Y.: Syracuse University Press, 1957), pp. 39–72.

32. "Doctrine for Fiction in the *North American Review:* 1815–1826," in Robert Falk, ed., *Literature and Ideas in America: Essays in Memory of Harry Hayden Clark* (Columbus: Ohio State University Press, 1975), pp. 20–39.

33. Samuel Gilman Brown, *The Works of Rufus Choate with a Memoir of his Life,* 2 vols. (Boston: Little, Brown, 1862), 1:320–21, 326.

34. May, p. 62.

35. They were eventually published as *Lectures on Moral Philosophy and Eloquence* (1800). May, who read notes taken by students in 1772, 1774, 1782 and 1795, found that variations in the lectures were minor: p. 367n25.

36. William Charvat, *The Origins of American Critical Thought 1810–1835* (1936; rpt. New York: Russell & Russell, 1968), p. 5.

37. May, pp. 348–49.

38. Charvat, *Origins,* p. 58.

39. Charvat, *Origins,* pp. 7–26.

40. Tocqueville, 2: 55–64.

41. Spencer, p. 33.

42. James Fenimore Cooper, *The Pioneers, or the Sources of the Susquehanna; A Descriptive Tale* (Albany: State University Press of New York, 1980), p. 6. See my discussion of Cooper's characterization in chapter 3.

43. "Foreword," in Matthew J. Bruccoli, ed., *The Profession of Authorship in America, 1800–1870: The Papers of William Charvat* (Columbus: Ohio State University Press, 1968), p. vi.

44. On Franklin as a cultural figure see Lewis P. Simpson, "The Printer as American Man of Letters," in his *The Brazen Face of History: Studies in the Literary Consciousness in America* (Baton Rouge: Louisiana State University Press, 1959), p. 34.

45. William Charvat, *Literary Publishing in America 1790–1850* (Philadelphia: University of Pennsylvania Press, 1959), p. 34.

46. Charvat, *Literary Publishing*, pp. 31–32.

47. Letter to John Neal, January 10, 1838, quoted in Benjamin Lease, *That Wild Fellow John Neal and the American Literary Revolution* (Chicago: University of Chicago Press, 1972), p. 195.

48. Earl L. Bradsher, *Mathew Carey, Editor, Author and Publisher: A Study in American Literary Development* (New York: Columbia University Press, 1912), p. 20.

49. Bradsher, p. 22.

50. Charvat, *Literary Publishing*, pp. 26 and 27.

51. Charvat, *Profession of Authorship*, p. 36.

52. Quoted in Charvat, *Literary Publishing*, p. 25.

53. *Cost Book of Carey & Lea*, pp. 30 and 52.

54. Quoted in Lease, p. 134. Longfellow's project was eventually realized in *Outre-Mer* (1834–35).

55. Charvat, *Profession of Authorship*, p. 45.

56. Bradsher, p. 25.

2. The Failure of Charles Brockden Brown

1. Charles Brockden Brown, "Advertisement for 'Sky Walk,'" in Harry R. Warfel, ed., *The Rhapsodist and Other Uncollected Writings* (New York: Scholars' Facsimiles & Reprints, 1943), pp. 135–36.

2. Max F. Schultz, "Brockden Brown: An Early Casualty of the American Experience," in Klaus Lanzinger, ed., *Americana-Austriaca: Beiträge zur Amerikakunde*, 2 vols. (Vienna: Wilhelm Braumuller, 1970), 2:81–90; Paul Witherington, "Benevolence and the 'Utmost Stretch': Charles Brockden Brown's Narrative Dilemma," *Criticism* (1972), 14:175–91; William Hedges, "Charles Brockden Brown and the Culture of Contradictions," *Early American Literature* (1974), 9:107–42; and Michael Davitt Bell, *The Development of American Romance: The Sacrifice of Relation* (Chicago: University of Chicago Press, 1980), pp. 40–61—a revised version of Bell's "The Double-Tongued Deceiver: Sincerity and Duplicity in the Novels of Charles Brockden Brown," *Early American Literature* (1974), 9:143–60.

3. William H. Prescott, "Charles Brockden Brown," in Jared Sparks, ed., *American Biography* (1839; rpt. New York: Harper, 1902), 7:9.

4. "The Rhapsodist, No. 1," from *The Universal Asylum and Columbian Magazine*, Philadelphia, August 1789; reprinted in *The Rhapsodist*, Warfel, ed., p. 2.

5. "The Rhapsodist, No. 1," pp. 1–2.

6. Prescott, p. 7.

7. Harry R. Warfel, "Charles Brockden Brown's First Published Poem," *American Notes and Queries* (1941), 1:19–20.

8. William Dunlap, *The Life of Charles Brockden Brown: Together With Selections from the Rarest of his Printed Works, from his Original Letters, and from his Manuscripts Before Unpublished*, 2 vols. (Philadelphia: James P. Parke, 1815), 1:17–18.

9. "A Series of Original Letters," in *The Rhapsodist,* p. 107. Further references to this work will be cited parenthetically.

10. Prescott, pp. 11–12. Dunlap made essentially the same point in his memoir; see 1:41–46. Cf. F. O. Matthiessen's brief comment: "Prescott's tribute to Brown . . . stressed the symbolic importance of this Philadelphian's repudiation of the study of law to become our first professional author." *American Renaissance: Art and Expression in the Age of Emerson and Whitman* (1941; rpt. Oxford: Oxford University Press, 1968), p. 202.

11. Harry R. Warfel, "Introduction," in *The Rhapsodist,* p. viii.

12. These fragments are printed in Dunlap, 1:170–396.

13. Warfel, "Introduction," p. viii.

14. Henry F. May, *The Enlightenment in America* (1976; rpt. New York: Oxford University Press, 1978), p. 234. May uses the Friendly Society as an example of the "paradoxes and complexities that hindered the development of the Revolutionary Enlightenment in America"; see pp. 233–36.

15. Alexander Cowie, "Historical Essay," in the Bicentennial Edition of *Wieland, or The Transformation, An American Tale* and *"Memoirs of Carwin the Biloquist"* (Kent, Ohio: Kent State University Press, 1980), p. 452.

16. George Gates Raddin, Jr., *Hocquet Caritat and the Early New York Literary Scene* (Dover, N.J.: Dover Advance Press, 1953), pp. 14–15; Allan Nevins and Henry Steele Commager, *A Short History of the United States,* 5th ed. (New York: Modern Library, 1969), p. 148.

17. Raddin, pp. 16 and 25.

18. The quotation is from the cover of Caritat's September 1800 catalogue, cited in Raddin, p. 28.

19. Raddin, pp. 26–27, 30.

20. Charvat, *Profession of Authorship,* p. 27.

21. Cowie, "Historical Essay," p. 321.

22. Joseph Katz, "Analytical Bibliography and Literary History: The Writing and Printing of *Wieland,*" *Proof* (1971), 1:11–12.

23. *The Diary of Elihu Hubbard Smith,* James E. Cronin, ed. (Philadelphia: America Philosophical Society, 1973), p. 457.

24. Katz, pp. 11 and 15.

25. Katz, p. 18.

26. Cowie, "Historical Essay," p. 323.

27. Katz, p. 23.

28. *Wieland,* p. 3. Further references to *Wieland* will be cited parenthetically.

29. Witherington, "Benevolence and the 'Utmost Stretch,'" p. 175.

30. Witherington, pp. 179, 181. For similar readings of Brown's career see Bell, *The Development of American Romance,* pp. 45–52, and Leslie A. Fiedler, *Love and Death in the American Novel,* revised ed. (1966; rpt. New York: Stein and Day, 1975), pp. 148–53.

31. Michael D. Butler, "Charles Brockden Brown's *Wieland:* Method and Meaning," *Studies in American Fiction* (1976), 4:131.

32. Quoted in *The American Review, and Literary Journal* (1801), 1:339.

33. Butler, p. 132.

34. Butler, p. 133. Butler does not connect this pattern of fire imagery with Clara's dream of the burning house.

35. Raddin, p. 52.

36. Cowie, "Historical Essay," pp. 454–55.

37. Quoted in Raddin, p. 53.

38. Quoted in Raddin, pp. 53–54.

39. Hans Borchers, "Introduction," in Charles Brockden Brown, *Memoirs of Stephen Calvert* (Frankfurt am Main: Peter Lang, 1978), p. xi.

40. Quoted in Raddin, p. 54.

41. Brown's letter is reprinted in George Perkins, ed., *The Theory of the American Novel* (New York: Holt, Rinehart and Winston, 1970), pp. 12–13.

42. *Jefferson Papers*, series 1, vol. 7, no. 305 (Library of Congress); quoted in David L. Butler, *Dissecting a Human Heart: A Study of Style in the Novels of Charles Brockden Brown* (Washington, D.C.: University Press of America, 1978), pp. 29–30.

43. Jefferson to Burwell, *The Works of Thomas Jefferson,* Paul Leicester Ford, ed. (New York: Putnam, 1899), 10:104–05. Bell quotes this letter on p. 17.

44. Quoted in Cowie, "Historical Essay," p. 459.

45. Charvat, *Profession of Authorship,* p. 19.

46. Quoted in Raddin, p. 59.

47. "On the Writings of Charles Brockden Brown, the American Novelist," *New Monthly Magazine and Universal Register* (December 1820), 14:609.

48. There is a minor controversy over whether Brown was the editor of the *American Review.* David Lee Clark claims that he was not: see his "Brockden Brown's First Attempt at Journalism," *University of Texas Bulletin,* No. 2743 (November 15, 1927), p. 174. It is certain, however, that he wrote for the *Review:* see his letter to John Blair Linn, July 8, 1802, in Ernest Marchand, "Introduction," to Brown's *Ormond* (1937; rpt. New York: Hafner, 1962), p. xii.

49. See Carl Van Doren, "Early American Realism," *Nation* (1941), 99:577–78. For a complete discussion of my reasons for regarding the review as Brown's work, see the appendix to this study.

50. "Article X. Wieland," *The American Review, and Literary Journal* (1801), 1:333. The review is on pages 333 to 339 of volume 1 and pages 28 to 39 of volume 2. Further references to the review will be cited parenthetically by volume and page.

51. Charvat, *Profession of Authorship,* p. 27.

52. "A Sketch of American Literature for 1806–7," *The American Register, or, General Repository of History, Politics and Science* (1806), 1:184.

53. "Sketch of American Literature," p. 185.

54. Charvat, *Profession of Authorship,* p. 28.

3. "An American Novel Professedly"

1. James Fenimore Cooper, *Notions of the Americans Picked Up by a Travelling Bachelor,* 2 vols. (1828; rpt. New York: Frederick Ungar, 1963), 2:111.

2. Susan Fenimore Cooper, *Pages and Pictures from the Writings of James Fenimore Cooper* (New York: W. A. Townsend, 1861), pp. 15–17; "Small Family Memories" (dated January 25, 1883), published as an introduction to *Correspondence of James Fenimore-Cooper,* edited by his grandson, James Fenimore Cooper, 2 vols. (New Haven: Yale University Press, 1922), 1:38–41; "A Glance Backward," *Atlantic Monthly* (February 1887), 59:199–206.

3. "Small Family Memories," p. 38.

4. Maurice Clavel, *Fenimore Cooper: Sa Vie et son œuvre: La Jeunesse* (Aix-en-Provence: Universitaire de Provence, 1938), pp. 251–56.

5. *The Letters and Journals of James Fenimore Cooper*, 6 vols., James Franklin Beard, ed. (Cambridge, Mass.: Harvard University Press, 1960–68), 1:4–5. Further references to these volumes will be cited parenthetically as *L/J* followed by volume and page numbers.

6. William Neill quoted by Beard in *L/J*, 1:5.

7. "Small Family Memories," p. 40.

8. "Small Family Memories," p. 38.

9. Wolfgang Iser, *The Act of Reading: A Theory of Aesthetic Response* (Baltimore: Johns Hopkins University Press, 1978), pp. 34 and 38.

10. Walter J. Ong, S.J., "The Writer's Audience Is Always a Fiction," *PMLA* (1975), 90:10.

11. Ong, p. 11.

12. Ong, pp. 12–14.

13. "Small Family Memories," pp. 39–40.

14. The case was made in George E. Hastings' meticulous study, "How Cooper Became a Novelist," *American Literature* (1940), 12:20–51.

15. James Fenimore Cooper, *Precaution: A Novel* (New York: W. A. Townsend, 1861), p. 52. All further references will be cited parenthetically.

16. Jane Austen, *Persuasion* (London: Oxford University Press, n.d.), p. 1.

17. Hastings, p. 45.

18. For example, the "Advertisement" to an American edition of *The Works of Mrs. Amelia Opie*, 3 vols. (Philadelphia: James Crissy, 1843), begins, "It is well known that the works of Mrs. Opie have always enjoyed a high degree of popularity, both in Europe and in this country" (1:3).

19. Margaret Eliot Macgregor, *Amelia Alderson Opie: Worldling and Friend* (Menasha, Wis.: Collegiate Press, n.d.), p. xi.

20. Austen, *Persuasion*, pp. 113–15.

21. *The Works of Mrs. Amelia Opie*, 3:139–40, *Temper* seems to have been Cooper's favorite among Opie's works. He met Opie in 1830 through Pierre Jeanne David, who wrote to her that Cooper had said, "Let us go see the author of *Temper*, I have a profound admiration for her works" (Macgregor, p. 110).

22. On changes in English society, see Harold Perkin, *The Origins of Modern English Society 1780–1880* (London: Routledge & Kegan Paul, 1969), and E. P. Thompson, *The Making of the English Working Class* (1963; rpt. New York: Random House, 1966). For a survey of the changes in ideal family structure and the use of the nuclear family as synechdoche for British and American culture, see Edwin G. Burrows and Michael Wallace, "The American Revolution: The Ideology and Psychology of National Liberation," *Perspectives in American History* (1972), 6:165–306.

23. William Cullen Bryant, "Discourse on the Life, Genius, and Writings of J. Fenimore Cooper," delivered at Metropolitan Hall, New York, February 25, 1852, and reprinted as a preface in *Precaution*, pp. v–xli; Hastings, p. 26. It is significant that Hastings developed his hypothesis about the connection between *Persuasion* and *Precaution* on the basis of the titles alone and before having read the latter.

24. The phrase is from the subtitle of *Home As Found: Authority and Genealogy in the American Imagination*, by Eric J. Sundquist (Baltimore: Johns Hopkins University Press, 1979). Sundquist is interested in the way that the conflict between the need for originality and the need for authority affects the presentation of incest, repetition, and parricide in the American imagination. A more nearly orthodox Freudian reading of Cooper's fatherless sons (and of Cooper) is found in Stephen Railton, *Fenimore Cooper: A Study of His Life and Imagination* (Princeton: Princeton University Press, 1978).

25. See Railton, pp. 82–89, for a perceptive discussion of Judge Temple's stray shot and its consequences.

26. Richard Slotkin, *Regeneration Through Violence: The Mythology of the American Frontier, 1600–1860* (Middletown, Conn.: Wesleyan University Press, 1973), p. 557. A similar argument is that of Sacvan Bercovitch, who locates an essential trait of the American character in the Puritan practice of turning "liminality" (a cultural no-man's-land where all social norms may be challenged) into a mode of socialization: see his *The American Jeremiad* (Madison: University of Wisconsin Press, 1978), pp. 25–26.

27. D. H. Lawrence, *Studies in Classic American Literature* (1924; rpt. New York: Viking Press, 1961), pp. 53 and 62.

28. "Small Family Memories," pp. 38–39.

29. William Charvat, *Literary Publishing in America 1790–1850* (Philadelphia: University of Pennsylvania Press, 1959), pp. 81 and 92.

30. *The Literary and Scientific Repository and Critical Review* (1821), 2:364, 371, 372.

31. *Literary and Scientific Repository*, pp. 374–75.

32. *The New Monthly Magazine and Literary Journal* (1821), 3:132.

33. *The Gentleman's Magazine: and Historical Chronicle* (1821), 91:345.

34. Charvat, *Profession of Authorship*, p. 73.

35. Robert E. Spiller, *Fenimore Cooper: Critic of His Time* (New York: Minton, Balch, 1931), p. 74.

36. James Fenimore Cooper, "Introduction," in *The Spy: A Tale of the Neutral Ground* (New York: W. A. Townsend, 1859), pp. ix–x. All further references to this edition of *The Spy* will be cited parenthetically.

37. James Franklin Beard, "Introduction," in *Tales for Fifteen*, by James Fenimore Cooper (Gainesville, Fla.: Scholars' Facsimiles & Reprints, 1959), pp. viii–ix.

38. Cooper's known reviews are reprinted in James Franklin Beard, ed., *Early Critical Essays (1820–1822)* (Gainesville, Fla.: Scholars' Facsimiles & Reprints, 1955).

39. Arvid Shulenberger, in *Cooper's Theory of Fiction: His Prefaces and Their Relation to His Novels* (Lawrence: University of Kansas Press, 1955), p. 14, charges that the 1921 preface is "written in a careless, helter-skelter style, with an air o[f] truculent good humor that is characteristic of his early critical remarks." Shulenberger misses entirely the anxiety that Cooper's air was designed to conceal. The style of the early prefaces (though not of the critical writings) is utterly unlike anything else that Cooper ever wrote—a fact that in itself is sufficient to indicate the extraordinary pressure Cooper felt.

40. The 1821 preface is in the first edition of *The Spy* (New York: Wiley and Halstead, 1821), pp. v–xii. It was reprinted in the second edition (1822) and then dropped from the third (also 1822).

41. George Dekker, *James Fenimore Cooper the Novelist* (London: Routledge & Kegan Paul, 1967), p. 33.

42. Sir Walter Scott, *Ivanhoe: A Romance* (New York: Mershon, n.d.), p. xix.

43. I am following Wolfgang Iser's analysis of Scott's technique in his "Fiction— The Filter of History: A Study of Sir Walter Scott's *Waverley*," in his *The Implied Reader: Patterns of Communication in Prose Fiction from Bunyan to Beckett* (Baltimore: Johns Hopkins University Press, 1974), pp. 81–100.

44. Iser, "Fiction—The Filter of History," p. 94. Georg Lukács treats Scott's "mediocre" heroes sympathetically as "unsurpassed in their portrayal of the decent and attractive as well as narrow-minded features of the English 'middle-class.'" *The Historical Novel*, Hannah and Stanley Mitchell, trs. (London: Merlin Press, 1962), p. 35.

45. Iser, "Fiction—The Filter of History," p. 99.

46. *Notions of the Americans,* 2:108. Here Cooper anticipates similar complaints by Hawthorne and James, but the idea was already in circulation in 1821; see my discussion of W. H. Gardiner's review of *The Spy* below.

47. James Franklin Beard, "Cooper and the Revolutionary Mythos," *Early American Literature* (1976), 11:85. See also John P. McWilliams, Jr., *Political Justice in a Republic: James Fenimore Cooper's America* (Berkeley: University of California Press, 1972), pp. 32–99.

48. *Notions of the Americans,* 2:188.

49. As Dekker notes (p. 33), the only wavering figure in *The Spy* is Mr. Wharton, and he is merely concealing his Tory sympathies to avoid the confiscation of his property.

50. Beard connects Harper/Washington with the *deus ex machina* of Euripidean tragedy—a figure who participates in the action "from an untouchable moral and physical height" ("The Revolutionary Mythos," pp. 88–89).

51. Cooper took ironic note of these complaints in his preface to the second edition of *The Spy,* quoted in Shulenberger, p. 15. See my discussion of the *Port Folio* review of *The Spy* below.

52. The most notable comments are James Franklin Beard, "Cooper and His Artistic Contemporaries," *New York History* (1954), 35:480–95; Donald A. Ringe, *The Pictorial Mode: Space and Time in the Art of Bryant, Irving, and Cooper* (Lexington: University of Kentucky Press, 1971); James T. Callow, *Kindred Spirits: Knickerbocker Writers and American Artists, 1807–1855* (Chapel Hill: University of North Carolina Press, 1967); Blake Nevius, *Cooper's Landscapes: An Essay on the Picturesque Vision* (Berkeley: University of California Press, 1976); Annette Kolodny, *The Lay of the Land: Metaphor as Experience and History in American Life and Letters* (Chapel Hill: University of North Carolina Press, 1975). In his *A World by Itself: The Pastoral Moment in Cooper's Fiction* (New Haven: Yale University Press, 1977), H. Daniel Peck discusses the "landscape of difficulty" in Cooper's early fiction, but Peck's commitment to subjecting Cooper's fiction to a mythopoeic "poetics of space" leads him to a very different reading than mine.

53. In his review of Catherine Sedgwick's *A New-England Tale* (1822), Cooper would argue that the "true historians" of the society are not the recorders of statutes, battles, and party politics, but Henry Fielding's describers of "society as it exists and men as they are" (*Early Critical Essays,* pp. 97–98). I discuss this review in chapter 4.

54. In *Lionel Lincoln* Cooper is particularly careful to present the indolence of the British generals who occupy Boston. In this respect, Howe, Gage, and Clinton are refinements of the portrayal of Mr. Wharton.

55. See Donald A. Ringe, "The American Revolution in American Romance," *American Literature* (1977), 49:352–65.

56. Observing the care Dunwoodie bestows on the wounded Singleton, one character remarks, "You speak of him as if he were your mistress." Dunwoodie replies, "I love him as one" (*Spy,* p. 118). Though the Dunwoodie-Singleton relationship is underdeveloped, it forecasts those later male bondings that earn Cooper's novels their place in critical controversies over anti-feminism in American culture.

57. Dekker, p. 35. Virtually every critic who has written on Cooper agrees that the genteel characters are boring.

58. Burrows and Wallace, "The American Revolution," *passim.*

59. Jay Fliegelman, *Prodigals and Pilgrims: The American Revolution against Patriarchal Authority, 1750–1800* (New York: Cambridge University Press, 1982), pp. 210–11.

60. It is also noteworthy that the only character from *The Spy* whom Cooper

mentions in his 1821 preface is Caesar, with whom Cooper affects to have spoken since finishing the book.

61. Harry B. Henderson, III, *Versions of the Past: The Historical Imagination in American Fiction* (New York: Oxford University Press, 1974), pp. 51–52.

62. Barton Levi St. Armand, "Harvey Birch as the Wandering Jew: Literary Calvinism in James Fenimore Cooper's *The Spy*," *American Literature* (1978), 50:348–68.

63. St. Armand, p. 349.

64. Kay Seymour House begins her *Cooper's Americans* (Columbus: Ohio State University Press, 1965) with this sentence: "Miles and years from Yoknapatawpha, James Fenimore Cooper created a coherent fictional world containing hundreds of characters that represented the possibilities of American life." Regional types were an important part of those possibilities.

65. See, for example, Cooper's discussion of "Crazy Bet" in his review of Sedgwick's *A New-England Tale*, in *Early Critical Essays*, pp. 107–8.

66. David Levin, *History as Romantic Art: Bancroft, Prescott, Motley, and Parkman* (1959; rpt. New York: Harcourt, Brace & World, 1963), p. 73.

67. The allegorical tradition also embraces the typological biographies of Cotton Mather's *Magnalia Christi Americana;* see Sacvan Bercovitch, *The Puritan Origins of the American Self* (New Haven: Yale University Press, 1976). For a discussion of the contributions of both Mather and Franklin to the biographical practice of depending on conceptions of personality and typical character, see David Levin, *In Defense of Historical Literature: Essays on American History, Autobiography, Drama, and Fiction* (New York: Hill and Wang, 1967), pp. 34–76.

68. The third (1832) preface to *The Pioneers, or the Sources of the Susquehanna; A Descriptive Tale* (Albany: State University of New York Press, 1980), p. 6.

69. James Fenimore Cooper, *A Letter to His Countrymen* (New York: John Wiley, 1834), pp. 13–14.

70. Slotkin, *Regeneration Through Violence*, pp. 485–86.

71. The text cited is a draft of a letter Cooper wrote for Griswold's use in preparing a biographical sketch which appeared in *Graham's Magazine* (August 1844), 26:90–93, with an engraved portrait of Cooper.

72. David Kaser, *The Cost Book of Carey & Lea, 1825–1838* (Philadelphia: University of Pennsylvania Press, 1963), p. 30. In 1828 the Arcade Book Store in Philadelphia printed an advertisement attempting to explain the situation to its customers:

> The new novel—The Red Rover, By Cooper. What's the price says one calling at the Arcade Book Store—Answer $1.50. Is not that very high—Answer we cannot help it. "You sell Canongate for 50 cents, which is quite as large a book and by a much greater author."—Answer, Canongate is not a *copyright book*—Mr. Cooper is a native American, and the most successful imitator of (till lately) "the great unknown of the North."

Quoted in David Kaser, *Messrs. Carey & Lea of Philadelphia: A Study in the History of the Booktrade* (Philadelphia: University of Pennsylvania Press, 1957), p. 69.

73. *The Cost Book of Carey & Lea*, pp. 249–70.

74. Kaser, *Messrs. Carey & Lea*, p. 78.

75. By comparison, Cooper's share of the profits from his whaling ship, the *Union*, was between $7,000 and $8,000 in 1820, but much of that profit had to be reinvested in fitting out for the next voyage (*L/J*, 1:59).

76. Charvat, *Profession of Authorship*, p. 74.

77. Charvat, *Profession of Authorship*, p. 77.

78. W. H. Gardiner, *"The Spy,"* from *The North American Review* (July 1822), 25:250–82; rpt. in George Dekker and John P. McWilliams, Jr., eds., *Fenimore Cooper: The Critical Heritage* (Boston: Routledge & Kegan Paul, 1967), p. 55.

79. Gardiner, pp. 56–57.

80. Gardiner, pp. 57–59.

81. Gardiner, pp. 63–65.

82. Gardiner, pp. 65–66.

83. *"The Spy," The Port Folio* (1822), 13:90, 95–96.

84. *"The Spy,"* p. 100.

85. *The Pioneers*, p. 3.

86. The extent of Cooper's revisions is obvious to anyone who has looked at both the first and the collected editions of his works. While Cooper never successfully overcame the fallibility of his printers, the publication of the State University of New York's *The Writings of James Fenimore Cooper*, of which eight volumes have thus far appeared, should lay to rest forever the myth of Cooper's careless, hasty composition.

87. *Correspondence of James Fenimore-Cooper*, 1:89.

88. *The Monthly Magazine; or, British Register* (1822), 53:549.

4. Educating the Imagination

(Page references for *The Pioneers* in text are to the State University Press of New York, 1980, edition.)

1. James Franklin Beard, ed., *Early Critical Essays* (Gainesville, Fla.: Scholars' Facsimiles & Reprints, 1955), p. 97. Further references will be cited parenthetically by page number.

2. John Murray, Irving's publisher in London, had paid him 1,000 guineas, a staggering sum, for *Bracebridge Hall;* see Ben Harris McClary, *Washington Irving and the House of Murray: Geoffrey Crayon Charms the British, 1817–1856* (Knoxville: University of Tennessee Press, 1969), pp. 41–42.

3. Robert Walsh, Jr., wrote an anti-Napoleonic tract, *A Letter on the Genius and Dispositions of the French Government, Including a View of the Taxation of the French Empire* (1809), that was praised in the *Edinburgh Review.* Subsequently he edited the *American Register* and the *National Gazette* of Philadelphia and became "a leader of the American magazinists in the battle with the English quarterlies." See John Neal, *American Writers: A Series of Papers Contributed to Blackwood's Magazine (1824–1825)*, Fred Lewis Pattee, ed. (Durham, N.C.: Duke University Press, 1937), p. 59n7 and p. 181n40.

4. For example, the first issue of *The New-York Mirror, and Ladies' Gazette* (August 2, 1823) carried the first chapter of a "Moral Novel" entitled *Whigs and Tories*, a Revolutionary War novel of love and adventure.

5. James Franklin Beard, ed., *The Letters and Journals of James Fenimore Cooper*, 6 vols. (Cambridge, Mass.: Harvard University Press, 1960–68), 1:86. Further references will be cited parenthetically as *L/J* followed by volume and page numbers.

6. Cooper, *Notions of the Americans*, 2 vols. (1828; rpt. New York: Frederick Ungar, 1963), 2:102.

7. See especially the chapters "On Demagogues," pp. 96–101, and "'They Say,'" p. 182, in Cooper, *The American Democrat; or, Hints on the Social and Civic Relations of the United States of America* (1838; rpt. New York: Vintage Books, 1956).

8. Note the use of the term "keeping" in the *Port Folio* reviews of *The Spy*, quoted in chapter 3 above, and of *The Pioneers*, quoted at the end of this chapter.

9. Cooper, *A Letter to His Countrymen*, (New York: Wiley, 1834), p. 100.

10. In England, of course, a novel was published in three volumes; in Cooper's calculation the third volume would begin with chapter 28 (the panther's attack) and would include Natty's arrest, trial, and escape, the fire on Mount Vision, and the skirmish at the cave.

11. D. H. Lawrence, *Studies in Classic American Literature* (1924; rpt. New York: Viking Press, 1961), p. 55.

12. Thomas Philbrick, "Cooper's *The Pioneers:* Origins and Structure," *PMLA* (1964), 79:581, 583.

13. Philbrick, p. 584.

14. Philbrick, p. 585.

15. Beard, "Historical Introduction," in *The Pioneers*, p. xxxiv.

16. "Historical Introduction," p. 1.

17. All Phillips' travel accounts are collected in one encyclopedic edition, *A Collection of Modern and Contemporary Voyages & Travels*, 11 vols. (London: Richard Phillips, 1805–1810).

18. Dorothy Dondore, "The Debt of Two Dyed-in-the-Wool Americans to Mrs. Grant's Memoirs: Cooper's *Satanstoe* and Paulding's *The Dutchman's Fireside*," *American Literature* (1940), 12:52–58.

19. Mrs. Grant, *Memoirs of an American Lady: With Sketches of Manners and Scenery in America, as They Existed Previous to the Revolution*, 2 vols. (1808; rpt. New York: Research Reprints, 1970), 1:16–23, 51–60, 126–40, 242–51.

20. "He was possessed of a very sound intellect, and used to declaim with the most vehement eloquence against our crafty and insidious encroachments on our old friends. His abhorrence of the petty falsehoods to which custom has too well reconciled us, and those little artifices which we all occasionally practice, rose to a height fully equal to that felt by Gulliver." Mrs. Grant, 1:244.

21. Quoted in Allan Nevins and Henry Steele Commager, *A Short History of the United States*, 5th ed. (New York: Modern Library, 1969), p. 209.

22. The text of this poem and its attribution to Adams are from Mark Anthony De Wolfe Howe, "The Capture of some Fugitive Verses," *Proceedings of the Massachusetts Historical Society* (1910), 43:237–41.

23. John P. McWilliams, Jr., *Political Justice in a Republic: James Fenimore Cooper's America* (Berkeley: University of California Press, 1972), p. 101. McWilliams' discussion (pp. 101–29) of *The Pioneers* is the most comprehensive treatment of this theme, but cf. James Grossman, *James Fenimore Cooper* (1949; rpt. Stanford: Stanford University Press, 1967), pp. 31–32; George Dekker, *James Fenimore Cooper the Novelist* (London: Routledge & Kegan Paul, 1967), p. 44; Henry Nash Smith, *Virgin Land: The American West as Symbol and Myth* (1950; rpt. New York, Vintage Books, n.d.), pp. 66–70; Donald A. Ringe, *James Fenimore Cooper* (New York: Twayne Publishers, 1962), pp. 32–37; Peter Valenti, "'The Ordering of God's Providence': Law and Landscape in *The Pioneers*," *Studies in American Fiction* (1979), 7:191–207.

24. This sense is reinforced by Cooper's additions of footnotes for Henry Colburn's Standard Novels edition of *The Pioneers* (1832). The effect of these notes is to update the reader's historical perspective and to identify (especially for the British reader) local customs, figures, and dialect.

25. Henry Fielding, *The History of Tom Jones: A Foundling* (New York: Modern

Library, 1950), p. 10. Note that Fielding's chapter is entitled, "The Reader's Neck Brought into Danger by a Description." Cooper literalizes Fielding's humor by staging the episode of the sleigh's narrow escape from plunging over a cliff in its descent into Templeton.

26. In *A World by Itself* (New Haven: Yale University Press, 1977), H. Daniel Peck notes Cooper's love of the "distant view": "from the perspective of literal and moral elevation, he can ignore the 'disgusting details.' (For Cooper, the disgusting details were part of objective reality, but the second impression [of a landscape] may have been spoiled for him by the surfacing of images of 'difficulty' from his interior landscape)" (p. 183). It seems to me that this argument graphically illustrates the limits of Peck's "pictorialist" approach to Cooper's fiction, which exploits the dynamics of the contrast between distant and near views.

27. The epigraph is attributed to "Duo." In an explanatory note Beard writes, "Diligent and repeated searching has failed to disclose the source of this epigraph." It is possible that Cooper wrote this epigraph (and those to chapters 12 and 25) himself, though that would be contrary to his usual practice.

28. William Cooper, *A Guide in the Wilderness; or, the History of the First Settlements in the Western Countries of New York, with Useful Instructions to Future Settlers* (1810), rpt. in *Jahrbuch für Amerikastudien* (1960), 5:308–39.

29. Beard, "Historical Introduction," in *The Pioneers,* pp. xxx–xxxi.

30. The name of Mount Vision may come from the "Mount of Vision" where Columbus receives his vision of the "Future Progress of society with respect to commerce, discoveries, the opening of canals," etc., in Joel Barlow's *The Vision of Columbus* (1787), though I know of no evidence that Cooper ever read Barlow.

31. See Richard Slotkin, *Regeneration Through Violence* (Middletown, Conn.: Wesleyan University Press, 1973), pp. 360–62.

32. Smith, *Virgin Land,* p. 67.

33. *L/J,* 1:39–41. Cf. Cooper's account of the gubernatorial election of 1824 in *Notions of Americans,* 1:262–63.

34. William W. Campbell, *The Life and Writings of De Witt Clinton* (New York: Baker and Scribner, 1849), pp. xxxi–xxxiv.

35. This centrifugal quality is all that remains of Natty in *Home As Found* (1838). The Effinghams go out on the lake to raise echoes from "the Speaking Rocks," echoes that "come from the spirit of the Leatherstocking, which keeps about its old haunts, and repeats everything we say, in mockery of the invasion of the woods." *Home As Found* (New York: W. A. Townsend, 1860), p. 230.

36. Richard Poirier, *A World Elsewhere: The Place of Style in American Literature* (London: Chatto and Windus, 1967), p. 71.

37. For a discussion of the circumstances of Logan's speech and its impact on American literature, politics, and education, see Edward D. Seeber, "Critical Views on Logan's Speech," *Journal of American Folklore* (1947), 60:130–46.

38. Thomas Jefferson, *Notes on the State of Virginia* (1787; rpt. Chapel Hill: University of North Carolina Press, 1955), p. 62.

39. Campbell, *Life and Writings of De Witt Clinton,* pp. 237–38.

40. Jefferson, *Notes on the State of Virginia,* p. 63.

41. The most complete of the numerous discussions of Cooper's use of Heckewelder is Edwin L. Stockton, Jr., *The Influence of the Moravians Upon the Leather-Stocking Tales,* a doctoral dissertation published in *Transactions of the Moravian Historical Society* (1964), 20:1–191.

42. *Notes on the State of Virginia,* p. 63.

43. Terence Martin, "Surviving on the Frontier: The Doubled Consciousness of Natty Bumppo," *South Atlantic Quarterly* (1976) 75:450.

44. Philbrick notes the motif of "volcanic passion" and "burning desire" that culminates in the burning of Mount Vision in "Cooper's *The Pioneers,* and Leatherstocking's Historical Function," *ESQ: A Journal of the American Renaissance* (1979) 25:7–8.

45. Edwin Fussell, *Frontier: American Literature and the American West* (Princeton: Princeton University Press, 1965), p. 37.

46. Roland Barthes, *S/Z,* Richard Miller, tr. (New York: Hill and Wang, 1974), p. 19.

47. Barthes, p. 19.

48. Barthes does not treat the five codes as either complete or forming an intelligible system that structures a text. Gerald Prince, for example, points out that one could as well posit a code of characters "to organize the narrative around heroes, false villains, helpers, and so on." "Notes on the Text as Reader," in Susan R. Suleiman and Inge Crossman, eds., *The Reader in the Text: Essays on Audience and Interpretation* (Princeton: Princeton University Press, 1980), p. 229n4. Barthes writes that the codes create a "*topos*"; "Thus, if we make no effort to structure each code, or the five codes among themselves, we do so deliberately, in order to assume the multivalence of the text, its partial reversibility" (*S/Z,* p. 20).

49. Person, p. 206.

50. Quoted in Beard, "Historical Introduction," p. xxxix.

51. Quoted in Beard, "Historical Introduction," p. xl.

52. On the difficulties occasioned by the lack of international copyright, see the introduction in Robert E. Spiller and Philip C. Blackburn, *A Descriptive Bibliography of the Writings of James Fenimore Cooper* (New York: Bowker, 1934), pp. 3–10.

53. Quoted in Lance Schachterle and Kenneth M. Anderson, Jr., "Textual Commentary," in *The Pioneers,* p. 472.

54. Schachterle and Anderson, p. 472.

55. Beard, "Historical Introduction," p. xli.

56. Beard, "Historical Introduction," p. xlii.

57. Quoted in Beard, "Historical Introduction," p. xlii.

58. *Niles' Weekly Register* (March 22, 1823), 24:34.

59. *The New-York Mirror, and Ladies' Literary Gazette* (August 9, 1823), 1:12.

60. *Port Folio* (1823), 15:230, 231.

61. Letter from James De Peyster Ogden to Cooper, London, September 6, 1823, quoted in Beard, "Historical Introduction," p. xlvi.

62. Spiller and Blackburn, p. 6.

63. Robert Lemelin, *Pathway to the National Character 1830–1861* (Port Washington, N.Y.: Kennikat Press, 1974), pp. 42–43.

64. *United States Gazette,* quoted in Beard, "Historical Introduction," p. xlvi.

65. Beard, "Cooper and His Artistic Contemporaries," and "Historical Introduction," pp. xlvi–xlvii.

66. *Correspondence of James Fenimore-Cooper,* 1:94.

67. Honoré de Balzac, "Cooper's *The Pathfinder,*" Auguste D'Avezac, tr. in Sidney D. Braun and Seymour Lainoff, eds., *Transatlantic Mirrors: Essays in Franco-American Literary Relations* (Boston: Twayne, 1978), p. 34.

5. Cooper's Audience

1. Reviews by these and other prominent figures are conveniently collected in George Dekker and John P. McWilliams, Jr., eds., *Fenimore Cooper: The Critical Heritage* (Boston: Routledge & Kegan Paul, 1973).

2. William Charvat, *The Profession of Authorship*, Matthew J. Bruccoli, ed. (Columbus: Ohio State University Press, 1968), p. 292.

3. Charvat, *The Profession of Authorship*, p. 78.

4. *Niles' Weekly Register*, New Series (June 8, 1822), 10:225.

5. Van Wyck Brooks, *The Flowering of New England* (1936; rpt. Dutton, 1952), p. 169.

6. Percival quoted in Beard, "Historical Introduction," in *The Pioneers*, p. xiv.

7. *The Minerva* (February 8, 1823), 1:348–49.

8. Kennedy Williams, Jr., "Cooper's Use of American History," in *James Fenimore Cooper and His Country, or Getting Under Way: Papers from the 1978 Conference at State University of New York College at Oneonta and Cooperstown, New York* (Oneonta, N.Y.: n.p., 1979), p. 5.

9. David Levin, *History as Romantic Art* (1959; rpt. New York: Harcourt, Brace & World, 1963), p. 73.

10. "The Importance of Illustrating New-England History," in Samuel Gilman Brown, *The Works of Rufus Choate*, 2 vols. (Boston: Little Brown, 1862), 1:321.

11. *Port Folio* (1823), 15:231n.

12. *Niles' Weekly Register*, New Series (February 8, 1823), 11:354. See Tremain McDowell, "The Identity of Harvey Birch," *American Literature* (1930), 2:119–34, for evidence of the persistent attempts to locate the "real" Harvey Birch.

13. *Port Folio* (1823), 15:232.

14. *Niles' Weekly Register*, 3d Series (December 3, 1825), 5:217.

15. Richard Slotkin, *Regeneration Through Violence* (Middletown, Conn.: Wesleyan University Press, 1973), pp. 313–68.

16. *Port Folio* (1823), 15:520.

17. All the vignettes were reproduced in a volume issued by the Port Folio office in Philadelphia in 1826: *Illustrations from* The Spy, The Pioneers, *and the Waverley Novels, with Explanatory and Critical Remarks.*

18. See James Franklin Beard, "Illustrations," in *The Pioneers*, pp. xiii–xvii.

19. Robert E. Spiller and Philip C. Blackburn, *A Descriptive Bibliography of the Writings of James Fenimore Cooper* (New York: Bowker, 1934), p. 211.

20. John D. Gordan, "*The Red Rover* Takes the Boards," *American Literature* (1938), 10:75.

21. Gordan, p. 75. Gordan remarks (p. 70) that *The Red Rover* was one of the few American novels to produce widely popular dramatizations before *Uncle Tom's Cabin.*

22. Richard Chase, *The American Novel and Its Tradition* (New York: Doubleday Anchor Books, 1957); Joel Porte, *The Romance in America: Studies in Cooper, Poe, Hawthorne, Melville, and James* (Middletown, Conn.: Wesleyan University Press, 1969); Edwin Fussell, *Frontier: American Literature and the American West* (Princeton: Princeton University Press, 1965); Leslie A. Fiedler, *The Return of the Vanishing American* (1968; rpt. London: Paladin, 1972); R. W. B. Lewis, *The American Adam: Innocence, Tragedy, and Tradition in the Nineteenth Century* (Chicago: University of Chicago Press, 1955); Harold Kaplan, *Democratic Humanism and American Literature* (Chicago: University of Chicago

Press, 1972); Marius Bewley, *The Eccentric Design: Form in the Classic American Novel* (New York: Columbia University Press, 1963).

23. *Niles' Weekly Register,* New Series (May 24, 1832), 12:178; *The New York Mirror, and Ladies' Literary Gazette* (August 2, 1823), 1:2 and 4.

24. Benjamin Lease, *That Wild Fellow John Neal and the American Literary Revolution* (Chicago: University of Chicago Press, 1972), pp. 39 and 41.

25. See Ellen Moers, *Harriet Beecher Stowe and American Literature* (Hartford, Conn.: The Stowe-Day Foundation, 1978).

26. W. C. Brownell, *American Prose Masters: Cooper—Hawthorne—Emerson—Poe—Lowell—Henry James,* Howard Mumford Jones, ed. (1909; rpt. Cambridge, Mass.: Harvard University Press, 1963), p. 5.

27. Samuel Finley Breeze Morse, quoted in Thomas Lounsbury, *James Fenimore Cooper* (1882; rpt. Detroit: Gale Research, 1968), pp. 76–77.

Appendix: The 1801 Review of *Wieland*

1. The review appeared in two parts: *The American Review, and Literary Journal* (1801), 1:333–39, and (1802), 2:28–39. All references to the review will be cited parenthetically as *1801* followed by volume and page numbers. For typical treatments of the review see Carl Van Doren, "Early American Realism," *Nation* (1941), 99:577–78; Harry R. Warfel, *Charles Brockden Brown: American Gothic Novelist* (Gainesville: University of Florida Press, 1940), p. 111; David Lee Clark, *Charles Brockden Brown: Pioneer Voice of America* (Durham, N.C.: Duke University Press, 1952), p. 168.

2. William Dunlap, *The Life of Charles Brockden Brown: Together With Selections from the Rarest of his Printed Works, from His Original Letters, and from His Manuscripts Before Unpublished,* 2 vols. (Philadelphia: James P. Parke, 1815).

3. Clark, *Charles Brockden Brown,* p. 196.

4. Letter to John Blair Linn, first printed in Ernest Marchand, "Introduction" to Brown's *Ormond; or the Secret Witness* (1937; rpt. New York: Hafner, 1962), p. xli. Further reference to *Ormond* will be cited parenthetically.

5. Scott's self-review incensed James Fenimore Cooper, who assailed the practice in his review of J. G. Lockhart's *Memoirs of the Life of Sir Walter Scott, Bart.;* see *The Knickerbocker or the New-York Monthly Magazine* (1848), 12:355–56. On Neal's self-reviews see Hans-Joachim Lang, "Drei Wurzeln der Wahrheit im Historischen Roman: John Neals *Rachel Dyer,*" in Karl Schubert and Ursula Müller-Richter, eds., *Geschichte und Gesellschaft in der amerikanischen Literatur* (Heidelberg: Quelle & Meyer, 1975), pp. 9–32.

6. Brown's letter is reprinted in George Perkins, ed., *The Theory of the American Novel* (New York: Holt, Rinehart and Winston, 1970), pp. 12–13. Jefferson's reply is quoted in David L. Butler, *Dissecting a Human Heart: A Study of Style in the Novels of Charles Brockden Brown* (Washington, D.C.: University Press of America, 1978), pp. 29–30.

7. George Gates Raddin, Jr., *Hocquet Caritat and the New York Literary Scene* (Dover, N.J.: The Dover Advance Press, 1953), p. 59.

8. *The Literary Magazine, and American Register* (1805), 3:16–17.

9. The advertisement is reprinted in Harry R. Warfel, ed., *The Rhapsodist and Other Uncollected Writings* (New York: Scholars' Facsimiles and Reprints, 1943), pp. 135–36. Further references will be cited parenthetically as *Rhapsodist.*

10. *The Literary Magazine, and American Register* (1804), 1:404. Further references to this dialogue will be cited parenthetically as "Diary."

11. *Wieland; or the Transformation. An American Tale* (Kent, Ohio: Kent State University Press, 1977), p. 3. Further references will be cited parenthetically as *Wieland.*

12. *Arthur Mervyn; or, Memoirs of the Year 1793* (Kent, Ohio: Kent State University Press, 1980), p. 3. Further references will be cited parenthetically as *Mervyn.*

13. *Edgar Huntly; or Memoirs of a Sleepwalker* (New Haven: College & University Press, 1973), p. 29. Further references will be cited parenthetically as *Huntly.*

14. "Introduction," in *Ormond,* p. xxxvi.

15. The variety of Brown's style is the subject of Butler's *Dissecting a Human Heart;* see especially chapter 7, "Brown's Theory of Style," pp. 35–38.

INDEX

Sutanstul 133

The Sky 108.09
Pioneers 1657

Emil 113.4

Melr 134-5

Bryant 23

Hawth 182.3

e Matmons e 10 last titles 141

Gaff 37

Barthes 151